GIORGIO LEVI DELLA VIDA CONFERENCES

Richard G. Hovannisian and Speros Vryonis, Jr., General Editors

---

Published for the

Gustave E. von Grunebaum Center for Near Eastern Studies

University of California

Los Angeles

EIGHTH CONFERENCE

Islam's Understanding of Itself

May 1-3, 1981

COMMITTEE

Speros Vryonis, Jr., University of California, Los Angeles, Chairman

Reverend G. C. Anawati, O.P., Dominican Institute, Cairo

Amin Banani, University of California, Los Angeles

Franz Rosenthal, Yale University

Bertold Spuler, University of Hamburg

Andreas Tietze, University of Vienna

Albert Hourani, University of Oxford

Recipient of the Seventh Giorgio Levi Della Vida Award in Islamic Studies

EIGHTH GIORGIO LEVI DELLA VIDA BIENNIAL CONFERENCE
May 1-3, 1981

Gustave E. von Grunebaum Center for Near Eastern Studies
University of California, Los Angeles

ISLAM'S UNDERSTANDING OF ITSELF

Edited by
RICHARD G. HOVANNISIAN and SPEROS VRYONIS, JR.

The Giorgio Levi Della Vida Medal of the Gustave E. von Grunebaum Center for Near Eastern Studies, University of California, Los Angeles, is awarded biennially to give recognition to an outstanding scholar whose work has significantly and lastingly advanced the study of Islamic civilization. The scholar is selected by a committee appointed by the chancellor of the University of California, Los Angeles, meeting under the chairmanship of the director of the Gustave E. von Grunebaum Center for Near Eastern Studies.

The award carries with it a bronze medal and a prize of money together with the obligation to present in person a formal lecture at the University of California, Los Angeles, as part of a conference. The recipient of the award chooses the theme and selects the other participants to the conference. The proceedings of each conference are published in a special series, of which this volume is the eighth.

The first award was made on May 12, 1967, to Professor Robert Brunschvig of the Sorbonne, Paris, by a committee under the chairmanship of Professor G. E. von Grunebaum, who originated the conference. Subsequent recipients were Professors Joseph Schacht of Columbia, Francesco Gabrieli of the University of Rome, posthumously G. E. von Grunebaum of the University of California, Shlomo Dov Goitein of the Institute for Advanced Study, Princeton, Franz Rosenthal of Yale University, and Albert Hourani, University of Oxford.

Seven volumes have been published to date: *Logic in Classical Islamic Culture* (1970), *Theology and Law in Islam* (1971), *Arabic Poetry: Theory and Development* (1973), *Islam and Cultural Change in the Middle Ages* (1975), *Individualism and Conformity in Classical Islam* (1977), *Society and the Sexes in Medieval Islam* (1979), and *Islamic Studies: A Tradition and Its Problems* (1980).

This volume and its predecessors owe what technical perfection they may possess to the care bestowed on them by Teresa Ruggieri Joseph, Principal Editor, Gustave E. von Grunebaum Center for Near Eastern Studies.

ISLAM'S UNDERSTANDING OF ITSELF

Giorgio Levi Della Vida
1886-1967

ISLAM'S UNDERSTANDING OF ITSELF

Edited by

RICHARD G. HOVANNISIAN and
SPEROS VRYONIS, JR.

1983

UNDENA PUBLICATIONS, MALIBU, CALIFORNIA

Library of Congress Card Number: 82-50987
ISBN: 0-89003-135-5

Undena Publications, P. O. Box 97, Malibu, CA 90265

CONTENTS

PRESENTATION OF AWARD TO EIGHTH RECIPIENT
W. MONTGOMERY WATT

SPEROS VRYONIS, JR.

University of California, Los Angeles

Central to the understanding of the great world religions and to the comprehension of the civilizations spawned within these religions is the figure of the religious founder, prophet, or messiah. The validity of this assertion is nowhere more evident than in the case of the prophet Muhammad and the Islamic religion and civilization. With the passage of time the figure of a Confucius, of a Buddha, or of a Christ becomes encrusted with the legends of the particular civilization to which the holy figure stands as father, and consequently it is very difficult for later generations to separate the original kernel-essence associated with the prophet-messiah-founder from the later encrustations that accumulate from piety, self-interest, or even carelessness. The historian's task when facing the problems of the rise of religion, prophecy, and of new civilizations is thus enormous. Though it is always historically easier to deal with some later phase in the development of a civilization or religion, nevertheless it is not as important as coming to grips with the problems of origin. For, as the ancient Greek thinkers postulated, ἀρχὴ ἥμισυ παντός, "the beginning is half of all."

It is precisely to the beginnings of Islam that Montgomery Watt has dedicated an important portion of his scholarly life with results that remain an object of abiding interest and consideration. In 1953 the Oxford University Press published his important *Muhammad at Mecca*, which was completed by the publication of a second volume in 1956, *Muhammad at Medina*. In these two fundamental works Watt set forth his attitude toward this crucial but sensitive subject and then established his evaluation and use of the sources. Both undertakings were fundamental, for, as he pointed out, there were no new major written sources to be taken into account in discussing the life of the prophet Muhammad. Aware of the various difficulties before him, Watt stated that he was writing for historians, Muslims, and Christians. Any scholar who attempts to write for an audience as varied as his acknowledged audience has a task that calls for constant awareness of its demands. He acknowledged that he wrote primarily as a historian but that he tried to observe neutrality on theological questions that could be considered common ground to Muslims and Christians. To Muslim readers he remarked: "I have endeavored, while remaining faithful to the standards of Western historical scholarship, to say nothing that would entail the rejection of any of the fundamental doctrines of Islam. There need be no unbridgeable gulf between Western scholarship and Islamic faith." Since he makes no theological judgment as far as Christianity is concerned, he tells his Christian reader that he may make his own theological conclusions from the materials that he is presenting in the book. He completed his scholarly declaration with his personal statement on the sources he was to follow. He followed basically the Koran and the traditional historical material (Ibn Hishām, aṭ-Ṭabarī, al-Wāqidī, Ibn Sa'd) and showed himself to lean more toward tradition than toward the school of skeptical scholars who tended to move farther away from this tradition. He allowed himself room for some qualification of what he termed "tendential shaping" of these earlier historians by later authors. Throughout his work Watt has followed these rigorous scholarly standards which ensure his results and which avoid doctrinaire and categoric declarations.

The breadth and versatility of his scholarly activity is immediately evident from his contributions to the Islamic Surveys series published by the University of Edinburgh Press. These contributions cover Islamic theology, philosophy, political thought, the history of Islamic Spain, and an account of the influence of Islam on Medieval Europe. Finally, he published in this series a completely revised and enlarged edition of his late teacher's (Richard Bell) *Introduction to the Qur'ān*.

The scholars who contributed papers to this volume have honored Watt's scholarly vision by offering to us a rich variety of communications on Islam's Understanding of Itself.

SELF-IMAGES OF ISLAM IN THE QUR'ĀN AND LATER

W. MONTGOMERY WATT

University of Edinburgh

The topic of this conference is "Islam's Understanding of Itself," a topic which may appear remote and academic, but which has some immediate practical relevance in our contemporary world. All human beings seek a meaningful life; and life is meaningful when the person has a meaningful role within a community which itself has a meaningful role in world history. A community's understanding of itself is its understanding of its role in history. Within this field my essay concentrates on certain aspects of Islam's understanding of itself or self-image which have been prominent in public statements or pronouncements by leading Muslims in recent years, and more particularly by those who may be called conservatives. A convenient point of reference is the First World Conference on Muslim Education held at Mecca from March 31 to April 8, 1977. This has produced a number of documents, including a series of seven volumes in English, which contain revised versions of papers read at the Conference.[1] The participants were rightly concerned at the growing extent of westernization and secularization in Islamic society and felt that in most Muslim countries life was in danger of losing its distinctive Islamic features and of being molded by many false beliefs and pernicious practices from the West. To reverse this trend they thought that what was above all necessary was to have a system of genuinely Islamic education. These points were clearly made in the publisher's announcement of the series of books, and from it a few paragraphs may be quoted.

> Muslims in the twentieth century are passing through a period of self-examination and self-awareness. The Muslim majority countries that extend from Morocco to Indonesia have adopted the Western system of education

[1] Islamic Education Series (Jeddah, 1979). The separate titles are: *Aims and Objectives of Islamic Education; Crisis in Muslim Education; Muslim Education in the Modern World; Social and Natural Sciences: The Islamic Perspective; Philosophy, Literature, and Fine Arts; Curriculum and Teacher Education; Education and Society in the Muslim World.*

> in order to acquire modern knowledge so that they may become intellectually and materially advanced. This system of education has long ago been separated from the sphere of the Divine and is at present secular in approach, since basic assumptions behind Natural, Applied, and Social Sciences and Humanities are not drawn from religion. Along with these concepts, a modern way of life which contradicts the traditional way of life governed by the Sharia is becoming established in Muslim society and is being encouraged by radio, television and other mass media programmes. A cultural duality has therefore appeared everywhere in the Muslim world. The traditional Islamic education that still persists is supporting the traditional Islamic group, whereas modern secular education is creating secularists who know or care little about their traditions and values or pay only lip-service to them.
>
> As the secular education system is dominant in Muslim countries, Muslim thinkers have become worried that gradually the Muslim world will lose its identity by losing its Islamic character and will thus suffer from the same moral disintegration and confusion as the West. It can preserve that identity and save the Ummah from the confusion and erosion of values and from the conflict between religious and secular groups only if Muslims receive a truly Islamic education. And education can be truly Islamic if Muslim scholars can produce Islamic concepts for all branches of knowledge and Muslim countries can disseminate them among Muslim intellectuals and students. This requires research projects, production of text-books, and properly devised teacher-training programmes.
>
> If Muslim scholars can evolve this system, formulate basic concepts from the religious point of view, and have text-books written on the basis of these concepts, even Western religious thinkers and educationists will find a new dimension to their thinking and thus they will be able to strengthen their efforts to stem the tide that has almost swept away religious values from their system and society.[2]

Non-Muslims who believe in God are bound to approve of the general aim of opposing secularizing and antireligious tendencies. Unfortunately, however, implicit in this thinking are some assumptions about Islam and its place in the world which make it more difficult, perhaps impossible, to realize that aim. These assumptions are essentially those of the conservative ulama who were the predominant group at the Conference. Other more liberal-minded groups attended, but it was the voice of the conservatives which prevailed. In this essay three of these assumptions, three aspects of this implicit self-image of Islam, are examined, and an attempt is made to show that they are exaggerated or one-sided developments of Qur'ānic truths. The three points are:

[2] Publisher's announcement.

1. Islam is self-sufficient, owing nothing to any other religious or philosophical system;
2. Islam is superior to Judaism, Christianity, and Western thought generally;
3. Islam alone has the final truth for humanity about everything.

The first of these aspects of the self-image of Islam–that it owes nothing to other forms of human thought–appears to be derived from the belief that God revealed the Qur'ān to Muḥammad. In the nineteenth century Western scholars discussed at great length whether Jewish or Christian influences were more important in the Qur'ān. Some went so far as to say that the whole teaching of the Qur'ān was not more than a selection from Jewish and Christian teaching. In reaction to this, Muslims emphasized their doctrine that the Qur'ān was the word or speech of God, and insisted that God could not be subject to influences of the kind alleged by the Western scholars. This line of argument, however, depends on a certain conception of the nature of revelation. It is this conception of revelation which has to be looked at more closely.

According to the Qur'ān God's revelations come to particular peoples through particular individuals. Thus the text of the Qur'ān was brought by an angel to the particular man Muḥammad, and was to be conveyed by him in the first place to the people of Mecca and then to other Arabs. Study of the earliest passages of the Qur'ān shows that their teaching was specially relevant to the situation in Mecca at the time.[3] The particularity of the Qur'ānic message is also shown by the fact that certain verses were abrogated, because the abrogation of a rule implies that it was relevant only in circumstances of a temporary character. At the same time, of course, it must be insisted that particularity does not exclude universality. A feature present in a particular people may be one which most other people also share. The fact that the Qur'ānic message was in the first place for the Meccans does not prevent Muḥammad being also "a mercy to the worlds," *raḥma li-l-'ālamīn* (21.107). Similarly Jesus preached in the first place to "the lost sheep of the house of Israel" in his time, and his teaching was specially relevant to their circumstances; but the essentials of his teaching were found to be of universal application.[4]

Next it is to be noted that a revelation is expressed in the language and thought forms of the particular people to whom it is first addressed. A language is something of human making, largely through the unconscious efforts of countless individuals over a period of centuries. Each language has distinctive features of its own. Even basic categories of thought may vary from language to language, such as the conception of time reflected in the various forms of the verb. Moreover the Arabic language contains words for various customs of the nomads of the

[3] W. Montgomery Watt, *Muhammad at Mecca* (Oxford, 1953), ch. III, 3.

[4] Matthew 15.24; cf. 10.56. Other Qur'ānic verses speaking of the universality of Muḥammad's mission are: 4.79, 7.158, 25.1, 34.28.

desert, which are only intelligible to those who know something about the customs. Many European translators have failed to understand the words *huwa yujīru wa-lā yujāru 'alay-hi* (23.88), which may be rendered "he gives protection, but no protection is given against him"; but even this translation is not intelligible unless one understands the nomadic practices of *ijāra*, "the giving of neighborly protection," and other practices connected with that.

Unless the speakers of a language have no contacts with other groups, the language does not develop in isolation from other languages. Arabic, when it has to deal with something novel, is probably better than most languages at producing a new word from its own resources; but, because Arab traders had many contacts with non-Arabs, it adopted a number of foreign words. These words were given an Arabic form, and many are found in the early poets. Of the foreign words in the Qur'ān a number deal with specifically religious practices found among non-Arabs, while several others denote types of buildings which would not be familiar to desert dwellers. Some early Muslim scholars denied the existence of foreign words in the Qur'ān, and tried to show how the alleged examples could be derived from Arabic roots. They may have been motivated chiefly by unwillingness to admit the Arabs' debt to other cultures. On the other hand, a few Muslim scholars admitted that the words had originally come from other languages, though they had now been fully accepted into Arabic.[5] In the light of modern linguistic studies it is certain that many words in the Qur'ān, though by Muḥammad's time fully arabized, had originally come from non-Arabic words and not from Arabic roots. This phenomenon is normal where there are cultural contacts between groups speaking different languages.

The assertion that God is not subject to literary or cultural influences seems cogent if considered in isolation. The Qur'ān itself, however, says that God never sent a messenger except with the language of his people (14.4); and when the divine message is expressed in a particular language, it inevitably becomes subject to whatever influences have been at work on that language. Thus, while there can be no question of God being subject to human influences, it is proper to consider influences upon the language in which the divine message is expressed. Indeed it is also proper and relevant to consider influences upon the people to whom the message is primarily addressed, since it has been adapted to their outlook and needs. The criticisms of Judaism and Christianity in the Qur'ān are not criticisms of these religions in general, but only of the particular forms of these religions with which the Arabs of Mecca and Medina had had contact. When the Qur'ān criticizes Jews for holding that 'Uzayr (or Ezra) is the son of God (9.30), and Christians for regarding Jesus and Mary as two gods (5.116), it is presumably because some Arabs in Mecca or Medina had met some Jews and Christians with these beliefs, even if the beliefs would be repudiated by the vast majority of Jews and Christians respectively.

[5] A. Jeffery, *The Foreign Vocabulary of the Qur'ān* (Baroda, 1938), esp. pp. 5-11.

A further point at which a human element may come in is in the interpretation of the revealed message. When any statement is made to human beings and they understand it, they are not merely passive recipients of an objective form of words which has only one possible meaning. To understand a statement the hearer has to link it up with his previous experience and his whole intellectual outlook. Those who first heard one of the Qur'ānic verses which speak of the earth being spread out like a bed or carpet (e.g., 2.22; 13.3; 78.6) were people who thought that the earth was flat, and so they would interpret the verse in accordance with this idea. On the other hand, those who know that the earth is spherical (like the commentator al-Bayḍāwī) interpret the verse as applying to an earth that is really round but is so large that it appears to be flat. Again, the Arabs of Muḥammad's day had very limited historical knowledge apart from their own traditions of "the days of the Arabs," and only a very vague chronological framework for general history within which to interpret the historical references in the Qur'ān. A century or two later, however, there were Muslim scholars who had an extensive knowledge of Biblical history and also knew something about the Greeks, Romans, and Persians, and these men had a much fuller understanding of the historical significance of the events mentioned in the Qur'ān. For example, they linked traditional Arab genealogies with those of the Bible, and showed how the northern Arabs were descended from Ishmael and the southern Arabs from one of Abraham's ancestors.[6]

A more serious question—and one that is common to Jews, Christians, and Muslims—is how God's work of creation is to be understood by one who accepts as a fact that human beings have evolved from "lower" forms of life over a period of millions of years. (This I take to be an established fact; disputes among scientists about Darwinism are concerned with details of the mechanisms of evolution, although conservative ulama make the disputes a ground for rejecting the whole idea of evolution.)[7] There has sometimes been a tendency for people to think of "creation" as the instantaneous origination or setting in motion of the cosmic process, which then continues in accordance with its own created nature. Those who hold such a view have probably come under the influence of the Aristotelian conception of the First Cause. Neither the Bible nor the Qur'an speaks of creation as a single momentary event, but as something spread over a period of time, described as "six days"; and they also speak of God as continuing to control the course of events. Specially relevant here is the Qur'ānic passage (23.14) which names several stages of the human embryo in the womb, and describes how God "created" (*khalaqa*) each out of the preceding stage. There can thus be no Biblical or Qur'ānic objection to thinking of creation as a continuous process; and so the modern Muslim, Christian, or Jew who accepts the established fact of

[6] R. A. Nicholson, *A Literary History of the Arabs* (Cambridge, 1930) p. xviii.

[7] Muhammad Qutb in S. N. al-Attas, ed., *Aims and Objectives of Islamic Education* (Jeddah, 1979), p. 52.

evolution is justified in interpreting creation as God's origination and continuing control of the evolutionary process. This practical conclusion is reinforced by the consideration that the purpose of these scriptures is not to convey scientific information but to enable humanity to understand its relationship to God. Some modern Muslims have tried to show that certain Qur'ānic statements are foreshadowings of recent scientific discoveries, just as some Biblical scholars have suggested that the "six days" of creation could be understood as aeons, each consisting of millions of years. Such speculations are pointless. The scriptures were revealed and written down for contemporaries, and no contemporary could have understood them in terms of twentieth-century science. Moreover, it cannot be too emphatically reiterated, the purpose of the scriptures is to give spiritual and moral guidance, not scientific knowledge.

With regard to the first assumption, then, the conclusion must be that whereas the Qur'ān as a message from God to men is essentially independent of human volition, nevertheless Muslims in the time of Muḥammad and later in every subsequent century cannot avoid sharing to some extent in the intellectual outlook of their time and culture, and interpreting their Islamic faith in accordance with elements in that outlook.

The second assumption frequently made now by Muslims is that Islam is superior to Judaism and Christianity and to Western thought generally, and has nothing to learn from them. It is, of course, only natural that a member of a religious community should consider his or her religion to be superior to all others, or at least not inferior to any of them; otherwise a change of religion would be indicated. Some Muslims today, however, especially among the conservative ulama, go further and are convinced that the religious and moral problems of the Islamic world are largely or entirely due to the corrupting influence of Western thought and Western practice, and that the solution of these problems lies in a return to a truly Islamic way of life, and in particular to a truly Islamic education. They further insist that, because of the inferiority of the West, this education must come entirely from Islamic roots.

This second assumption has some support in the Qur'ān. On the one hand, the Qur'ān teaches that Moses, Jesus, and Muḥammad all were sent with a revelation that was the same in essentials, and that the Qur'ān confirmed the previous revelations. On the other hand, however, the Qur'ān criticizes Judaism and Christianity on certain points. In the course of the first Islamic century, too, Muslims came to hold that as a whole the Jewish and Christian scriptures were corrupt. This doctrine is thought to be based on the Qur'ān, but all that can be found there are verses which speak of how Jews (and perhaps also Christians) played verbal tricks on the Muslims, and some similar matters.[8] The doctrine of the

[8] W. Montgomery Watt, *Islam and the Integration of Society* (London, 1961), p. 260, with further references.

corruption of the scriptures was, of course, a useful "defence" for simple-minded Arabs who had to argue with more sophisticated Jews and Christians, since it prevented the latter arguing on their own ground, and forced them to go to ground of the Muslims' choosing. Despite this doctrine of corruption the Muslims continued to accept Jews and Christians as People of the Book and as such to give them privileges in Islamic states.

There is no simple criterion by which religions can be arranged in an order of superiority and inferiority. If one takes some such definition of religion as that it is "a set of symbolic forms and acts which relate man to the ultimate conditions of his existence,"[9] then it is found that, because religious truth is expressed in symbolic or nonliteral form it is not subject to the usual logical rules. Symbols which superficially are completely different, even contradictory, may in effect relate men to ultimate conditions in much the same way. Thus the symbolic character of religious assertions virtually excludes the intellectual comparison of religions. Another type of criterion, however, is put forward in the Sermon on the Mount (Matthew 7.16,20): "You shall know them by their fruits." The term "fruits" here is taken to mean the practical consequences of religious teaching, such as the quality of life of the adherents of a religion and its ability to guide them to a solution of the various problems they encounter in the course of centuries. This further means that the essential truth of a religion is not something that can exist of itself in written documents. It can only exist effectively in the life of a community that treasures these documents as its scriptures, whose experience of God is similar to that of its earliest members, and which has the vitality in every generation to find guidance in the scriptures to deal with the contemporary problems confronting it.

The question of the superiority or otherwise of Islam is thus not an intellectual question, but a practical one. Not only Islam, but Christianity, Judaism, and every other world religion is today confronted with much the same problems of how to promote peace and justice in a world unified by modern technology. Christians must certainly admit that they have not been entirely successful in dealing with their problems during the last two or three centuries, and their failures have contributed to the rise of secularism. Yet they have had some successes, and have maintained their communities in existence despite the inroads of secular thought. The chief concern, however, must be with the future. The great religions are now in contact with one another to a greater extent than ever before. This means that they are also in competition with one another, though in a sense it is friendly competition to see who can do most for the promotion of peace and justice. These are the fruits for which the whole human race is desperately longing, and it is by such fruits that the superiority or otherwise of each will be known.

[9] R. N. Bellah in Roland Robertson, ed., *Sociology of Religion: Selected Readings* (Harmondsworth, 1969), p. 263, quoting from *American Sociological Review*, 29 (1964), 358-374.

The third assumption follows from the second but goes beyond it. It is that Islam and Islam alone has the final truth about everything–or at least everything concerned with the ultimate conditions of human existence–and that it is capable of giving true guidance to the human race about all their problems from now to the end of time. In Iran at the present time we see an attempt to base a modern state on this assumption; but the assumption goes back almost to the beginning of Islam. A story is told which refers to the Arab capture of Alexandria, then capital of Egypt, in the year 642. The general in command wrote to the caliph 'Umar asking how he was to dispose of the books in the great library. He got the reply: "If they are in agreement with the Qur'ān, they are unnecessary and may be destroyed; if they do not agree with the Qur'ān, they are dangerous and must certainly be destroyed." This story is almost certainly not true as fact, but it is an illustration of the undoubted tendency among Muslims to believe in the self-sufficiency of Islam.[10]

The Qur'ān gives little support to the idea that Islam is self-sufficient in this sense; and there is a famous saying of Muḥammad's, telling his followers to "seek knowledge even from as far away as China." Contemporary Muslims unanimously interpret the Qur'ānic description of Muḥammad as "the seal of the prophets" (33.40) as meaning that he is the last of the prophets and supersedes the previous ones; but to the first hearers this probably meant no more than that his revelation confirmed previous ones, and this interpretation is given by early commentators.

Some of the members of the First World Conference on Muslim Education called for the working out of an Islamic basis for all the natural and social sciences. One can have some sympathy with this demand, since it is attempting to deal with the apparent denial of religious truth by certain scientists, but it is based on a serious misunderstanding of the proper autonomy of the sciences and of their general relation to religious truth. Each of the particular sciences has a special field of study within which it operates. It has to take account of the results of other sciences where their fields impinge on its own, but otherwise it is autonomous within its field, and cannot be controlled by wider cosmological theories derived from religion or philosophy. There is no Buddhist biology or Christian chemistry or Islamic astronomy or Marxist mathematics, but only biology, chemistry, astronomy, mathematics; and both the religious believer and the Marxist philosopher must accept the results of the sciences in their proper sphere. There is the notorious case of the Soviet biologist Lysenko who adopted a particular theory not because of the biological evidence but because it fitted in better with Marxist philosophy. In the end, however, the evidence proved too strong, and Lysenko and his theory were discredited, even though for a time the theory had been official Marxist doctrine. On the other hand, revelation and religious truth

[10] Edward Gibbon, *The Decline and Fall of the Roman Empire*, chap. 51; P. K. Hitti, *History of the Arabs* (London, 1943), p. 166.

have also their proper sphere, namely, the relationship of humanity to God, and within this sphere they are supreme.

The difficulty is that there is a certain overlap between the proper sphere of the sciences and that of religious truth. This is in respect of what may be called cosmology. Beyond the proper spheres of the particular sciences there is some scope for science-based speculation attempting to give a general picture of the world (or the cosmic process), that is, a cosmology; but the cosmological speculations of scientists do not have behind them the same authority as the assured results of the particular sciences in their proper spheres. Revelation, again, in speaking of the relation of the human race to God, usually speaks in terms of the cosmology current at the time of the revelation. The idea that the human race is descended from a single pair, Adam and Eve, is a primitive cosmological theory. The fact that it is now outdated as cosmology does not mean that the believer has to reject the religious truth implicit in the Biblical account of creation, namely, that humanity owes its being to a beneficent creator. When this is understood, it can be seen that what Muslim educators—and likewise Christian—are justified in seeking is a cosmology within which the assured results of physics, astronomy, geology, and other sciences have a place, but which at the same time is in harmony with belief in God and does not contradict it. In the social sciences the problems are somewhat different, but the same general approach is valid.

The main problem confronting Muslim and Christian alike is how to produce such a cosmology and to get it generally accepted. Many Christians think that some progress toward this goal was made by Teilhard de Chardin, but his views are far from being accepted by all Christians. Muslims have before them the example of al-Ghazālī. At the end of the fifth Islamic century (about A.D. 1090) he was aware of the conflict between religious truth derived from revelation and the science-linked philosophy of the day, which was the form of Neoplatonism developed by Ibn Sīnā (Avicenna); and his critique of that philosophy showed that the points of cosmology on which it was contrary to Islamic teaching were no more than dubious and indeed self-contradictory speculations, which gave no rational grounds for abandoning the cosmology based on revelation. Part of what al-Ghazālī did was to examine the various scientific or philosophical disciplines in order to determine how far their results were compatible with religious belief. Probably the most important result of his work here was the incorporation of Aristotelian logic into the main stream of Islamic thought.

The difficulties confronting all believers in God today are more complex than those dealt with by al-Ghazālī. While different estimates may be given of the results attained in the social sciences, there can be no doubt that the achievements of the natural sciences in the last two centuries have been such that the general soundness of their methods is massively confirmed. Just as al-Ghazālī accepted Aristotelian logic, the believer in God today must accept the assured results of the sciences, that is, those matters on which scientists themselves are in agreement, as distinct from theories or hypotheses about which there is some dispute.

In general these assured results of science are neutral in respect of religious truth, neither confirming it nor discrediting it. In one or two points, however, they may appear to contradict scriptural statements, such as the account of creation in Genesis. In such cases it is necessary for the modern believer to distinguish between the kind of truth found in the scriptures and that attained by science; and this takes one deep into the discipline of epistemology. In the sphere proper to the sciences it is clear that truth is discovered by the sciences working autonomously, and that neither Islam nor any other religion can claim to be the source of truth here.

Since religion also, however, has a proper sphere, the important question becomes whether within this sphere Islam and Islam alone has the final truth. Two aspects of the question may be distinguished: the ethical or practical, and the spiritual or theological. These are looked at in turn.

With regard to the ethical or practical aspect the main point to consider is whether the Islamic Sharī'a provides a perfect and all-embracing ideal of human conduct for both individuals and communities. Ayatollah Khomeini and his associates apparently claim that it does, and they have attempted to set up a modern state on this basis. Unfortunately, very little thinking has been done by the conservative ulama to take account of the differences between medieval and modern states, such as those brought about by the adoption of modern technology. One important difference is in respect of communications, where modern means of transport have resulted in there being vastly more contacts between Muslims and non-Muslims than was the case in the Middle Ages. In medieval times the Sharī'a was worked out to deal with situations where only a handful of non-Muslims (other than dhimmīs) visited or lived in an Islamic state and where official contacts between Islamic and non-Islamic states were minimal. It was unnecessary to consider what the Sharī'a said about Muslim attitudes to the norms followed by other peoples. The affair of the American diplomats held as hostages by Iranians for seventeen months in 1980 and 1981 shows that it has become an urgent matter for a Muslim to know whether the Sharī'a tells him to accept international diplomatic conventions or to reject them. Presumably the Sharī'a would recommend something not unlike the existing conventions; but, because this has not been considered and stated publicly by the ulama, Iranian Muslims seemed to think they were permitted to flout the existing conventions.

A similar case of even greater importance is the Universal Declaration of Human Rights adopted by the General Assembly of the United Nations on 10 December 1948. Again, presumably, if Muslim ulama considered matters of human rights, they would come to the conclusion that the Sharī'a led to rules very similar to those of the Universal Declaration; but, so far as I know, no widely supported public statements of this kind have been made, and consequently some violations of human rights by Muslims in positions of authority have not been felt to be infringements of the Sharī'a. There is indeed a small book entitled *Islam and Human Rights* (London, ? 1967), but unfortunately the author Muhammad Zafrulla Khan belongs to the Aḥmadiyya community which has been declared to be outside Islam. Yet he does say that "Islam lays down broad values and standards which clearly endorse the spirit and purpose of the Declaration" (p. 17).[11] The basic question implicit in this matter of Human Rights is how Muslims are to deal with non-Muslims in the various fields where international cooperation now takes place. The ethical norms followed by masses of human beings cannot simply be neglected because they are based on religions or philosophies allegedly inferior to Islam. Muslims have to decide to what extent the Sharī'a permits or obliges them to cooperate with these non-Muslims.

Even if it is provisionally admitted that in principle the Sharī'a is applicable to all matters in which contemporary individuals or states may need guidance, there are still some complexities to be noted. Various forward-looking Muslim scholars have realized that there has always been an important human and rational factor in the working out of how the Sharī'a applies to some novel problem. This is primarily at the level of theory. For example, human judgment enters in when ulama are applying analogical reasoning (*qiyās*) and have to decide what is the ground (*'illa*) of an established rule. A further point is that some account must also be taken of human experience and that there may even be cases where the experience of non-Muslims is relevant, which is no more than saying that one must see how a theory works out in practice. By way of example one might consider the Third Universal Theory of the President of Libya, Muammar al-Qathafi (Gaddafi). It includes a political system that claims to be derived from Islamic principles, that is, to be based on the Qur'ān and the Sharī'a. Briefly, it consists of a series of assemblies usually called popular congresses and people's committees. At the lowest level are village assemblies and factory assemblies in which every individual has a place. Above these basic congresses are others composed of the secretariats of the basic congresses; and there are also professional and craft unions. The summit is occupied by the General People's Congress for the whole state. This system is now being put into practice in Libya, and in a few years it should be possible to know how it is going to work. Even if it works up to a point in Libyan conditions, that is no guarantee that it will work elsewhere; and one suspects that few Muslims in the more populous Islamic countries will be enamored of it.[12]

The need to know how a thing works in practice is also apparent in considering whether divorce should be made easy or difficult. In Islam divorce has traditionally been very easy, especially for husbands; and the system seems to have worked well in the past, since there has been no obvious instability in Islamic

[11] Abul A'la Maududi has a book entitled *Fundamental Rights of Man* and a section on the topic in his *Islamic Way of Life* (3d ed.; Lahore, 1965), pp. 58-62, but most of the points in the Universal Declaration are not touched on.

[12] Al-Qathafi, *The Green Book*, Part One, *The Solution of the Problem of Democracy* (Tripoli, n.d. [c. 1979]).

societies. It is arguable, however, that this state of affairs owes much to the fact that in traditional Islamic societies the extended family was strong and important. Where the extended family is small, lacking in cohesion, and perhaps widely scattered, as in modern Western states, easy divorce may well lead to instability in society. This appears to be the case in some Western-developed societies, and so there is a tendency to make divorce more difficult and to take other steps to prevent marital breakdown. That is the sort of experience of which Muslims could profitably take cognizance when they are adapting the Sharīʻa to modern conditions.

Let us now turn to the theological or spiritual aspect of the religious sphere. Here it is not obvious that the Islamic conception of God, for example, is superior to the Jewish or Christian conception in so far as they differ, an aspect that I have already discussed. All that is needed now is to reinforce the suggestion that contemporary Islam requires someone like al-Ghazālī to defend its conception of God from a scientific or pseudoscientific attack. Beyond that, of course, is the ultimate criterion: "By their fruits you shall know them." Only the future can show whether one of the present world religions or perhaps some new or minor religion is going to be successful in establishing peace and justice in a unified world.

To a sympathetic observer, then, it is by no means clear that Islam alone has all truth, even in the specifically religious sphere. The future will undoubtedly bring greater clarity, but for the moment some questions cannot be answered. The Sufis sometimes use the illustration of a candle reflected in a number of different mirrors of varying quality. Though the reflections differ considerably, the candle is one and the same. What I have been trying to show in this lecture is that the mirror of the conservative ulama is not a particularly good one. Rather better is that of those liberal-minded Muslims who are aware of the modern secular and scientific outlook and yet remain faithful to the basic teachings of the Qur'ān. In conclusion, a quotation from a Christian theologian may be appropriate, since it applies equally to all religions: "Religions which are not open to new experiences and cannot integrate them critically grow old and in the long run can even die away."[13] May we all be open to new experiences and in this way enable our mirror to reflect the candle better.

[13] Edward Schillebeeckx, *Interim Report* (London, 1980), p. 58.

MUHAMMAD'S UNDERSTANDING OF HIMSELF: THE KORANIC DATA

ALFORD T. WELCH

Michigan State University

> He was given to sadness, and there were long periods of silence when he was deep in thought; yet he never rested but was always busy with something. He never spoke unnecessarily. What he said was always to the point and sufficient to make his meaning clear, but there was no padding. From the first to the last he spoke rapidly. Over his feelings he had a firm control. When he was annoyed he would turn aside; when he was pleased, he lowered his eyes. His time was carefully apportioned according to the various demands on him. In his dealings with people he was above all tactful. He could be severe at times, though in the main he was not rough but gentle. His laugh was mostly a smile.

In these words William Montgomery Watt has described the manner and character of Muhammad.[1] This description and, indeed, all of Professor Watt's studies of Muhammad are based on the conviction that the Koran is the primary source for the life of the Prophet and that at least the material in the early biographies is also to be accepted as trustworthy, except where there are particular reasons for suspecting that an anecdote was distorted or invented through legal, theological, or political motives.[2] On the extent of the reliability of the Sira and Hadith accounts as historical sources I am not yet prepared to render a final judgment. I can, however, speak with some confidence about the Koran as our primary historical source for the life of the Prophet and the origins of the Muslim community and Islamic faith and practice. I am confident that the contents, although not the final arrangement, of the Koran date from the time of Muhammad, and that the Koran is utterly reliable as a historical source, if it is properly interpreted. The Koran is an unusual historical source. It is a contemporary and authentic record that responds constantly to Muhammad's situation, and yet it contains no historical

[1] *Muhammad Prophet and Statesman* (Oxford, 1961), p. 229.
[2] Ibid., pp. 241 f.

narrative or description, and it does not have as its purpose the recording of history or biography. It is a literary work that took on a life of its own in oral and written form during Muhammad's lifetime, and, as Kenneth Cragg has stressed, it became a historical event itself, interacting with and influencing the life of Muhammad and the rise of the Muslim community.[3]

I have dared to ask of the Koran the question: What was Muhammad's understanding of himself? And I have not been disappointed. If the Koran contained only a few verses relevant to this question, then it might be difficult to reach firm conclusions. But this is not the case. In fact, there are several hundred verses that speak to the question I have posed. Furthermore, when I began collecting these verses, it immediately became clear that the answers they give are radically different from some of the views presented by the Sira and Hadith literature, which seems to answer a different question, that question being: What was the early Muslim community's understanding of Muhammad? This difference of perspective posed a problem in terms of the method and scope of the present study, since it is usually assumed that the Koran by itself is of little use as a historical source, that is, without the framework and details provided by the Sira and other early Islamic historical writings. Still, since the Koran provided so much material in response to the question posed, I have limited this study to the Koranic data, thus leaving the second stage of the inquiry for another occasion.

One other issue must be addressed in these opening remarks: How can the Koran, which presents itself as the speech of God, be taken as a source for the views of Muhammad? Quite simply, I think. Regardless of what view may be taken as to the authorship of the Koran, that is, whether God or Muhammad is regarded as its author, all would agree that as the Prophet and recipient of the revelation Muhammad must have known what the Koran says and must have agreed with the views it espouses. In other words, even if the traditional Islamic view of revelation is accepted, that is, that God is the author and speaker of the Koran, still it must be admitted that the revelation also reflects the views of the Prophet through whom it was imparted to man. And for the same reason, any development of ideas in the Koran can be taken as reflecting at least roughly the stages in Muhammad's own progression of ideas. The task of reconstructing this development is complicated by the fact that the Koran is not in any chronological order, and critical studies have shown that most of the suras contain material from various dates, making it impossible to date most passages precisely or to arrange the suras as wholes in chronological order. Still, it is possible to reconstruct the sequence of the main stages, and sometimes the approximate dates, in the development of the Koran's major themes and teachings.[4]

[3] *The Event of the Qur'ān* (London, 1971).

[4] All statements on dating in this article are my own conclusions. They do not always agree with the traditional dating systems, but usually support the conclusions reached by Richard

In passages quoted from the Koran the translation of A. J. Arberry[5] has been used unless otherwise indicated. The second person singular forms thou, thee, and thy have been retained to show that these passages are addressed specifically to Muhammad. Taking this characteristic of the dramatic form of the Koran into consideration is essential for any precise understanding of its meaning and message. A survey of the dramatic form of the entire Koran shows that in most cases the use of the second person singular indicates that Muhammad is being addressed. Where this is not the case the meaning is usually clear, for instance, in some rhetorical questions such as *wa-mā adrā-ka mā* ______ ?, "And what has let thee know what ______ is?" (86.2, 97.2, 101.3/2, 104.5), and in about thirty questions beginning with *a-lam tara*, "Hast thou not seen," which could also be translated "Has one not seen."[6] The second person singular, *tarā*, "thou seest," is in most contexts probably also best translated in the indefinite sense, "one sees."[7] In all of the passages quoted in this article it is the view of the author that the second person singular refers to Muhammad.

Muhammad's Personal Experience

A large number of passages reveal something of Muhammad's understanding of himself in terms of his personal experience and human limitations, especially regarding times of trial and persecution in Mecca and times of triumph in Medina. In most cases the exact dates and even chronological order of the passages cannot be known with any degree of certainty.

MUHAMMAD IS COMFORTED IN TIMES OF PERSECUTION

93.1 By the white forenoon
2 and the brooding night!
3 Thy Lord has not forsaken thee nor hates thee

Bell in his *The Qur'ān, Translated, with a critical re-arrangement of the Surahs* (2 vols.; Edinburgh, 1937, 1939), where tentative dates are given for individual pericopes rather than for entire suras. On the problems regarding the chronology of the Koran, see A. T. Welch, "al-Ḳur'ān," *Encyclopaedia of Islam*, 2d ed., V (1981), 414-419.

[5] *The Koran Interpreted* (London and New York, 1955).

[6] See, e.g., Bell's translations of 3.23/2, 4.44/7, 51/4, 14.19/22, 22.18, 63/2, 65/4, 24.41, 43, 31.29/8, 31/0, and 35.27/5. Throughout this article verse numbers are given according to the Egyptian standard edition first, and then after a virgule the number according to Flügel's system, where they differ. Identical digits are not repeated except for 10 to 19. This method should cause no confusion since the difference between the two numbering systems is never more than seven verses.

[7] See again Bell's translations of 5.52/7, 62/7, 80/3, 83/6, 8.50/2, 14.49/50, 16.14, 18.17/16, 49/7, 20.107/6, 22.5, 24.43, 27.88/90, etc.

93.4 and the last shall be better for thee than the first.[8]
5 Thy Lord shall give thee, and thou shalt be satisfied.
6 Did He not find thee an orphan, and shelter thee?
7 Did He not find thee erring (*ḍāllan*), and guide thee?
8 Did He not find thee needy, and suffice thee?
9 As for the orphan, do not oppress him,
10 and as for the beggar, scold him not,
11 and as for thy Lord's blessing, declare it.

With the possible exception of the last three verses, which are out of rhyme, this sura is probably a unity dating from fairly early in Muhammad's Meccan ministry, although at some point after opposition and persecution arose. This sura reflects among other things Muhammad's human limitations and his complete dependence upon God. Verse 4 may mean that the latter part of his life would bring better times than the present. The term *ḍāllan* has the root meaning "to go astray" and is the same term that occurs in the plural at the end of Sura 1 where Muslims are to pray "Guide us on the straight path, . . . not (the path) of those who go astray (*aḍ-ḍāllīn*)." The last three verses seem to indicate Muhammad's need for admonition.[9]

94.1 Did We not expand thy breast for thee
2 and lift from thee thy burden (*wizra-ka*),
3 the burden that weighed down thy back?
4 Did We not exalt thy fame?
5 So truly with hardship comes ease.
6 truly with hardship comes ease,
7 So when thou art empty, labour,
8 and let thy Lord be thy quest.

When the interpretation of this sura came to be combined with the legend of the opening of Muhammad's breast, sometime after aṭ-Ṭabarī (d. 310/923),[10] the term *wizra-ka* in verse 2 came to be interpreted as "thy sin" and was identified with polytheism.[11] This interpretation was, of course, later rejected by the majority of religious authorities after the rise of the doctrine of the sinlessness (*'iṣma*) of the Prophet. Birkeland has shown, however, that the oldest known interpretation of 94.1-3, most likely indicating the meaning this passage had for Muhammad and his Companions, was that the burden lifted from the Prophet was that of poverty and worldly distress, no doubt as a result of his marriage to

[8] Arberry has "Last" and "First," suggesting an eschatological interpretation.
[9] On this sura see Harris Birkeland, *The Lord Guideth* (Oslo, 1956), pp. 13-37.
[10] See Harris Birkeland, *The Legend of the Opening of Muhammad's Breast* (Oslo, 1955), esp. pp. 40-47.
[11] See, e.g., Fakhr ad-Dīn ar-Rāzī, *Mafātīḥ al-ghayib al-mushtahir*, on this verse.

Khadīja.[12] This interpretation is also consistent with the Koranic usage of the term *wizra*.[13]

108.1 Surely We have given thee abundance (*al-kauthar*);
2 so pray unto thy Lord, and sacrifice (*wa-nḥar*).
3 Surely he who hates thee, he is the one cut off.

Although *al-kauthar* in verse 1 came to be interpreted by most Muslim commentators as the name of a river in Paradise, thus giving the verse an eschatological meaning, Birkeland has shown that the oldest interpretation of this expression gave it its simple, lexical meaning, "abundance," and took it to refer to the good things of this life (*al-khair al-kathīr* or *khair ad-dunyā*). Another problem of interpretation of this short but important sura about Muhammad involves the command to sacrifice in verse 2, *wa-nḥar*. The classical commentators are virtually unanimous in interpreting this command as referring to the actual sacrifice (*naḥr*) of animals as a religious ritual. This verse eventually came to be interpreted as referring to the Islamic ritual sacrifice that takes place annually during the Pilgrimage ceremonies in Minā on the 10th of Dhū l-Ḥijja. But the older interpretation, most likely the original one, is that this command referred to ritual sacrifice in general, probably involving a ceremony Muhammad performed regularly at the Ka'ba in Mecca before the Hijra.[14] The setting and general purpose of this sura are essentially the same as those of suras 93 and 94: Muhammad is comforted in times of persecution or disappointment by being reminded that his life is in God's hands and that he should be thankful for the abundance and good fortune God has already given him.

Many verses in the Koran bear witness to Professor Watt's statement about Muhammad: "He was given to sadness, and there were long periods of silence when he was deep in thought." A variety of accusations were made against Muhammad by his opponents, and these caused him much grief, especially during the Meccan years. For instance, he was accused of being a liar:

6.33 We know indeed that it grieves thee (*yaḥzunu-ka*) the things they say; yet it is not thee they cry lies to (*yukadhdhibūna-ka*), but the evildoers–it is the signs of God they deny.

And he was mocked in other ways:

21.36/7 When the unbelievers behold thee, they take thee only for mockery (*huzu'*), [saying:] "Ha, is this the one who makes mention of your gods?"

43.30/29 And when the truth came to them, they said, "This is sorcery, and in it we are unbelievers."

[12] *The Lord Guideth*, pp. 38-55.
[13] See 6.164, 17.15/16, 35.18/19, 39.7/9, and 53.38/9.
[14] See Birkeland, *The Lord Guideth*, pp. 56-99.

31/0 They say, "Why has this Koran not been sent down upon some man of importance in the two cities?"

Muhammad was comforted by being informed that he was not alone and that God would support him:

6.34 Messengers indeed were cried lies to before thee, yet they endured patiently that they were cried lies to and were hurt, until Our help came to them. . . .

15.10 We sent Messengers before thee among the factions of the ancients,
11 and not a single Messenger came to them but they mocked him.

25.31/3 Even so We have appointed to every Prophet an enemy among the sinners; but thy Lord suffices as a guide and as a helper.

After the Hijra it was mainly the continuing unbelief of Muhammad's opponents that hurt him deeply:

5.41/5 O Messenger, let them not grieve thee (*lā yaḥzun-ka*) that vie with one another in unbelief; such men as say with their mouths, "We believe," but their hearts believe not. . . .

So Muhammad was mocked and ridiculed by his opponents, and he seemed powerless to stop this harassment. The only comfort given to him was God's assurance that all prophets had been mocked the same way, and that God would support him against his enemies.[15]

MUHAMMAD IS URGED TO BE PATIENT

This theme occurs fairly frequently in the Koran in passages dating from fairly early Meccan times up until about the time of the battle of Badr in 624. These patience passages are important for understanding Muhammad's life and character during the difficult period prior to his spectacular military and diplomatic successes in Medina. A fairly early Meccan example:

74.1 O thou shrouded in thy mantle,
2 arise and warn!
3 Thy Lord magnify
4 Thy robes purify
5 and defilement flee!
6 Give not, thinking to gain greater
7 And be thou patient (*fa-ṣbir*) unto thy Lord.

These seven verses are sometimes said to have been the first or second revelation

[15] On the personal grief Muhammad suffered, see also 3.176/0, 4.113, 10.65/6, 16.127/8, 26.3/2, 31.23/2, and 33.48/7.

Muhammad received, but this can hardly be the case. The passage simply reflects one of those times when Muhammad had to be roused from a mood of discouragement. Verse 6 is probably better translated by Bell: "Bestow not favour to gain many" meaning "do not speak smooth things in order to gain adherents."[16] Verse 7 shows that Muhammad had already had time to become impatient, probably at his failure to win converts. A somewhat later context, probably dating from the last years before the Hijra, also stresses Muhammad's impatience and urges him not to falter:

30.60 So be thou patient (*fa-ṣbir*); surely God's promise is true; and let not those who have not sure faith make thee unsteady.[17]

In a number of passages this call to Muhammad to be patient is associated with his role as worship leader:

11.114/16 And perform the Salat at the two ends of the day and the near part of the night; surely the good deeds will drive away the evil deeds. . . .

115/17 And be thou patient (*wa-ṣbir*); God will not allow to waste the wage of the good-doers.

40.55/7 So be thou patient (*fa-ṣbir*); surely God's promise is true. And ask forgiveness for thy sin, and proclaim the praise of thy Lord at evening and at dawn.

This close connection between patience and worship (at dawn and in the evening) occurs in at least four others passages,[18] making this a significant theme of Meccan parts of the Koran. One striking point in all of these passages is that the imperative verbs are consistently in the second person singular. It was Muhammad himself who needed repeatedly to be called to patience, indicating that he often became impatient or that he remained impatient over an extended period of time. Another obvious point is that the call to patience is closely related to a call to continue to worship, suggesting that from time to time Muhammad was tempted to discontinue the daily Salats. Throughout the Meccan period the Salat was performed twice daily, at dawn and at sunset, and a long vigil was kept during the night. Again the imperative verbs are consistently in the second person singular in these Meccan passages, suggesting that only the Prophet was commanded to perform this ritual.[19] Whether it was a private or public ritual at this time is not certain from these contexts. Other Meccan passages and other evidence give the

[16] *Qur'ān*, p. 617.

[17] See also 16.125/6-127/8, which may be early Medinan.

[18] See 20.130, 50.39/8, 52.48 f., and 76.24-6.

[19] The imperative verbs change to the plural at about the time of the battle of Badr when the daily Salats became obligatory for all Muslims. On the Koranic evidence regarding the origin and early development of the Salat, see W. M. Watt and A. T. Welch, *Der Islam I: Mohammed und die Frühzeit–Islamisches Recht–Religiöses Leben* (Stuttgart, 1980), pp. 264-271.

impression that Muhammad performed the ritual publicly, while his followers participated mainly by their presence, listening in silence and possibly reciting set formulas such as the *takbīr*, the *taḥmīd*, and the *tasbīḥ* at various points. In any case, these passages show that one of Muhammad's primary roles within the community during the Meccan period was as worship leader, and that he continued to perform the Salat in spite of persecution and the temptation to discontinue it.[20]

MUHAMMAD'S HUMANITY

A theme of later Meccan and Medinan parts of the Koran that seems to have arisen out of accusations made against Muhammad by his opponents stresses the humanity and mortality of Muhammad and God's other messengers. The following passages can be taken as accurately reflecting the challenges made to Muhammad and the accusations made against him by his opponents:

17.90/2 They say, "We will not believe thee till thou makest a spring to gush forth from the earth,
91/3 or till thou possessest a garden of palms and vines . . .
92/4 or till thou makest heaven to fall . . .
93/5 or till thou possessest a house of gold ornament, or till thou goest up to heaven; and we will not believe thy going up till thou bringest down on us a book that we may read." Say: "Glory be to my Lord! Am I aught but a human being (*bashar*), a Messenger (*rasūl*)?"

25.7/8 They also say, "What ails this Messenger that he eats food and goes about in the markets? Why has an angel not been sent down to him to be a warner with him?
8/9 or why is a treasure not thrown down to him, or why has he not a garden to eat of?" The evildoers say, "You are only following a man bewitched!"

The same charge is made against former prophets. The unbelievers among Noah's people say:

23.24 "This is naught but a human being (*bashar*) like ourselves, who desires to gain superiority over you. And if God willed, He would have sent down angels. We never heard of this among our fathers, the ancients.
25 He is naught but a man bedevilled; so wait on him for a time."[21]

The Koran's response to this charge is, Yes, prophets are only human beings:

[20] On *ṣabr* in the Koran, see Cragg, *The Event*, pp. 157-160.

[21] Similar statements are recorded regarding Ṣāliḥ in 26.154, Shu'aib in 26.186, and prophets in general in 64.6.

14.11/13 Their Messengers said to them, "We are only human (*bashar*) like you; but God is gracious unto whomever He will of His servants. It is not for us to bring you an authority save by the leave of God; and in God let the believers put all their trust."

And Muhammad is told in identical terms in 18.110 and 41.6/5:

Say: "I am only a human being (*bashar*) like you; it is revealed to me that your God is One God. . . ."

One important aspect of Muhammad's humanity or human nature was his need to ask forgiveness for his sins:

47.19/21 Know thou that there is no god but God, and ask forgiveness for thy sin (*wa-staghfir li-dhanbi-ka*),[22] and for the believers, men and women. God knows your going to and from and your lodging.

48.1 Surely We have given thee a manifest victory,
2 that God may forgive thee (*li-yaghfira la-ka*) thy former and thy latter sins (*mā taqaddama min dhanbi-ka wa-mā ta'akhkhara*), and complete His blessing upon thee, and guide thee on a straight path,
3 and that God may help thee with mighty help.

Again Muhammad is comforted by being told that earlier prophets were in the same situation regarding their need to ask forgiveness for sins:

3.146/0 Many a prophet there has been, with whom thousands manifold have fought, and they fainted not for what smote them in God's way, neither weakened, nor did they humble themselves. . . .
147/1 Nothing else did they say but, "Lord, forgive us our sins (*ighfir la-nā dhunūba-nā*), and that we exceeded in our affair, and make firm our feet, and help us against the people of the unbelievers."

The doctrine of the sinlessness of Muhammad and other prophets, which became part of later Islamic belief, has no foundation in the Koran, where the sins (*dhunūb*) of Muhammad and former prophets and their need to ask forgiveness (*ghafr*) are openly and repeatedly acknowledged.[23]

The ultimate test of Muhammad's human nature was his mortality, the certainty that he would die, a theme that also came to be treated in the wider context of the human nature of prophets in general:

3.144/38 Muhammad is naught but a Messenger; Messengers have passed away

[22] See also 40.55/7, quoted above, where the same statement occurs in reference to Muhammad.

[23] Muhammad's need to ask forgiveness for his sins is also acknowledged in the canonical Hadith collections; for references, see A. J. Wensinck, *A Handbook of Early Muhammadan Tradition* (Leiden, 1927), pp. 162 and 165.

before him. Why, if he should die or be slain, will you turn about on your heels? . . .

39.30/1 Thou art mortal (*mayyit*), and they are mortal (*mayyitūn*);
31/2 then on the Day of Resurrection before your Lord you shall dispute.[24]

At the same time that the Koran stressed Muhammad's human nature and mortality, it also attempted to bring down to the level of mortal man certain earlier prophets who had been exalted too high by their followers:

5.75/9 The Messiah, son of Mary, was only a Messenger; Messengers have passed away before him; his mother was a just woman; they both ate food. . . .[25]

These passages provide a strong sense of Muhammad's understanding of himself as having all of the limitations of human nature, and being supported in this with references to former prophets who had the same limitations.

One other aspect of Muhammad's human nature needs to be mentioned: his family life and his attraction for the good things of this life, including women, wealth, and children. It is typical of the complete candor of the Koran that it alludes to Muhammad's attraction for women, as for instance in:

33.50/49 O Prophet, We have made lawful for thee thy wives to whom thou hast given their dowries, and what thy right hand owns [i.e., female slaves], spoils of war that God has given to thee. . . .
51 Thou mayest put off whom thou wilt of them and whom thou wilt thou mayest take to thee; and if thou seekest any thou hast set aside there is no fault in thee. . . .
52 Thereafter women are not lawful to thee, neither for thee to take other wives in exchange for them, though their beauty (*ḥusnu-hunna*) please thee (*a'jaba-ka*), except what thy right hand owns.

The Koran refers several times, especially in suras 33 and 66, to Muhammad's wives and problems he had with them. Here we see the Prophet deeply involved in everyday family matters and enduring, not always patiently, troublesome disputes and intrigues not untypical of Oriental haram life through the centuries. Closely related to Muhammad's family life was his attraction for wealth and children, alluded to a number of times in the Koran and mentioned explicitly occasionally:

9.85/6 And let not their wealth (*amwāl*) and their children (*aulād*) please

[24] See also 21.34 f./35 f.

[25] This last statement distinguishes Mary and Jesus from angels, as for instance in the story of the angelic messengers who visited Abraham to announce the birth of his son and the destruction of the cities of Lot (11.69 ff./72 ff., 51.24 ff.).

thee (*tu'jib-ka*); God only desires thereby to chastise them in this present world. . . .[26]

The term *amwāl* also means simply "possessions," but here and in 34.35/4 the meaning is certainly "wealth." The term *aulād* could also be translated "sons," which would render a more poignant meaning for Muhammad since all of his sons died in infancy, but the more common meaning is simply "children." It is no doubt children at least, and possibly also wealth, that are alluded to in other passages on Muhammad's attraction for the good things of this life:

20.131 Stretch not thine eyes to what We have given pairs of them to enjoy, the flower of the present life, that We may try them therein; but thy Lord's provision (*rizq*) is better and more enduring.[27]

The well-known *kauthar* (abundance) verse, 108.1, discussed above, needs to be interpreted in the light of these *amwāl* and *rizq* contexts. The meaning must be that Muhammad went from a life of poverty to one of sufficiency, but that he still was tempted to look longingly at the wealth of others. These passages provide amazing insight into Muhammad's character and situation, as we see him accepting the admonition that God's "provision is better and more enduring."

Muhammad's Prophetic Experience

The Koran has much to say about various aspects of Muhammad's prophetic experience, including the process of revelation, its source and intermediary agents, Muhammad's visions and dreams, and even his human informants. Also relevant here are passages involving the limitations of his knowledge and power, and others that show significant changes that took place after divine/prophetic knowledge and power were given to him by God.

MUHAMMAD'S EXPERIENCE OF REVELATION

During the Meccan period of Muhammad's prophetic activity he frequently encountered accusations that his messages were "inspired by jinn" (*majnūn*) or were brought down by demons (*shayāṭīn*). These accusations also involved the charge that he was a poet (*shā'ir*), a soothsayer (*kāhin*), and a sorcerer (*sāḥir*). During the same period Muhammad's antagonists also demanded that angels (*malā'ika*) be sent down to confirm the truth of his message. The responses the Koran made to these accusations provide a running commentary on the development of the view of the Koran and Muhammad's own understanding of the process of revelation. Among the earliest passages on this topic are the following:

[26] See also 34.34/3-37/6.
[27] See also 15.88.

81.15 No! I swear by the slinkers,
16 the runners, the sinkers,
17 by the night swarming,
18 by the dawn sighing,
19 truly this is the speech of a noble Messenger (*rasūl karīm*)
20 having power with the Lord of the Throne secure,
21 obeyed, moreover trusty.
22 Your companion is not possessed (*majnūn*):
23 he truly saw Him/him on the clear horizon;[28]
24 he is not niggardly of the Unseen.
25 And it is not the speech of an accursed satan (*shaiṭān rajīm*).

69.38 No! I swear by what you see
39 and by what you do not see,
40 truly this is the speech of a noble Messenger (*rasūl karīm*).
41 It is not the speech of a poet (*shā'ir*) . . .
42 nor the speech of a soothsayer (*kāhin*). . . .
43 [It is] a sending down from the Lord of the worlds.
44 Had he [i.e., Muhammad] invented against Us any sayings,
45 We would have seized him by the right hand,
46 then We would surely have cut his life-vein
47 and not one of you could have defended him.

Note that 69.40 is a verbatim duplication of 81.19. In 69.40 it is clear that the expression *rasūl karīm*, which could also be translated "honorable messenger"[29] refers to Muhammad. Richard Bell has argued that in Sura 81 verse 19 originally referred to Muhammad, but then verses 20, 21, and 23 were added to make the expression *rasūl karīm* refer to an intermediary agent of revelation, later identified as Gabriel. Whether or not such a revision was made is difficult to determine, but the consistent use of *rasūl karīm* as an expression for a prophet in other parts of the Koran (referring to Muhammad in 69.40 and Moses in 44.17/16) supports the view that it referred at least originally to a prophet, Muhammad, in 81.19. The expression *shaiṭān rajīm* in 81.25 can also be translated "stoned satan" or "pelted demon,"[30] and is most likely an allusion to the Koranic versions of the ancient Near Eastern shooting-star myth, in which jinn and demons attempt to overhear what is being said in heaven but are pelted with flaming missiles.[31] The purpose of the Koranic versions of this myth is to deny the charge that Muhammad was receiving messages from heaven delivered by jinn and demons.

[28] Arberry has "he truly saw him," interpreting this verse as referring to Gabriel, but the reference may be to God. See the discussion of Muhammad's visions below.

[29] See Bell, *Qur'ān*, p. 602.

[30] Ibid., p. 639.

[31] See 15.16-18, 26.210-12, 37.6-10, 67.5, and 72.8 f.

Assurance to Muhammad and his opponents that he was not *majnūn* was given several times, for instance:

52.29 Therefore remind! By thy Lord's blessing thou art not a soothsayer (*kāhin*), neither possessed (*majnūn*).

39 Or do they say, "He is a poet for whom we await Fate's uncertainty"?[32]

The *majnūn* contexts give the impression that this term means "jinn-possessed" or "inspired by jinn" in the Koran. This concept is no doubt based on the ancient Arabian belief that poets were inspired by their individual jinn,[33] similar to the European idea of Muses who inspire poets and musicians. The Koran sometimes gives the impression that Muhammad needed to be assured that he was not jinn-possessed at times.[34] It is striking that the only response the Koran gives to these accusations that Muhammad was inspired by jinn or demons consists of simple denials of the charge and affirmations that the revelation came from God. There are no references to any intermediary agents of revelation. What appears to be the earliest such reference in the Koran occurs toward the end of Sura 26:

26.192 Truly it is the revelation (*tanzīl*) of the Lord of the worlds.[35]
193 With it came down the faithful spirit (*ar-rūḥ al-amīn*)
194 upon thy heart, that thou mayest be one of the warners,
195 in a clear, Arabic tongue.
196 Truly it is in the scriptures (*zubur*) of the ancients.

Verse 193 contains the only Koranic occurrence of the expression *ar-rūḥ al-amīn*, and the immediate context provides no indication of its identity. The term *al-amīn* seems to be simply an adjective meaning that the spirit was "faithful" in delivering the messages of God, so that what Muhammad recited was to be accepted as the truth from God. This spirit (*rūḥ*) is referred to again in:

17.85/7 They ask thee about the *rūḥ*. Say: "The *rūḥ* is of the bidding of my Lord (*min amri rabbī*). . . ."

This vague explanation was apparently accepted for a time as a sufficient answer to questions about the *rūḥ*. Similar expressions occur in other contexts involving the process of revelation: *ar-rūḥ min amri-hi* in 40.15 and *rūḥan min amri-nā* in 42.52.

[32] See also 15.6-9, 37.35/4-37/6, and 68.51 f.

[33] Cf. 37.36/5.

[34] On the relationship between the concept *majnūn* and the ancient Arabian poets and soothsayers, see Paul Eichler, *Die Dschinn, Teufel und Engel im Koran* (Leipzig, 1928), pp. 24-29.

[35] Here and throughout the Koran, Arberry translates *rabb al-'ālamīn* as "Lord of all Being" or "Lord of all beings"; see the final section below.

The context of this last expression contains a significant late Meccan or early Medinan statement on the process of revelation:

42.51/0 It is not fitting that God should speak to any human being (*bashar*) except by inspiration (*waḥy*)[36] or from behind a veil,

51 or by sending a messenger to inspire (*yūḥiya*) whatever He wills, by His leave; surely He is All-high, All-wise.

52 Thus We have inspired thee with a spirit of Our bidding (*rūḥan min amri-nā*). Thou knewest not what the Book was, nor belief; but We made it a light, whereby We guide whom We will of Our servants. . . .

This statement represents an intermediate stage in the development of the Koranic portrayal of the process of revelation. According to this passage there appear to be three methods: (1) God inspires a prophet by means of *waḥy*, that is, by "suggesting" or "giving rise to ideas," (2) God speaks to a prophet "from behind a veil" (*min warā'i ḥijāb*), apparently meaning that the prophet hears the voice but does not see its source, and (3) God sends a messenger (*rasūl*), that is, some heavenly being, to inspire (*yūḥiya*) whatever God wills. Note that terms from the same root, *w-ḥ-y*, are used regarding both the first and the third methods, indicating that the difference between the two is the agent of revelation. In the Koran *waḥy* and its cognates do not normally have their later technical, theological meaning.[37] It is not unreasonable to assume that Muhammad experienced at various times all three of these methods of revelation.

In one isolated verse, which appears to be early Medinan and later than the passage just quoted from Sura 42, the intermediary agent of revelation is called "the spirit of holiness" or possibly "the Holy Spirit" (*rūḥ al-qudus*):

16.102/4 Say: "The *rūḥ al-qudus* has sent it down (*nazzala-hu*) from thy Lord in truth to confirm those who believe, and to be a guidance and good tidings to those who surrender (*li-l-muslimīn*)."

Here *nazzala-hu* could be interpreted "brought it down," but "sent it down" seems to be the usual Koranic meaning of this term. The term *muslimīn* could be taken in the technical sense of "Muslims," but this is a later meaning that most likely was not known when this verse was first recited. Since *rūḥ al-qudus* in the Koran is usually associated with Jesus (2.87/1, 253/4, 5.110/09) it is reasonable to conclude that this expression was influenced by the Christian concept "Holy Spirit" (usually *ar-rūḥ al-qudus* in Christian Arabic usage, but sometimes *rūḥ al-qudus* as in the Koran), but for Muhammad its usage in 16.102/4 probably

[36] Arberry has "except by revelation" here, and "reveal" and "revealed" in the following two verses.

[37] On the Koranic usage of *waḥy* and its cognates, see W. M. Watt, *Bell's Introduction to the Qur'ān* (Edinburgh, 1970), pp. 20 f. This work is hereafter cited as Bell-Watt. On the use of *waḥy* as a technical term in the Sira and Hadith, see A. J. Wensinck, "Waḥy," *Shorter Encyclopaedia of Islam* (Leiden, 1965), pp. 622-624.

connoted little more than the terms *rūḥ* and *ar-rūḥ al-mīn* in the other revelation contexts cited above.[38]

What appears to be the final stage in the Koran's portrayal of Muhammad's experience of revelation is the designation of the intermediary agent as Gabriel:

2.97/1 Say: "Whoever is an enemy to Gabriel–he it was who sent it down (*nazzala-hu*)[39] upon thy heart by the leave of God, confirming what was before it, and for a guidance and good tidings to the believers."

The verbatim duplication of certain phrases suggests that this verse was based on 16.102/4. The earlier verse seems to have been adapted so that the expression *rūḥ al-qudus*–which may have led to confusion and misunderstanding if this had been the final Koranic statement on Muhammad's experience of revelation–was replaced by the name Gabriel. A careful reading of all of these contexts gives the strong impression that the identification of the intermediary agent of revelation as Gabriel was a new idea when it was mentioned in this early Medinan passage for the first (and only) time in the Koran. It is highly unlikely that Muhammad and his Companions identified the expressions *rūḥ min amr*, *rūḥ al-qudus*, and *ar-rūḥ al-amīn* in the earlier contexts with Gabriel until after the revelation of 2.97/1. The evidence of the Koran does not support the later Hadith accounts that place Gabriel at the very beginning of Muhammad's prophetic experience.[40] Thus, in attempting to comprehend the development of Muhammad's own understanding of his experience of revelation it is best to set aside these later accounts and the statements of the commentators identifying the *rūḥ* throughout the Koran with Gabriel.[41]

Additional insight into Muhammad's experience of revelation comes from an analysis of Koranic passages that mention or allude to his human informants. The earlier relevant contexts involve accusations made against Muhammad by his opponents:

25.4/5 The unbelievers say, "This is naught but a fraud (*ifk*) he has forged, and other folk have helped him at it." So they have committed wrong and falsehood.

[38]On *rūḥ al-qudus* in the Koran and in Christian usage, along with a survey of the views of the Muslim commentators, see T. O'Shaughnessy, *The Development of the Meaning of Spirit in the Koran* (Rome, 1953), pp. 42-51. For references to parallels in other Semitic languages, see Arthur Jeffery, *The Foreign Vocabulary of the Qur'ān* (Baroda, 1938), p. 232.

[39]Arberry, influenced by later Islamic belief, has "brought it down," but out of 26 occurrences of this term in the Koran this is the only time he translates it this way.

[40]For the references see Wensinck, *Handbook*, p. 163.

[41]See, e.g., aṭ-Ṭabarī, az-Zamakhsharī, ar-Rāzī, and al-Baiḍāwī on 16.102/4 and 17.85/7.

5/6 They say, "Fairy-tales of the ancients that he has written down (*iktataba-hā*);[42] they are recited to him morning and evening."

6/7 Say: "He sent it down, who knows the secret in the heavens and the earth; He is the All-forgiving, All-compassionate."

16.103/5 And We know very well that they say, "Only a human being (*bashar*) is teaching him." But the speech of him at whom they hint is barbarous, and this is clear, Arabic speech.

Except for the element of fraud the Koran does not deny what is reported from Muhammad's opponents in these passages. The Koranic response to the first accusation does not deny that stories were dictated to Muhammad "morning and evening," nor that he made copies of them (*iktataba-hā*). It merely asserts that whatever Muhammad recited as revelation was inspired by God. Similarly, the Koranic response to the second accusation does not deny that Muhammad had human informants. In fact, the Koran seems to acknowledge the truth of this charge by mentioning that one such person was a foreigner, while at the same time insisting that the actual wording of the Koran, since it is "clear, Arabic speech," did not come from this informant. Several Medinan passages give the impression that Muhammad actively sought information from the scriptures of the Jews, since they are condemned for concealing their Book from him. Some mention written copies that certain Jews showed to Muhammad or his followers (e.g., 6.91), while others accuse the Jews of writing out passages of their own and then claiming that they were from their scriptures (e.g., 2.79/3; see also 2.77/2, 140/34, 174/69, 3.71/64, and 5.15/18). In these passages it is not difficult to see Muhammad receiving stories and other information from various informants and then in moments of inspiration (*waḥy*) reworking the material into its Koranic form.

MUHAMMAD'S VISIONS AND DREAMS

Related to Muhammad's experience of revelation and significant for understanding his relationship to God are several visions and dreams that are described or alluded to in the Koran. Best known among these are the two visions described at the beginning of the Sura of the Star:

53.1 By the star when it plunges,
2 your comrade is not astray, neither errs,
3 nor speaks he out of caprice.
4 This is naught but a revelation revealed,
5 taught him by one terrible in power,

[42] Arberry, influenced by later Islamic belief, has "he has had written down."

6 very strong; He/he stood poised,[43]
7 being on the higher horizon,
8 then drew near and suspended hung,
9 two bows-length away, or nearer,
10 then revealed to His servant what He revealed,
11 His heart lies not of what he saw (*mā ra'ā*);
12 what, will you dispute with him what he sees (*mā yarā*)? [44]

13 Indeed, he saw Him/him (*ra'ā-hu*) another time
14 by the Lote-Tree of the Boundary
15 nigh which is the Garden of Refuge,
16 when there covered the Lote-Tree that which covered;
17 his eye swerved not, nor swept astray.
18 Indeed, he saw (*ra'ā*) one of the greatest signs of his Lord.

The interpretation of these visions has been much discussed, both in the classical commentaries and in modern literature. The first is usually interpreted by the Muslim commentators as a vision of Gabriel,[45] but it is highly unlikely that it was so taken when first recited. The idea of an intermediary agent of revelation had not yet been introduced into the Koran, and other passages dating from the earlier Meccan years state that Muhammad received the revelation from God (73.5, 87.6, and elsewhere; see also 15.9, a clear, but somewhat later, verse). The fact that verse 10 clearly refers to God provides additional support for the view that at least in the beginning Muhammad understood this first account as reporting a vision of God. The "Lote-Tree of the Boundary" and the "Garden of Refuge" were most likely well-known landmarks in the vicinity of Mecca, but the commentators gave this account a celestial setting, often relating it to the story of Muhammad's Night Journey and Ascension to heaven. Regardless of the setting of this vision, the pronominal suffix *hu* in verse 13 most likely was taken originally as referring to God.[46]

Important references to visions Muhammad had also occur in two other passages:

17.60/2 And when We said to thee, "Surely thy Lord encompasses men,"[47] and We made the vision (*ru'yā*) that We showed thee and the tree

[43] Here and in verse 13 Arberry has "he" and "him," following the traditional interpretation.

[44] Another brief reference to this vision occurs in 81.23, quoted above.

[45] See, e.g., al-Baiḍāwī and az-Zamakhsharī on this passage.

[46] See Richard Bell, "Muhammad's Visions," *Muslim World*, 24 (1934), 145-154; Rudi Paret, *Mohammad und der Koran* (Stuttgart, 1957), pp. 44-46; and Tor Andrae, *Mohammad the Man and His Faith* (New York, 1960), pp. 43-47.

[47] This statement does not occur elsewhere in the Koran, raising the interesting question

cursed in the Koran to be only a trial for men; and we frighten them, but it only increases them in great insolence.

48.27 God has indeed fulfilled the vision (*ru'yā*) He vouchsafed to His Messenger truly: "You shall enter the Holy Mosque, if God wills, in security, your heads shaven, your hair cut short, not fearing." He knew what you knew not, and appointed ere that a nigh victory.

Some commentators say the vision mentioned in 17.60/2 is one of the visions described at the beginning of Sura 53. Others relate it to 17.1 and Muhammad's Night Journey,[48] which from the beginning has been regarded by some Muslims as a vision. The reference to "the tree cursed in the Koran" is not very helpful for identifying the vision; this tree is probably the Zaqqūm mentioned in 37.62/0, 44.43, and 56.52. The vision mentioned in 48.27 is consistently regarded by the commentators as one Muhammad had inspiring him to undertake the journey toward Mecca that resulted in the Treaty of al-Ḥudaibiya.[49]

These "visions" should be compared with another type of experience Muhammad had that is called a "dream":

8.43/5 (Recall) when God showed thee them in thy dream (*manām*) as few; and had He shown them as many you would have lost heart and quarrelled about the matter, but God saved; He knows the thoughts in the breasts.

This verse occurs in the context of a long discussion about the battle of Badr, and the meaning of the verse is fairly clear. Just before the battle Muhammad must have had a dream in which he saw the Meccan forces as much fewer than they actually were, thus encouraging him to encounter them in battle. The fact that the Muslim forces of about 300 men defeated the much larger Meccan army was taken as a clear sign that God was on the side of the Muslims. One key point regarding this dream is that God showed Muhammad something that was not consistent with the facts. This does not mean, however, that a distinction should be made between prophetic visions and dreams on this basis, since elsewhere in the Koran the terms "vision" (*ru'yā*) and "dream" (*manām*) are used interchangeably regarding a prophetic experience.[50]

We can thus conclude that Muhammad had visions and dreams through which he experienced God's guidance, but that these experiences were distinct from the process of revelation, which resulted in the Koran. Muhammad seems to have

---

of the relationship between the Koran and other divine and prophetic sayings. On this see William A. Graham, *Divine Word and Prophetic Word in Early Islam* (The Hague, 1977).

[48] See, e.g., al-Baiḍāwī on 17.60/2.

[49] See Watt, *Muhammad Prophet and Statesman*, pp. 182 f.

[50] I.e., in 37.102/1-106, regarding Abraham's dream (v. 102/1) or vision (v. 105) in which he saw himself sacrificing his son; this also, of course, did not take place. See also 12.5 and 12.100/1 on Joseph's vision (*ru'yā*).

believed at first that the earlier experiences described in Sura 53 were visions of God, in the same way that he believed at first that the revelation of the Koran came directly from God. Later, as God came to be portrayed in more exalted terms, and as the concept of intermediary agents of revelation was introduced into the Koran and developed there, Muhammad may have come to believe that the Sura 53 visions were of Gabriel rather than God. This conclusion is supported by the fact that the brief reference to one of these visions in 81.23 (see above) seems to identify the object of the vision as the intermediary agent of revelation. Regarding the later (i.e., Medinan) experiences, there seems to be no essential difference between the "vision" reported in 48.27 and the "dream" reported in 8.43/5. In any case, the function of the later visions and dreams is clear: Muhammad saw himself as having received instructions and guidance from God through experiences that were distinct from the process of revelation.[51]

MUHAMMAD'S KNOWLEDGE

Important for understanding Muhammad's prophetic experience are a number of Koranic passages that stress limitations of certain aspects of his knowledge, and others that mention prophetic knowledge being given to him. Belonging to the first category are the following examples:

6.50 Say: "I do not say to you, 'I possess the treasuries of God'; I know not the Unseen (*al-ghaib*). And I say not to you, 'I am an angel'; I only follow what is revealed (*mā yūḥā*) to me."

7.187/6 They question thee concerning the Hour. . . . Say: "The knowledge of it (*'ilmu-hā*) is only with my Lord; none shall reveal it (*yujallī-hā*) at its proper time but He. . . . "

These passages, and several others cited below, involve demands from Muhammad's opponents that he prove his prophethood by displaying some type of supernatural knowledge. The Koran responded at first simply by affirming that Muhammad knew only what God had revealed to him, and that up to that time God had not given to him knowledge of *al-ghaib* (see also 7.188 and 72.26). This term occurs frequently in the Koran, usually meaning simply "the invisible" or "that which is hidden (from human sight or knowledge)," for instance whether an unborn child in the womb of the mother is male or female (13.8 f./9 f.). Such knowledge, that is, supernatural knowledge, was reserved only for God, who knew everything, the visible (*ash-shahāda*) and the invisible (*al-ghaib*).[52]

[51] These visionary experiences of Muhammad should be compared with the phenomenon of the *ḥadīth qudsī*, treated in the valuable study by William A. Graham cited above in note 47. See especially his thought-provoking analysis of "Revelation in Early Islam," pp. 9-39.

[52] See, e.g., 6.73, 13.9/10, 23.92/4, 32.6/5, and 39.46/7.

Specifically Muhammad was said to have been given no knowledge of future events, either eschatological or temporal: he did not know when the end of time, "the Hour," would come (see 33.63, 43.85, and 79.42-5), nor whether the threatened punishment of the Meccans was near (72.25/6-27). Also, he had no knowledge of events that took place in "the High Council [i.e., the heavenly council of angels] when they disputed" (38.69), referring probably to the story of the angels being consulted by God just before the creation of Adam (see 2.30/28-33/1).[53] It is significant that neither in these passages nor elsewhere in the Koran is the claim ever made that Muhammad had knowledge of future events.

Muhammad's claim to prophethood lay in another type of knowledge, the stories and other information contained in the Koran regarding the past. In the introduction and conclusion to the Joseph story in Sura 12 Muhammad is told:

12.3 We will relate to thee the fairest of stories in that We reveal (*auḥainā*) to thee this Koran, though before it thou wast one of the heedless (*al-ghāfilīn*).

12.102/3 That is [one] of the tidings of the Unseen (*al-ghaib*) that We reveal (*nūḥī-hi*) to thee; thou wast not with them when they agreed upon their plan, devising. . . .

And at the conclusion of the Noah story in Sura 11 Muhammad is told:

11.49/51 That is of the tidings of the Unseen (*al-ghaib*) that We reveal (*nūḥī-hā*) to thee; before this neither thou nor thy people knew them. . . .[54]

These verses seem on the surface to say that Muhammad's knowledge of the stories of earlier prophets came only through revelation from God, thus denying any role to human informants. But a closer analysis shows that this is not necessarily the meaning of these passages. The verb *auḥā* seems to mean "inspire" or "suggest" in the Koran, rather than "reveal" in a later, theological sense,[55] and could in these three verses refer to the process of achieving the final literary product. The term *al-ghāfilīn* in 12.3 could indeed be rendered "those who were unaware," but Arberry's translation, "the heedless," reflects the usual meaning of this term, which may mean that Muhammad had heard the stories before but had paid no attention to them. Likewise, 12.102/3 says Muhammad was not

[53] It is perhaps significant that this disclaimer to knowledge about the High Council in 38.69 f. occurs just before an account of the Iblīs story, thus occupying the same position as the High Council story in the later Sura 2 account. Could this mean that Muhammad had heard of the High Council story or had been questioned about it prior to the time of the revelation of the Sura 38 Iblīs account, but did not yet have sufficient knowledge of the story to include it there?

[54] See also 3.44/39 regarding the story of Mary, and 11.100/2 regarding the stories of Hūd, Ṣāliḥ, Abraham, Lot, and Shu'aib.

[55] See Bell-Watt, pp. 20-22.

present when Joseph's brothers plotted against him, but does not deny the possibility that Muhammad had previously heard this story from some human informant. And 11.49/51 says only that Muhammad and his people, meaning the Quraish or possibly the pagan Arabs in general, had not known the stories before. This verse must be interpreted in light of 16.103/5, discussed above, which seems to acknowledge that one of Muhammad's informants was a foreigner.

The stories of former prophets took on a higher meaning in the Koran, and knowledge of them came to be equated with the truth (*al-ḥaqq*):

11.120/1 And all that We relate to thee of the tidings of the Messengers is that thereby We strength thy heart; in these there has come to thee the truth (*al-ḥaqq*) and an admonition, and a reminder to the believers.[56]

Having this prophetic knowledge carried with it a new responsibility that Muhammad was more than once warned not to shirk:

13.37 Even so We have sent it down as an Arabic judgment. And if thou followest their caprices after the knowledge (*al-'ilm*) has come to thee, thou shalt have no protector against God, and no defender.[57]

Thus we see again a progression of ideas, from the earlier Meccan contexts where, in response to his opponents, Muhammad is said to have no knowledge of the Unseen (*al-ghaib*), to the later Meccan and early Medinan contexts where he is said to have been given "the tidings of the Unseen" or "the knowledge" (*al-'ilm*). Again it should be stressed that Muhammad's claim to prophethood lay not in his ability to foretell the future, a common characteristic of prophets in other traditions, but in his knowledge of the past, the very information he is likely to have received from Jewish and Christian informants. It was because of this vulnerability and the question of the source of Muhammad's knowledge that later Muslims attempted to protect the Prophet and the process of revelation by arguing that he was illiterate, a claim that is not supported by the Koran.[58]

MUHAMMAD'S POWER AND RESPONSIBILITIES

Parallel to the Koranic treatment of Muhammad's growing knowledge is its treatment of his power and responsibilities, which at first are said to be limited in various ways, but later are portrayed as being greatly increased. The passages that stress the limitations of Muhammad's power and responsibilities are mainly late Meccan and early Medinan. In some passages it is clear that Muhammad strongly

[56] See also 2.119/13.
[57] See also 2.120/14.
[58] See Bell-Watt, pp. 33-36, and Welch, "Ḳur'ān," p. 403.

desired to guide the people to the truth, and even to coerce them to become believers, but he was told that he would not be given the power to do as he wished:

10.99 . . . Wouldst thou then constrain (*tukrihu*) the people until they are believers?

100 It is not for any soul to believe save by the leave of God. . . .

16.37/9 Though thou art ever so eager (*taḥriṣ*) to guide them, God guides not those whom He leads astray; they have no helpers.

28.56 Thou guidest not whom thou likest (*man aḥbabta*), but God guides whom He wills, and God knows very well those who are guided.[59]

These passages reflect an intermediate stage in Muhammad's prophetic career, between the time when some earthly punishment or destruction was threatened against the Meccans (apparently with the hope of a dramatic rescue of Muhammad and his followers like those of Noah, Lot, and the other prophets of the Koranic punishment-stories) and the period of Muhammad's impressive victories in the fields of battle and diplomacy.

During the same period, Muhammad was repeatedly challenged to perform some miracle, like those of Moses, to prove that he was sent by God. Most of the Koranic contexts on this issue seem to be early Medinan, and those who issued the challenges seem to have been Muhammad's Jewish opponents there. Some passages, however, such as 17.90/2-93/5 and 25.7/8, quoted above in the discussion of Muhammad's humanity, and 15.7 and 16.33 f./35 f., in which he is challenged to bring down angels, may be late Meccan. Typical of the early Medinan contexts are the following:

3.183/79 Those same men said, "God has made covenant with us that we believe not any Messenger until he brings to us a sacrifice devoured by fire [from heaven]."

183/0 Say: "Messengers have come to you before me bearing signs (*al-bayyināt*) and what you spoke of. Why then did you slay them, if you speak truly?"

28.48 Yet when the truth (*al-ḥaqq*) came to them from Ourselves, they said, "Why has he [i.e., Muhammad] not been given the like of what Moses was given?" But they, did they not disbelieve also in what Moses was given aforetime? . . .[60]

These passages and those mentioned just above report a number of occasions in which Muhammad's opponents challenged him to perform a variety of miracles as proofs (*bayyināt*) or signs (*āyāt*) of the truth of his message. The Koranic

[59] See also 43.40/39-42/1 and the two-verse passage that occurs verbatim in 27.80 f./82 f. and 30.52 f./51 f.

[60] See also 29.50 f./49 f.

responses to these challenges never say that Muhammad did not have the power to perform such miracles; they simply affirm that all such power is in the hands of God. The possibility was thus left open that this power might be granted to him at some point in the future. The Koran acknowledged that certain earlier prophets, particularly Moses and Jesus, did have the power to perform miracles (see, e.g., 3.45 ff./40 ff. and 7.103 ff./101 ff.). Thus Muhammad was under pressure to produce some clear sign of his own. Before the battle of Badr the only such sign the Koran cited was what is mentioned in 29.51/0: "What, is it not sufficient for them that We have sent down upon thee the Book (*al-kitāb*) that is recited to them?" The wider context of this verse (see verses 45/4-49/8) and other passages that refer to the revelation as the Book (*al-kitāb*) give the impression that Muhammad began to prepare a written scripture for the Muslim community.[61] At the same time, early Medinan parts of the Koran began to associate the task of bringing or producing a Book or scripture with the role of prophet or messenger of God.[62] Since the Book became in a sense Muhammad's verifying miracle, the particulars of its production remained somewhat mysterious, while the Koran continued to affirm that it was being "sent down" by God. Sometime after the battle of Badr the challenge that angels be sent down was answered in a way in the statement in 3.123/19-126/2 that three thousand angels reenforced the Muslims at that battle. But this, like the Book, was a response of a different sort from the challenge, since the angels who are said to have participated in the battle of Badr were invisible.[63] By this time, it should be noted, Muhammad no longer needed the type of verifying miracle his opponents demanded. There is no evidence in the Koran that Muhammad ever claimed to have the power to perform miracles like those of Moses.[64]

The Koran is explicit about limitations placed on Muhammad's responsibilities regarding those who rejected his message:

2.272/4 Thou art not responsible for guiding them (*hudā-hum*); but God guides whomever He will. . . .

6.107 . . . And We have not appointed thee a watcher (*ḥafīẓ*) over them, neither art thou their guardian (*wakīl*).

13.40 Whether We show thee a part of what We promise them, or We call

[61] See Bell-Watt, pp. 135-144, and Welch, "Ḳur'ān," pp. 403 f.

[62] See, e.g., 2.129/3, 151/46, 3.79/3, 164/58, 6.84-9, 29.27/6, and 57.26.

[63] See A. T. Welch, "Allah and Other Supernatural Beings," *Journal of the American Academy of Religion*, 47/Suppl. (December 1979), 747-749.

[64] Such powers probably came to be attributed to Muhammad soon after his death. For references in the Hadith, see Wensinck, *Handbook*, pp. 166-168. Ibn Sa'd has a long section on Muhammad's miracles in his *Kitāb aṭ-ṭabaqāt al-kabīr* (Leiden, 1905), I/i, 112-126; English translation by S. M. Haq (Karachi, 1967), pp. 195-219. Another English translation is given in Arthur Jeffery, *A Reader on Islam* (The Hague, 1962), pp. 309-330.

> thee to Us, it is thine only to deliver the message, and Ours is the reckoning.[65]

These repeated assurances to Muhammad that he was not responsible for those who rejected him give the impression that he felt a need to do more than just deliver the message. These late Meccan and early Medinan passages may also have been intended to comfort Muhammad in times of disappointment over his lack of success in winning converts.

Then the picture changes dramatically beginning about the time of the battle of Badr as Muhammad is portrayed more and more as one who has considerable power and authority. Two motifs that typify his new position are the requirements that the believers "obey God and His Messenger" and "believe in God and His Messenger," both of which occur frequently in post-Badr contexts. The change in Muhammad's position exemplified by these two motifs can be seen clearly in a survey of the development of Koranic creedal statements, which often include short lists of recommended, and later required, religious duties. Before Badr the Koran frequently made general statements such as "believe in God and the Last Day and do deeds of righteousness" (e.g., in 2.62/59). At about the time of the battle of Badr the lists of required beliefs and practices became more specific, and references to obeying Muhammad or believing in him were added:

4.136/5 O believers, believe (*āminū*) in God and His Messenger and the Book He has sent down on His Messenger and the Book He sent down before. Whoever disbelieves in God and His angels and His Books and His Messengers and the Last Day has surely gone astray far into error.

9.71/2 And the believers, the men and the women, are friends one of the other; they bid to honour, and forbid dishonour; they perform the prayer (*aṣ-ṣalāt*), and pay the alms (*az-zakāt*), and they obey (*yuṭī'ūna*) God and His Messenger. . . .[66]

Sometimes the "obey God and His Messenger" and "believe in God and His Messenger" motifs are accompanied with promises of Paradise and threats of the hellfire:

4.13/17 Whoever obeys (*yuṭi'i*) God and His Messenger, He will admit him to gardens in which rivers flow, therein dwelling forever. . . .

14/18 But whoever disobeys (*ya'ṣi*) God and His Messenger and transgresses His bounds, him He will admit to a Fire, therein dwelling forever.

48.13 Whoever believes not (*lam yu'min*) in God and His Messenger, We have prepared for the unbelievers a Blaze.[67]

[65] See also 4.80/2, 6.66, 104, 10.108, 17.54/6, 39.41/2, 42.6/4, 48/7, and 88.21f.

[66] See also 24.56/5, 49.15, 58.13/14, etc.

[67] Cf. 9.63/4 and 57.19/18-21.

At the height of Muhammad's position in Medina his power and authority are portrayed in the Koran in a variety of ways. Sometimes the believers are gently chided or counseled on matters of etiquette when in his presence:

33.53 O believers, enter not the houses of the Prophet, except leave is given you for a meal, without watching for its hour. But when you are invited, then enter; and when you have had the meal, disperse, neither lingering for idle talk; that is hurtful to (*kāna yu'dhī*) the Prophet, and he is ashamed (*yastaḥyī*) before you. . . .

49.2 O believers, raise not your voices above the Prophet's voice, and be not loud in your speech to him, as you are loud one to another, lest your works fail while you are not aware.

3 Surely those who lower their voices in the presence of God's Messenger, those are they whose hearts God has tested for godfearing; they shall have forgiveness and a mighty wage.[68]

In some verses there are ambiguous pronouns that could refer either to God or to Muhammad, for instance:

8.20 O believers, obey (*aṭī'ū*) God and His Messenger, and do not turn away from Him/him even as you are listening.

49.14 . . . If you obey God and His Messenger, He/he will not diminish you anything in [the reward for] your works. . . .

57.28 O believers, fear God and believe in His Messenger, and He/he will give you a twofold portion of His/his mercy, and He/he will appoint you a light whereby you shall walk, and forgive you. . . .[69]

In these passages the pronouns in question are usually taken by the commentators as referring to God, but it is likely that some of Muhammad's followers took some of them as referring to the Prophet. This ambiguity, characteristic of Koranic style in many places, provided a subtle, rhetorical device for elevating the position of Muhammad in the minds of his followers. Other passages present clear statements on Muhammad's position and authority:

4.80/2 Whoever obeys the Messenger thereby obeys God. . . .

33.36 It is not for any believer, man or woman, when God and His Messenger have decreed a matter, to have a choice in the affair. Whoever disobeys God and His Messenger has gone astray into manifest error.

48.10 Those who swear fealty to thee swear fealty in truth to God. . . .

The height of Muhammad's power is portrayed nowhere more clearly than in

[68] See also 8.20, quoted below, which may also refer to Muhammad.

[69] On Muhammad as a "light-giving lamp," see 33.46/5, quoted below.

several passages in which he was told to be harsh in his treatment of those who opposed him:

5.33/7 This is the recompense of those who fight against God and His Messenger and hasten about the earth to do corruption there: They shall be slaughtered (*yuqattalū*), or crucified (*yuṣallabū*), or their hands and feet on opposite sides (*min khilāfin*) shall be struck off (*tuqaṭṭaʿa*), or they shall be banished from the land. . . .

34/8 except for such as repent before you have power over them. . . .

And the following verse that occurs verbatim in 9.73/4 and 66.9:

> O Prophet, struggle with the unbelievers and hypocrites, and be thou harsh with them; their refuge is Gehenna, an evil homecoming!

Whether Muhammad took up the reins of power willingly or reluctantly has been much debated. In any case the Koran makes clear that his power and responsibilities changed dramatically after the battle of Badr, and there is no reason to dispute the Koranic evidence suggesting that he saw this change as being brought about by God, thus reenforcing his confidence in himself as God's Messenger to the Arabs.

Did Muhammad see himself as having the power to influence people's eternal destiny? Or to put the question in Islamic terms, did he see himself as having the power of intercession (*shafāʿa*), and, if so, were there any limits to this power? As is well known, Islamic tradition affirmed that the Prophet was given the power to intercede on the Day of Judgment. There is difference of opinion as to whether this power extends to nonbelievers. The majority view is that Muhammad's power of intercession applies only for the lesser sins of believers. Many Muslims find support for their belief in Muhammad's power of intercession on the Day of Judgment in several verses of the Koran:

4.64/7 . . . If, when they wronged themselves, they had come to thee and asked forgiveness of God, and the Messenger had asked forgiveness for them (*wa-staghfara la-hum*), they would have found that God turns, All-compassionate.

4.85/7 Whoever intercedes (*yashfaʿ*) with a good intercession (*shafāʿa*) shall receive a share of it; whoever intercedes with a bad intercession shall receive the like of it; God has power over everything.

20.109/8 Upon that day no intercession (*shafāʿa*) shall profit, save for him to whom the All-merciful gives leave, and whose speech He approves.[70]

47.19/21 Know thou therefore that there is no god but God, and ask forgiveness for thy sin (*wa-staghfir li-dhanbi-ka*), and for the believers, men and women. . . .

[70] See also 19.87/90.

Although these passages can be interpreted so as to support the Islamic doctrine of Muhammad's power of intercession, the "ask forgiveness" contexts seem to refer only to Muhammad's contemporary situation, and the *shafā'a* contexts (of which only two of twelve in the Koran have been quoted here) are so vague that no clear impression of Muhammad's understanding of intercession can be derived from them. A third group of passages, for example, 9.113/14 and 63.5 f., state that Muhammad's intercession on behalf of nonbelievers is of no avail. These are interpreted by some as implying that his intercession for believers will be efficacious. A survey of all of the relevant passages in the Koran shows that the Islamic doctrine of the Prophet's intercession is nowhere clearly stated. The Koran does, however, leave open the possibility that Muhammad will have the power to intercede on behalf of believers on the Day of Judgment, and he very well may have come to accept this belief toward the end of his life.

MUHAMMAD'S ROLES

Closely connected with the question of Muhammad's understanding of himself are the various terms used in the Koran to designate his roles or functions. Most common are the terms "warner," "messenger," and "prophet," but in addition to these well-known designations many others occur, providing a rich portrayal of Muhammad's roles within the Meccan and Medinan communities.

WARNER

The most frequent designation of Muhammad's role in Meccan parts of the Koran is "warner," usually *nadhīr* but sometimes *mundhir*. This role is mentioned also in Medinan contexts, usually along with others (see below). One of the most frequent usages of *nadhīr* is in the statement "I am/He is a clear warner (*nadhīr mubīn*)" (e.g., 7.184/3, 29.50/49, 38.70). Surprisingly the role of warner is very seldom associated with the numerous versions of the Koranic "punishment-stories," and it is seldom applied explicitly to anyone other than Muhammad (see 11.25/7 and 26.115, both involving Noah). The role of warner is sometimes associated with individual cities:

34.34/3 We sent no warner (*nadhīr*) into any city except its men who lived at ease said, "We disbelieve in the message you have been sent with."[71]

Sometimes it is associated with peoples and communities:

32.3/2 ... It is the truth from thy Lord that thou mayest warn a people (*qaum*) to whom no warner (*nadhīr*) came before thee, that perhaps they may be guided.[72]

[71] See also 25.51/3 and 43.23/2.
[72] See also 28.46.

35.24/2 Surely We have sent thee with the truth, a bearer of good tidings (*bashīr*) and a warner (*nadhīr*);[73] not a community (*umma*) is but there has passed away in it a warner (*nadhīr*).

38.4/3 Now they marvel that a warner (*mundhir*) has come to them from among them; and the unbelievers say, "This is a lying sorcerer."[74]

The term *qaum* in 32.3/2 and the subject "they" in 38.4/3 were probably taken originally as referring to Muhammad's tribe, the Quraish. Later, these terms came to be interpreted as referring to all Arabs.

Other important *nadhīr* contexts involving the question of Muhammad's prophetic function and his understanding of himself include:

46.9/8 Say: "I am not an innovation among the Messengers, and I know not what shall be done with me or with you. I only follow what is revealed (*yūḥā*) to me; I am only a clear warner (*nadhīr mubīn*)."

53.56/7 This [i.e., Muhammad] is a warner (*nadhīr*) of the warners of old.[75]

Although the relevant passages cannot be dated precisely, it seems fairly certain that the term "warner" does not occur in the earliest revelations or in the latest ones, but that this function was basic to the Koran's portrayal of Muhammad throughout most of his prophetic career, both in Mecca and in Medina. The object of Muhammad's warning is usually not specified or otherwise indicated by the contexts. From other passages it can be concluded that it included both temporal and eschatological punishment. Since some of the relevant Meccan passages seem to have been revised in Medina (probably omitting specific threats of some imminent natural catastrophe like those experienced by the people of Noah, Lot, and the others in the punishment-stories), we cannot reconstruct a clear picture of the Meccan development of Muhammad's message of warning.[76]

MESSENGER

By far the most common designation for Muhammad in Medinan parts of the Koran is *rasūl*, "messenger," usually in the expressions "God and His Messenger" (about eighty times) and "the Messenger" (about sixty times). The term *rasūl* occurs a number of times in Meccan contexts in reference to earlier messengers, for instance Noah in 7.61/59 and 26.107, Hūd in 7.67/5 and 26.125, Ṣāliḥ in 26.143 and 91.13, and Moses in 7.104/2, 26.16/15, and 43.46/5. In the verses cited from Sura 7 each messenger is called *rasūlun min rabbi l-'ālamīn*, "a

[73] A.berry has "good tidings to bear, and warning."

[74] Muhammad is called a *mundhir* also in 13.7/8 and 50.2.

[75] See also 34.28/7, discussed below on the universality of Muhammad's mission, and the verses cited below in which "warner" is one of several roles.

[76] See Bell-Watt, pp. 89 ff., 127 ff., and 158 f.

messenger from the Lord of the worlds," and in the last two verses cited above Moses is called *rasūlu rabbi l-'ālamīn*, "the messenger of the Lord of the worlds." Neither of these titles, the second of which could be used as a claim to a universal mission, is applied to Muhammad anywhere in the Koran. The most likely reason for this is that references to God as *rabb al-'ālamīn* are typically Meccan, while Muhammad is not commonly referred to as *rasūl* until after the Hijra. There are, in fact, few if any Meccan contexts that refer explicitly to Muhammad as *rasūl*. The frequently occurring expression "God and His Messenger" is exclusively Medinan, with the possible exception of one occurrence in 72.23/4.[77] The only other clear references to Muhammad as *rasūl* in contexts that might be Meccan occur in 25.7/8 (quoted above in the discussion of Muhammad's humanity), 25.30/2, 41/3, and 73.15.[78] A survey of all of the *rasūl* contexts gives the impression that it was at first simply the general Arabic term for "messenger" or "one sent by God" and was synonymous with *mursal*, which occurs about thirty-five times, usually in the plural, *mursalūn*. In Medinan contexts the term *rasūl*, usually definite, either in construct or with the definite article, took on something of a technical meaning as a title, usually for Muhammad.

PROPHET

Medinan parts of the Koran refer to Muhammad as *nabī*, "prophet," about thirty-five times, almost half of which occur in Sura 33. As applied to Muhammad this term usually occurs as a title with the definite article, *an-nabī*, "the Prophet." Thirteen times Muhammad is addressed "O Prophet . . ." (*yā'ayyuhā n-nabī*) (8.64/5, 65/6, 70/1, 9.73/4, and others, including six in Sura 33). There are no explicit references to Muhammad as *nabī* in Meccan parts of the Koran. Indirect references such as "We appointed for every prophet an enemy" (6.112 and 25.31/3) occur in four passages that are traditionally regarded as Meccan, but may be Medinan.[79] Did Muhammad see any distinction between his function as a *nabī* and his function as a *rasūl*? The relationship between these two terms has been much discussed, both in the Islamic theological treatises and in modern European literature on Islam.[80] Medieval Muslim theologians distinguished between the two terms, giving *nabī* a wider connotation than *rasūl*. They spoke of thousands and even hundreds of thousands of prophets, of whom only a small number were sent as messengers to specific communities. The Koranic evidence, however, does not

[77] This expression occurs also in 7.158, but this verse is certainly Medinan.

[78] Indirect references to Muhammad as *rasūl* occur in a few contexts that may be late Meccan: 13.38, 15.10 f., 17.93/5, 21.25, 40.78, and 81.19.

[79] See Bell, *Qur'ān*, on these two verses and also 7.94/2 and 43.6 f./5 f.

[80] For references see Arthur Jeffery, "The Qur'ān as Scripture," *Muslim World*, 40 (1950), 116, and W. A. Bijlefeld, "A Prophet and More Than a Prophet?" *Muslim World*, 59 (1969), 1.

support this or any other theory of a special distinction between the two terms in which they are said to represent different lists of men.[81] Their Koranic usages are not identical: *rasūl* occurs earlier and much more frequently and has a more general usage,[82] while *nabī* seems to be more closely associated with the Biblical characters of the Koran.[83] But later parts of the Koran show that the two terms became synonymous in their Koranic usage. This can be seen in Sura 33, where Muhammad is addressed or referred to fifteen times as *nabī* and fourteen times as *rasūl*. Note the consistent usage of these two terms in the following examples:

v.6	The Prophet is nearer to the believers than their selves
v.12	"God and His Messenger promised us only delusion"
v.13	Part of them were asking leave of the Prophet
v.21	You have had a good example in God's Messenger
v.22	This is what God and His Messenger promised us
	God and His Messenger have spoken truly
v.29	But if you desire God and His Messenger
v.30	Wives of the Prophet, whoever among you commits a flagrant indecency
v.31	But whoever of you is obedient to God and His Messenger
v.32	Wives of the Prophet, you are not as other women
v.33	Obey God and His Messenger
v.36	When God and His Messenger have decreed a matter
	Whoever disobeys God and His Messenger

Whenever the context connects God and Muhammad the term *rasūl* is used, either in construct (*rasūlū llāh*) or with a pronominal suffix (*Allāhu wa-rasūlu-hu*); whenever Muhammad is addressed or mentioned alone the term *nabī* is used with the definite article (*an-nabī*). This usage is not always followed in the Koran, but it became standard in the later passages. This also explains why the term *nabiyyīn* occurs in the list of required beliefs in 2.177/2, while *rusul* occurs in the parallel list in 4.136/5:

2.177/2 True piety is this: to believe in God, and the Last Day, the angels, the Book, and the Prophets (*an-nabiyyīn*), to give of one's substance, however cherished, . . .

4.136/5 . . . Whoever disbelieves in God and His angels and His Books and His Messengers (*wa-rusuli-hu*) and the Last Day has surely gone astray far into error.

[81] Cf. Jeffery, "The Qur'ān as Scripture," pp. 115 f.

[82] E.g., in reference to angels (6.61, 7.35/5, 10.21/2, 11.69/72, 77/9, 81/3, 19.19, and others) and a messenger of the king in the Joseph story (12.50); also it is applied specifically to the Arabian heroes, Hūd, Ṣāliḥ, and Shu'aib (26.125, 143, 178, 91.13, and others).

[83] For other differences in their Koranic usages see Bijlefeld, "A Prophet," pp. 16-22.

For Muhammad and his contemporaries the expressions "the prophets" and "His messengers" must have had the same meaning in these two passages.[84] Those who have argued that these terms designate two different lists of men, with distinct functions, are either reading later ideas into the Koran,[85] or placing too much emphasis on differences that happen to occur in the contexts of the two terms.[86] *Rasūl* is simply the general Arabic term for "a messenger," which is also used in the specific sense, "God's messenger," while *nabī* came into the Koran as a borrowed, technical term for "God's messenger"; their Koranic usages are similar in this respect to those of *ṣadaqa* and *zakāt*, which are also used synonymously. Thus there is no reason to assume that Muhammad distinguished between his identity and function as a *rasūl* and his identity and function as a *nabī*. He saw himself as continuing a long line of prophet-messengers that went back to Noah (see 33.7 and 42.13/11).

Did Muhammad see himself as greater than the other prophets? The Koranic verse that came to have this meaning for many later Muslims is:

33.40 Muhammad is not the father of any one of your men, but the Messenger of God, and the Seal of the Prophets (*khātam an-nabiyyīn*); God has knowledge of everything.

As is well known, the expression *khātam an-nabiyyīn* came to mean for many Muslims that Muhammad was "the last and greatest of the prophets." While this expression may have had some connotation of "last" in a line of prophets,[87] it is very unlikely that it meant "greatest" for Muhammad and his contemporaries. Some ranking of the prophets does seem to be implied in the special attention the Koran devotes to Abraham, Moses, and Jesus, and in statements such as "We have given some of the prophets preference over others" (17.55/7); but the Koran gives the impression that Muhammad only gradually came to see himself as equal to these great prophets of earlier generations, and it never suggests that he ever saw himself as superior in any way to the earlier prophets.

[84] Bijlefeld (ibid., p. 13) is thus not completely justified in his criticism of Jeffery, among others, for using the term "Prophets" instead of "Messengers" for this category of essential beliefs in his *Islam: Muhammad and His Religion* (New York, 1958), p. 130. Jeffery's use of "His Prophets" is not precisely correct according to Koranic usage; but see *anbiyā'a llāhi* in 2.91/85.

[85] E.g., A. J. Wensinck, *The Muslim Creed* (Leiden, 1932), pp. 203 f.

[86] E.g., Bijlefeld, "A Prophet," whose study is also flawed by his overzealous dependence on the European dating system of Gustav Weil and his followers, notably Nöldeke and Blachère. On this problem, see Welch, "Ḳur'ān," pp. 416-418.

[87] Even this connotation seems to be negated by 5.19/22: "People of the Book, now there has come to you Our Messenger . . . upon an interval between the messengers (*'alā fatratin mina r-rusul*)."

OTHERS

One of the most important functions Muhammad had as a prophet-messenger, that of "warning," has already been discussed. A number of others are mentioned, some repeatedly, in the Koran, mainly in Medinan passages. Some of the most important of these functions are seen in the following verses:

2.119/13 We have sent thee with the truth, a bearer of good tidings (*bashīr*)[88] and a warner (*nadhīr*). Thou shalt not be questioned touching the inhabitants of Hell.

2.151/46 We have sent among you of yourselves a Messenger, to recite (*yatlū*) Our signs to you and to purify you (*yuzakkī-kum*), and to teach you (*yu'allimu-kum*) the Book and the Wisdom, and to teach you what you knew not.[89]

5.48/52 And We have sent down to thee the Book with the truth, confirming the Book that was before it, and assuring it. So judge (*fa-ḥkum*) between them according to what God has sent down, and do not follow their caprices, to forsake the truth that has come to thee. . . .[90]

33.45/4 O Prophet, We have sent thee as a witness (*shāhid*),[91] a bearer of good tidings (*mubashshir*),[92] a warner (*nadhīr*),

46/5 one who invites (*dā'ī*)[93] unto God by His leave, and a light-giving lamp (*sirāj munīr*).[94]

So Muhammad was a bearer of good tidings, warner, reciter, purifier, teacher, judge, witness, inviter, and a light-giving lamp. In addition to these specific functions attributed to Muhammad in the Koran, there are many other descriptions that also reflect something of his understanding of himself, for instance:

9.128/9 Now there has come to you a Messenger from among yourselves; grievous to him is your suffering; anxious (*ḥarīṣ*) is he over you, gentle (*ra'ūf*) to the believers, compassionate (*raḥīm*).

Taking these Koranic verses on Muhammad's functions and character as their starting point, Muslims have formulated lists of Attributes of the Prophet, similar

[88] Muhammad is called a *bashīr* also in 5.19/22, 7.188, 11.2, 34.28/7, and 35.24/2. See also Bell, *Qur'ān*, p. 477, on 41.4/3.

[89] These same three functions are attributed to Muhammad also in 2.129/3, 3.164/58, and 62.2.

[90] The role of judge is attributed to Muhammad also in 4.105/6, 5.42/6, 49/54, and 24.48/7, 51/0.

[91] Muhammad is called a *shāhid* also in 48.8 and 73; he is called a *shahīd* in 2.143/37, 16.89/91, and 22.78.

[92] Muhammad is called a *mubashshir* also in 17.105/6, 25.56/8, and 48.8.

[93] See also 46.31 f./30 f.

[94] This is my own translation of these two verses, following Bell rather than Arberry.

to the lists of Ninety-nine Names of God. It is interesting that some of these Attributes occur in the Koran in reference to other prophets, but not to Muhammad, for example, "Faithful" (*amīn*), referring to Noah in 26.107, Hūd in 7.68/6 and 26.125, and Moses in 44.18/17; "Friend (of God)" (*khalīl*), referring to Abraham in 4.125/4; and "Chief" (*sayyid*), referring to John (the Baptist) in 3.39/4. It is also significant that many of the terms that later became Attributes of the Prophet are applied in the Koran only to God, for example, the two paris, "First" (*awwal*) and "Last" (*ākhir*), and "Outward" (*ẓāhir*) and "Inward" (*bāṭin*), listed together in 57.3. This elevation of Muhammad in later Muslim belief was part of the same process that seems to have affected the issue of the universality of his prophetic role.

The Universality of Muhammad's Mission

Opposing views have been expressed on the question: Did Muhammad feel summoned as a prophet to his people or as a prophet to the world? The Koran has much to say on this complex issue and appears to express a variety of views. The best way to derive a consistent picture from the Koranic data is to attempt to reconstruct the main lines of development of this issue by determining the approximate chronological order of the main statements. In the earlier passages it is clear that Muhammad's message was addressed to his own city and tribe:

26.214 And warn thy clan (*'ashīrata-ka*), thy nearest kin (*al-aqrabīn*).

27.91/3 I have only been commanded to serve the Lord of this territory which He has made sacred; to Him belongs everything.

106.1 For the composing of Quraish
2 their composing for the winter and summer caravan!
3 So let them serve the Lord of this House
4/3 who has fed them against hunger
4 and secured them from fear.

Then the concept of "an Arabic recitation (*qur'ān*)" was introduced in contexts that suggest that Muhammad's message was an Arabic version of what was in the earlier scriptures. A key theme is that Muhammad was sent to a people to whom no warner came before. Some passages give the impression that Muhammad's message was for all Arabs, while others continue to stipulate geographical limitations:

20.113/12 Even so We have sent it down as an Arabic Koran . . . that perhaps they [i.e., the Arabs] may be godfearing, or it may arouse in them remembrance.

26.194 . . . that thou mayest be one of the warners,
195 in a clear, Arabic tongue.

196 Truly it is in the scriptures of the ancients.[95]

32.3/2 . . . It is the truth from thy Lord that thou mayest warn a people (*qaum*) to whom no warner came before thee, that perhaps they may be guided.

42.7/5 And so We have revealed to thee an Arabic Koran, that thou mayest warn the Mother of Cities and those who dwell about it. . . .

Similar concepts, placing the theme within a broader context, occur a number of times in the Koran. Each nation or community is sent its own messenger who delivers the message in the language of his people:

10.47/8 Each community (*umma*) has its Messenger; then, when their Messenger comes, justly the issue is decided between them, and they are not wronged.

14.4 And We have sent no Messenger except with the tongue of his people (*qaum*), that he might make all clear to them. . . .

28.59 Yet thy Lord never destroyed the cities until He sent in their mother-city [i.e., their capital or main city] a Messenger, to recite Our signs to them. . . .[96]

In these Meccan passages the situation is fairly clear: Muhammad saw himself as God's Messenger to the Arabs, bringing a message that had not been delivered to them before, a message in their own language that was the same as that delivered by earlier messengers in their languages.

Early Medinan parts of the Koran give a somewhat different picture. A number of passages, usually addressed to the "People of the Book," give the impression that Muhammad's mission was extended to include the Jewish people living in Medina and some Christians as well:

5.15/18 People of the Book, now there has come to you Our Messenger, making clear to you many things you have been concealing of the Book. . . .

5.19/22 People of the Book, now there has come to you Our Messenger, making clear to you, upon an interval between the Messengers lest you should say, "There has not come to us any bearer of good tidings (*bashīr*) nor any warner (*nadhīr*)." Indeed there has come to you a bearer of good tidings and a warner. . . .

It must be remembered, however, that the Jewish tribes and possibly individual Christians to whom these verses were addressed were Arabs. Some passages refer to some of the Jews and Christians as believers or righteous ones, but still

[95] Cf. 87.18 f., which mentions the "ancient scrolls" of Abraham and Moses.

[96] See also 4.41/5, 16.36/8, 38.4/3, and 50.2.

distinguish them from the Muslims (see 2.62/59, 3.113 f./109 f., 5.66/70 and 69/73). These verses date from the first year or two in Medina when Muhammad was appealing to the Jews and Christians to accept him and the Koran as having been sent by God, just as he had openly accepted their prophets and scriptures. But the People of the Book in Medina only argued with Muhammad and rejected him. What seems to be a final appeal for accommodation with them appears in:

3.64/57 Say: "People of the Book! Come now to a word common between us and you, that we serve none but God, and that we associate not aught with Him, and do not some of us take others as Lords, apart from God. . . .

With the rejection of this plea, the Koran made clear that the close relationship between the Muslims and the People of the Book was to be broken off and that the Muslims would constitute a third, distinct religious community with Muhammad as its prophet and leader (see especially 5.44/8-53/8). The basis for the establishment of Islam as a separate community, superior to the Jewish and Christian communities, was twofold: the Muslims were the true followers of Abraham (3.65/58-68/1), and the Jews and Christians refused to give up their "polytheism" (9.30 f.). In the many passages that treat these complex issues, there is no indication that Muhammad saw himself as more than God's Messenger to the Arabs. He does seem to have expected all Arabs, including those who had previously converted to Judaism and Christianity, to accept him as their prophet and leader.

Two groups of passages are often cited as evidence for the view that Muhammad's mission had a universal scope from the beginning.[97] One group involves the expression *an-nās*, which is taken to mean "mankind," as for instance in Arberry's translations of the following examples:

7.158/7 Say: "O mankind (*yā 'ayyuhā n-nās*), I am the Messenger of God to you all,

158 of Him to whom belongs the kingdom of the heavens and the earth. There is no god but He. . . ."

14.52 This is a message to be delivered to mankind (*li-n-nās*) that they may be warned by it. . . .

39.41/2 Surely We have sent down upon thee the Book for mankind (*li-n-nās*) with the truth. . . .

But this interpretation seems to be reading a later idea into the Koran. It seems much better to take *an-nās* to mean simply "the people," as is done by Bell and

[97] See, e.g., T. Nöldeke, *Wiener Zeitschrift für die Kunde des Morgenlandes*, 21 (1907), 307 f.; I. Goldziher, *Introduction to Islamic Theology and Law* (Princeton, 1981), pp. 27 f. (translation of the 1st ed. of *Vorlesungen über den Islam* [Heidelberg, 1910]), and T. W. Arnold, *The Preaching of Islam*, 2d ed. (London, 1913), pp. 27-31.

others. This more likely interpretation can be seen more clearly in such contexts as:

9.3 A proclamation from God and His Messenger to the people (*ilā n-nās*) [assembled] on the day of the Greater Pilgrimage. . . .

17.106/7 And a Koran We have divided for thee [Muhammad] to recite to the people (*'alā n-nās*) at intervals. . . .

The *an-nās* context that comes closest to supporting the universal claim is 34.28/7, which seems best translated:

> We have sent thee not except to all of the people (*illā kāffatan li-n-nās*), a bearer of good tidings, and a warner; but most of the people (*akthara n-nās*) have no knowledge.

The expression *kāffatan li-n-nās*, literally, "inclusively to the people," can be interpreted variously in this late Meccan or early Medinan verse. It does seem to indicate an extension of Muhammad's mission beyond the limited confines stipulated by some of the earlier verses of the Koran; but it does not necessarily extend to people beyond Muhammad's world of experience, or even beyond the Arabs. That is, this verse is not necessarily inconsistent with those that suggest that his mission was to the Arabs. After Muhammad's death and after the rapid spread of Islam this verse naturally took on a wider meaning. For Muhammad, however, the expression *kāffatan li-n-nās* almost certainly did not mean "all of mankind," as it later came to be interpreted.

The other group involves the term *'ālamūn*, "worlds." The precise meaning of this term in the Koran is uncertain. The commentators usually took it to mean the two or three species of rational beings, men and jinn, or men, jinn, and angels. The Koran itself, however, gives no indication that it ever refers to beings other than people. The expression *rabb al-'ālamīn*, which occurs frequently in Meccan portions of the Koran as a title for God, is not at issue since according to the Koran there is only one true God, who is the Lord of all of creation, which would thus include whatever specific connotations *'ālamīn* may have had. The question as to whether Muhammad saw himself as a prophet to the entire world involves mainly the passages in which the expression *li-l-'ālamīn*, "to the worlds," occurs. Mecca is said to be "a guidance to the worlds" (3.96/0); Abraham and Lot were delivered "to a land blessed for the worlds" (21.71); and Mary and her son are said to have been "a sign to the worlds" (21.91), as is Noah's ark (29.15/14). The message Muhammad brought is several times said to be "a reminder to the worlds" (6.90, 12.104, 38.87, 68.52, and 81.27). But Muhammad's message is also said to have been the same as was brought earlier by other prophets, so that it is this changeless message, brought by many messengers, that is "a reminder to the worlds" or "a reminder to man." The *li-l-'ālamīn* context that is most often cited in support of the view that Muhammad's mission was universal is 21.107: *wa-mā arsalnā-ka illa raḥmatan li-l-'ālamīn*, which is usually translated "We have not sent thee, save as a mercy to the worlds." This verse took on special meaning for later Muslims, and cosmic meaning for the Sufis. But it is very unlikely that it had special meaning for Muhammad, who probably took it to mean "We sent thee [along with the other messengers] out of [Our] mercy for man." Regardless of the various connotations the verse may have had for Muhammad and his contemporaries, the expression *raḥmatan li-l-'ālamīn* was certainly not intended to elevate Muhammad above the other prophets or assign to him a unique mission the other prophets did not share.[98]

Muhammad became in time a prophet to the world, the prophet of hundreds of millions of Muslims representing every major race and culture. To what extent he foresaw this development is difficult to say; the many verses of the Koran that say he could not foretell the future may be relevant here. Despite the views of earlier, eminent scholars, it now seems extremely doubtful that Muhammad felt a world mission during the years of struggle and persecution in Mecca before the Hijra.[99] Toward the end of his life his vision of his mission no doubt widened, but it is unlikely that he ever conceived anything like a "world religion" or saw himself as a prophet to the world. Many verses of the Koran came to be interpreted as supporting the belief that Muhammad's mission was to the entire world, but there are good reasons for concluding that these verses did not have this meaning for him.

This study has shown that much can be known about Muhammad and his understanding of himself from the Koran. For a complete picture one must, of course, go to the Sira and Hadith literature; but these sources introduce new problems into the discussion, and, as was stated at the beginning, seem to involve a different basic question. As a general rule the surest knowledge about Muhammad is what is supported by the Koran, which remains our most reliable source, but also the most difficult to interpret. The present survey has shown that there is very little Koranic foundation for certain Islamic beliefs such as the sinlessness of Muhammad, his superiority over other prophets, and his proclivity and even ability to perform miracles. Other Islamic beliefs such as those regarding Muhammad's power of intercession and the universality of his mission developed in later thought far beyond the ambiguous Koranic statements on these issues.

The Koran presents Muhammad as a great man, but also as a very human one.

[98]Cf. 9.61/2, which in the Kūfan texts seems to refer to Muhammad as "a mercy to those who believe." But in other texts, where this phrase begins a new verse, it seems best translated "there is mercy for those who believe." Cf. also 10.57/8 and 16.64/6.

[99]The conclusion reached by Nöldeke, Goldziher, and others that Muhammad felt a universal mission from the beginning is based on the traditional Muslim and older European dating of certain key verses such as 21.107 and 34.28/7. But these verses now appear to be late Meccan or early Medinan, and in any case their universalist theme is not clear.

In the generations after his death historical fact gave way to an idealized Muhammad of pious legend, a miracle worker, a hero, and a paragon of virtue and of all other human traits of excellence. From the Koran it appears that Muhammad himself did not wish this to happen. He saw himself as a warner, a messenger of God, a prophet, and also as a worship leader, a teacher, and a judge. But he is not portrayed in the Koran as a model for all Muslims to imitate, except in his submission to God and his diligence in worship and prayer. The Koran gives no indication that Muhammad saw himself as a saint or that he wanted his followers to regard him as one. He seems to have been fully aware of his human limitations, including his need for seeking forgiveness for his sins. In this he served as a model for all who are fully surrendered to God. These conclusions do not lessen Muhammad's significance in any way, but serve to place him within the perspective of his own time and place. It is to be hoped that the issues raised here will be pursued further by others and that the conclusions reached will be refined or corrected where needed in the continuing quest for the historical Muhammad.

ISLAM IN THE MIRROR OF RITUAL

WILLIAM A. GRAHAM

Harvard University

Any study of religious ritual, and particularly ritual in Islam, must begin with the work of W. Robertson Smith, the predecessor in Arabic studies and fellow countryman of the 1981 Levi Della Vida medalist, W. Montgomery Watt. It is now nearly a century ago that Smith delivered his famous Burnett Lectures at Aberdeen, on "The Religion of the Semites."[1] In the first of these, Smith made clear that he saw religion as fundamentally a composite of "beliefs" and "practices," the latter being always and everywhere the primary of the two. For him, "institutions, ritual practices and rules of conduct" are the determinants of "myths," "dogmas," and "theories" in religious life.[2] In his evolutionary view, the more primitive or ancient the religious tradition, the more completely does it consist of ritual and custom; thus rite precedes explanation or, to use the terminology of Jane Harrison (whom Smith influenced), *drōmena* are prior to *legomena*, "things done" precede "things said."[3] Closely allied to this principle is a second, even more portentous premise of Smith's approach: The way in which any religious datum is best understood is by reference to its historical and linguistic origins and antecedents. Accordingly, he sought to lay the foundation for understanding the great Semitic monotheisms of more recent history through reconstruction and analysis of the archaic, primitive practices of the ancient Semites. For him, these practices themselves could be traced to the primordial centrality of the rite of sacrifice: "the origin and meaning of sacrifice constitute the central problem of ancient religion."[4]

Smith's ideas have long been and remain still influential in a variety of scholarly

[1]Published as *The Religion of the Semites. First Series: The Fundamental Institutions* (1889). Smith's poor health after 1889 precluded the completion of the second and third lecture series, but he was able, with the assistance of J. S. Black, to complete revisions of the first series which were incorporated in a revised edition (London: A. and C. Black, 1894; repr. New York: Schocken Books, 1972).

[2]*Religion of the Semites*, rev. ed., pp. 16 ff.

[3]Jane Ellen Harrison, *Themis: A Study of the Social Origins of Greek Religion*, rev. ed. (Cambridge: University Press, 1927; repr. London: Merlin Press, 1963), pp. 42-45, 328-331.

[4]*Religion of the Semites*, rev. ed., p. 27.

fields. The stress upon the primacy of social and religious institutions among anthropologists and sociologists, the concern with ritual and its interpretation among both social scientists and students of religion, and the emphasis among orientalists upon tracing origins and influences in older cultures—all of these trends have found in Smith's work either a seminal or a corroborative influence. In this respect, Arabists and Islamicists have been no exceptions, and in order to deal with Muslim ritual we must look at least briefly at this "Smithian" orientation that has been characteristic of most work on Islam.

The dominant focus in study of Muslim institutions has certainly been upon historical background and sources. This is amply demonstrated by a survey of examples from some of the major studies of that most complex of Muslim rituals, the ḥajj.

Robertson Smith himself, in his magisterial treatment of "holy places" in lectures III, IV, and V of *The Religion of the Semites*, explains the donning of special *iḥrām* garments for the ḥajj as a holdover from pagan Arab custom regarding the tabooed character of the *ḥaram* or *ḥimā*, the sacred territory. His argument is that "the forfeiture of clothes in Islamic law is only a continuation of the old rule attested for the sanctuary of Mecca, that common raiment worn in the sacred place had to be cast off and left behind. . . ."[5]

Julius Wellhausen, writing at the same time as Smith (1887), sought to explain the iḥrām in a slightly different way. He saw it as the continuing Arab practice of ritual purification in preparation for the presentation of a blood sacrifice.[6] Like Smith, he stressed the importance of sacrifice in pre-Islamic paganism, emphasizing the practice of joint or communal sacrificial offerings (*Gesamtopfer*). Accordingly, he saw the two *wuqūf*s at 'Arafāt and Muzdalifa during the ḥajj as no-longer-comprehensible rituals of waiting on a god's answer to a petition offered up with sacrifice.[7]

Two Dutch scholars, C. Snouck Hurgronje[8] and M. Th. Houtsma,[9] similarly looked to pre-Islamic pagan practices as the prototypes and sources for the actions of ḥajj. Houtsma followed Snouck Hurgronje in seeing in the two wuqūfs and subsequent ritual "flights" (*ifāḍas*) of the Muslim ceremonies a somewhat altered pagan practice connected with worship of sun and thunder deities at 'Arafāt and Muzdalifa.[10] Some years later, Maurice Gaudefroy-Demombynes would in similar fashion see the details of *ṭawāf* around the Ka'ba as extensions or modifications

[5]Ibid., p. 146. Cf. pp. 446 ff., esp. p. 451.

[6]*Reste arabischen Heidentums* (1887), 2d ed. (Berlin: Georg Reimer, 1897), pp. 122-123.

[7]Ibid., p. 120.

[8]*Het Mekkaansche feest* (Leiden: E. J. Brill, 1880).

[9]"Het skopelisme en het steenwerpen te Mina," in *Verslagen en Mededeelingen der Koninklijke Akademie van Wetenschappen* (Afdeeling letterkunde), ser. 4, pt. VI (Amsterdam: Johannes Müller, 1904), pp. 185-217.

[10]"Het skopelisme," pp. 196 ff. Cf. Hurgronje, *Het Mekkaansche feest*, pp. 147-159.

of pagan Arab practices.[11]

Another trend in ḥajj interpretation that antedates all of these preceding treatments is exemplified by Reinhart Dozy: the identification of Hebrew prototypes for the Muslim observances. Dozy, writing in 1864, presents an extreme example in his interpretation (much of it based on arcane linguistic parallels) of the ḥajj rites as the unwitting continuation by the Arabs of the ritual celebrations of an Israelite "Gilgal" festival commemorating the conquest of Canaan![12] Houtsma also saw Israelite tradition behind the wuqūf at 'Arafāt, linking this "standing" with the "waiting upon the Lord" at Sinai (Exodus 19 ff.).[13]

Perhaps the greatest student of Muslim rituals, including the ḥajj, was Arendt Jan Wensinck, who stressed in his work the many parallels in Western Semitic tradition to Muslim usages. An example from his early work is his relating of the Ka'ba's cubic shape and the quadrangular form of the stone of the *maqām Ibrāhīm* to the ancient Semitic link between the square-sided altar and the "navel" sanctuary" (such as Mecca).[14] He also saw in the ancient concept of the link between rites at the earthly sanctuary and those in heaven, around the divine throne, a basis for the Muslim practices associated with the Ka'ba in Mecca.[15]

Such examples could be multiplied. What is important for us, however, is the general tendency to see the ḥajj (and other Islamic rites) as Gaudefroy-Demombynes does when he describes the ḥajj as primarily of interest "because it is a revival and syncretism of ancient rites common throughout the Semitic East."[16] The presumption at one level beneath all of this impressive searching for precedents in earlier practice to explain these rites is the familiar scholarly belief that essence lies in origins. The modern study of the Ṣalāt and the Ramaḍān fast, as well as less central ritual practices, is further testimony to this prevailing conviction.[17]

[11] *Le pèlerinage à la Mekke. Étude d'histoire religieuse* (Paris: Paul Geuthner, 1923), pp. 205-224.

[12] *De Israëlieten te Mekka van Davids tijd tot in de vifde eeuw onzer tijdrekening* (Haarlem: A. C. Kruseman, 1864), pp. 113 ff.; German trans. *Die Israeliten zu Mekka von Davids' Zeit bis in's fünfte Jahrhundert unsrer Zeitrechnung* (Leipzig: W. Engelmann; Haarlem: A. C. Kruseman, 1864), pp. 103 ff.

[13] "Het skopelisme," p. 195.

[14] "The Ideas of the Western Semites concerning the Navel of the Earth," no. 1 of *Verhandelingen der Koninklijke Akademie van Wetenschappen te Amsterdam* (Afdeeling letterkunde), n.s., Pt. XVII (Amsterdam: Johannes Müller, 1916), pp. 41-43.

[15] "Some Semitic Rites of Mourning and Religion: Studies on Their Origin and Mutual Relation," no. 1 of ibid., Pt. XVIII (Amsterdam: Johannes Müller, 1917), pp. 43-58.

[16] *Muslim Institutions*, trans. John P. MacGregor (New York: Barnes & Noble, 1950, orig. French ed., *Les institutions musulmanes*, 1945), p. 81.

[17] For a sense of the general orientation of such study, see A. J. Wensinck, "Ṣalāt," and M. Plessner, "Ramaḍān," in *The Encyclopaedia of Islam* (4 vols. and suppl.; Leiden and London, 1913-38), s.v. [both also reproduced in the *Shorter Encyclopaedia of Islam* (London and Leiden, 1961)], which remain the standard reference sources. For more specific, "classic"

At another level, however, we can discern in the tendency to try to isolate pre-Islamic or extra-Islamic sources for the discrete rites of the ḥajj a kind of suppressed frustration of the scholar who is confronted here with a series of ritual acts that elude comprehensive, rational systematization under any one interpretive rubric. The great Muslim thinker Ghazzālī recognized this centuries ago when he remarked that the ḥajj rites individually do not satisfy either the reason (*al-'aql, al-'uqūl*) or the senses (*an-nufūs*, lit. "desires"), but can only be seen as meaningful in their performance as acts of obedient service and worship.[18] (Ghazzālī went on, we may note, to make as beautiful and coherent sense of the "mysteries" of ḥajj symbolism as has ever been done.) Non-Muslim scholars have not had the benefit of Ghazzālī's faith perspective, nor would perhaps any of them claim his extraordinary intellectual gifts. Thus the modern scholar, faced with a seeming hodge-podge of loosely related activities, has taken refuge in etiology and "originology" as his or her only escape from frustration. This frustration is apparent even in statements of sensitive and erudite Islamicists like Gustave von Grünebaum, who remarks with respect to the ḥajj: "The very tenuous relation between the old [pagan] ritual and the new religion [Islam] is striking. Aside perhaps from the ceremonies centering on the Ka'ba, there is no attempt at an ideological or even mythological integration."[19]

Nor have Islamicists and Arabists been the only ones frustrated by interpretation of the ḥajj and other major Muslim institutions. The dearth of symbols, ideological elaboration, and mythical constructs in Islamic usage and practice generally has proven an even greater obstacle to comparativists and social scientists in dealing with the central, "orthoprax" ritual and piety of Islam.[20] If the "myth and ritual" school of interpretation had not foundered on other shoals, its ultimate nemesis would surely have been Muslim "myth and ritual" (a subject

studies of Muslim ritual which discuss Islamic practice in a Judeo-Christian framework, see J. Horovitz, "Bemerkungen zur Geschichte und Terminologie des islamischen Kultus," *Der Islam*, XVI (1927), 249-263; C. H. Becker, "Zur Geschichte des islamischen Kultus," *Der Islam*, III (1912), 374-399 (repr. in C. H. Becker, *Islamstudien* [2 vols.; Leipzig: Quelle & Meyer, 1924], I, 472-500); and E. Mittwoch, "Zur Entstehungsgeschichte des islamischen Gebets und Kultus," *Abhandlungen der Preussischen Akademie der Wissenschaften* (Berlin) (1913), no. 2.

[18] Abū Ḥamīd Muḥammad al-Ghazzālī (d. 505/1111), *Iḥyā' 'ulūm ad-dīn* (5 vols.; Cairo, 1356-1357/1935; repr. Beirut: Dār al-ma'rifa li-ṭ-ṭabā'a wa-n-nashr, n.d.), I, 266 (in "Kitāb asrār al-ḥajj," section 3).

[19] *Muhammadan Festivals* (1950; repr. London: Curzon Press, 1976), p. 35.

[20] The use of "orthoprax" instead of "orthodox" as an appropriate designation for mainstream Muslim thought and traditional Muslim practice follows that of Wilfred C. Smith in *Islam in Modern History* (Princeton, N.J.: Princeton University Press, 1957); cf. p. 20 for discussion of this usage. In this study the term is used to refer to the "Sharī'a tradition" of legal and religious interpretation that emerged as early as the second/eighth century and has ever since, in the hands of the 'ulamā', served the Muslim community as a kind of yardstick for faith and normative practice, however many additional ideas and practices have been

I am certain none of the proponents of this school ever even considered taking up).[21] Phenomenologists of religion and other comparativists have fared but little better in their efforts to make sense of Muslim rite and symbol. The relative scarcity of Islamic examples in the works of Gerardus van der Leeuw, W. Brede Kirstensen, or Mircea Eliade is striking,[22] as is the inability of scholars such as Eliade or R. C. Zaehner to integrate Islam convincingly into their larger schemes of interpretation.[23] A comparativist theologian, Hendrik Kraemer, can write of Islam as "comparatively poor in thought and feeling" even while recognizing "a

superadded at various times in various places or sectors of the community. Historically, Islamic "orthopraxy" has been represented especially by what Marshall G. S. Hodgson calls the "Jamā'ī-Sunnī" tradition (*The Venture of Islam: Conscience and History in a World Civilization* [3 vols; Chicago and London: University of Chicago Press, 1974], I, 278-279).

[21] The "myth and ritual" school of thought in religion, anthropology, and various special fields of study has found in ritual action the primordial form of religiousness and specifically the origin of myth and mythmaking. W. Robertson Smith and Émile Durkheim may be described as patron saints of this orientation and James G. Frazer its true progenitor. Seminal figures in its development were Arnold van Gennep and the so-called "Cambridge school" of classicists–Gilbert Murray, A. B. Cook, F. M. Cornford, and especially Jane Harrison–along with S. H. Hooke in his work on divine kingship in the ancient Near East and Bronislaw Malinowski in his work on Melanesia. A more recent scholar whose ideas about myth and ritual place him in the same tradition is Mircea Eliade. Lesser lights among its exponents have been Lord Raglan and Stanley Hyman, both of whom are the focus of the telling criticism of the whole "school" by Joseph Fontenrose in *The Ritual Theory of Myth* (Berkeley and Los Angeles: University of California Press, 1966). To this latter scholar's sharp critique should be added the more broadly conceived attack on the "myth and ritual" premises and theories launched by G. S. Kirk in *Myth: Its Meaning and Functions in Ancient and Other Cultures* (Cambridge: University Press; Berkeley and Los Angeles: University of California Press, 1971), especially Chaps. I and VI (where Kirk's general critique tends to be more telling than his own counterinterpretations of specific myths in Chaps. II-V). Even aside from the criticisms of Fontenrose and Kirk, the "myth and ritual" orientation is generally not taken seriously any longer, having gone the way of most other sweeping and facile general theories of religion and culture as more careful study of particular religious and cultural traditions has deepened our awareness of the unique aspects of each. Cf. Clyde Kluckhohn, "Myths and Rituals: A General Theory," *Harvard Theological Review*, 35 (1942), 45-79.

[22] Gerardus van der Leeuw, *Religion in Essence and Manifestation*, J. E. Turner, trans., with additions from the 2d. German ed. by Hans H. Penner (New York and Evanston: Harper and Row, 1963 [German orig., 1933]); W. Brede Kristensen, *The Meaning of Religion: Lectures in the Phenomenology of Religion*, John B. Carman, trans. (The Hague: Martinus Nijhoff, 1960); and Mircea Eliade, *Patterns in Comparative Religion*, Rosemary Sheed, trans. (Cleveland and New York: World Publishing Company, Meridian Books, 1963 [French orig., 1949]). Cf. also the other, more specific, comparative studies of Eliade on a variety of topics.

[23] Mircea Eliade, *Cosmos and History: The Myth of the Eternal Return*, Willard R. Trask, trans. (1954; repr. New York: Harper & Row, 1959 [French orig., 1949]), esp. pp. 102-162; and R. C. Zaehner, *The Comparison of Religions* [orig. title, *At Sundry Times* (London, 1958)] (Boston: Beacon Press, 1962), esp. the appendix, "The Qur'an and Christ," pp. 195-217. Eliade simply ignores Islam in his discussion of the unique character of Christian and Jewish ideas of history and theophany; Zaehner struggles rather lamely in a special appendix to explain how his interpretation of non-Christian religious traditions as parts of a

colossal power which is rooted in its faith in God."[24] The social scientists on the other hand, from Edward Westermarck to Clifford Geertz, have had to gravitate almost exclusively to the practices of "folk" or "local" Islam and have not taken Islamic "orthopraxy" very seriously.[25] Even Victor Turner can only draw upon the ḥajj for his work on pilgrimage in the most partial fashion—primarily to illustrate his concept of *communitas*.[26]

In short, "orthoprax" Muslim ritual and symbolism have eluded or confounded the generalist even more visibly than the orientalist. Where the latter at least has had recourse to a quest for Semitic "sources," the former has most often had to turn to other traditions altogether for his or her data in these subject areas. Charles J. Adams, himself an Arabist as well as an historian of religion, describes this general scholarly frustration very clearly:

> There are, of course, mythological elements and ritual practices in the historical stream of Muslim religiosity. There is data for the investigator in these realms to consider, but in comparison with the Hindu tradition or that of the ancient Near East, it is very much less *in both quantity and significance* [italics mine]. In this connection it is important to realize that some of the most elaborately developed and structured ritual activities of the Muslims—such as those surrounding the Hajj—are survivors from pre-Islamic times. The prospects are no more optimistic for the approach to Islam through myth and ritual. Study of the relation of these two does not seem to offer access to the heart of Islamic experience as it has in so many other cases.[27]

praeparatio evangelica can still hold despite the appearance and spread of Islam subsequent to the appearance of Christ.

[24] Quoted by G. van der Leeuw, *Religion in Essence and Manifestation*, p. 641, from a letter sent to him by Kraemer.

[25] Edward Westermarck, *Ritual and Belief in Morocco* (2 vols.; London: Macmillan, 1926); Clifford Geertz, *Islam Observed: Religious Development in Morocco and Indonesia* (New Haven and London: Yale University Press, 1968). Even though Geertz does give some attention to orthoprax tradition (to which he refers as "scripturalist"), he clearly does not see it as central to the two regional cultures with which he deals. On the general tendency of anthropologists in particular to ignore mainstream orthopraxy in favor of "the unique, the esoteric, and the exotic," see the penetrating critique by Richard T. Antoun in the section entitled "The Social Anthropologist and the Study of Islam" on pp. 159-172 of his chapter "Anthropology" in Leonard Binder, ed., *The Study of the Middle East: Research and Scholarship in the Humanities and the Social Sciences* (New York, London, Sydney, Toronto: John Wiley & Sons, 1976), pp. 137-213, esp. pp. 159-172.

[26] "The Center Out There: Pilgrim's Goal," *History of Religions* (Chicago), 12 (1973), 191-230, passim, esp. pp. 193, 200-201, 218-219.

[27] "The Study of Religions and the Study of Islam," in J. M. Kitagawa, ed., *The History of Religions: Essays on the Problem of Understanding* (Chicago and London: University of Chicago Press, 1967), p. 182.

Here we reach the crux of our concerns. Descriptively we have immense detail about major Muslim ritual activities such as the ḥajj. Historically we have a similarly detailed array of information about the possible sources and prototypes for the discrete forms of Muslim ritual. Yet neither in terms of rich comparative study nor in terms of interpretive study of Muslim ritual *on its own* terms–namely those of Muslim interpretation and understanding themselves–do we have any really significant work to build upon. Our present task is thus necessarily more of a reconnaissance of the field than an effort at conquest, since the problem of taking Muslim ritual seriously as a central and ultimately intelligible expression of Muslim faith has hardly been posed, let alone solved. Our orientalist tradition has worked on the specifically *non-Islamic* sources and parallels for orthoprax Muslim ritual. Our religionist and social scientific traditions have worked to some degree on *popular, regional,* and *folk* rituals of Islam and their comparison with similar ritual phenomena around the world. Our task is to make a beginning of the work of seeing what the peculiarly *Islamic* character of Muslim ritual might be.

To do this we must first take seriously the unity of faith and action, "beliefs" and "practices," in Islam in a way that scholars before and especially since Robertson Smith have not been much inclined to do. If we are to approach Muslim ritual as a source for a Muslim "self-image," we shall not find the separation of ritual from doctrine, "actual practice" from "theoretical ideals," very relevant. Instead, we propose to presume that Muslims who are at all thoughtful about their faith and action have never seen the ḥajj, the ṣalāt, or other basic ritual duties and practices of Islam as inconsistent with their faith–however they may have chosen to interpret the consistency that they *have* seen, or however many other devotional practices they may have cultivated in addition to these basic rituals. I presuppose here that such ritual practice is a valid self-expression of Islam, a symbolic articulation of Muslim ideals and values, a kind of "discourse" in which it should be possible to "hear" the ways in which Islam as a way of living "speaks" intelligibly and presumably eloquently to the Muslim. Thus rites are not to be seen merely as products of a particular religiocultural substrate out of which old practices repeatedly appear in new garb, but much more as the enactments of religious convictions and ideals, the embodiments as well as the results of conscious or unconscious sentiments. If the Qur'ān, or a Ṣūfī manual, presents us with a Muslim "self-image," so too does Muslim ritual generally, or any single rite in particular. My purpose is to explore central characteristics of Muslim thought and action as they may be reflected in the mirror of ritual–not only for the eyes of the outside observer, but also for those of the Muslim observer. In this way ritual may become a new "primary text" through which Muslims can tell us as outsiders about Islam.

This purpose demands that we be at least generally clear about what we mean by "Muslim ritual" and by "ritual" itself. The generic concept "ritual" is, to be sure, only slightly more susceptible to definition than "religion."[28] Several comments and qualifications, however, can provide us with a working usage to serve our present purposes. First, ritual is limited here to religious ritual–action with some transcendent reference.[29] Further it always involves some communal relationship, even if performed alone (private, obsessive "rituals" belong to psychopathology, private devotions to religion).[30] Third, it is understood as formalized, patterned behavior that involves both repetition and a quality that is recognizably "special" or different from that of ordinary, nonritual acts.[31] Fourth, it is presumed to be representational, expressive, dramatic, or symbolic in character–in other words, it is meaningful, or potentially meaningful, activity (*pace* those observers who may not see any intelligible meaning in it).[32] Finally,

[28] On the complexities of defining both, see Jack Goody, "Religion and Ritual: The Definitional Problem," *British Journal of Sociology*, 12 (1961), 142-164. Cf. Edmund R. Leach, "Ritual," in *International Encyclopaedia of the Social Sciences*, s.v.

[29] For the present purposes I part company here with the many social scientists who have appropriated "ritual" to designate virtually any formal, repeated action, even those of the animal world. In this regard, J. H. M. Beattie's definition of a rite as "a dramatic, symbolic expression of man's awareness of his dependence on forces outside himself" seems particularly apt ("On Understanding Sacrifice," in M. F. C. Bourdillon and Meyer Fortes, eds., *Sacrifice*, [New York and London: Academic Press, 1980], p. 32). In his preface to the volume just cited, Meyer Fortes also stresses the religious dimension of ritual. He emphasizes that ritual is activity tailored to the need to relate "the profane world of Durkheimian sociology" to the supramundane world of "the Durkheimian sacred." While the dichotomization of the Durkeimian world view is certainly to be questioned because of its inherent reductionist quality, it does rest upon the same premise that I am stressing here: that religious activity presupposes an awareness of transcendence of some kind.

[30] A point made forcefully by Margaret Mead in "Ritual and Social Crisis," in James D. Shaughnessy, ed., *The Roots of Ritual* (Grand Rapids, Mich.: Wm. B. Eerdmans, 1973), where she notes that ritual is "social behavior" (p. 88) and that "ritual is concerned with relationships, either between a single individual and the supernatural, or among a group of individuals who share things together" (p. 89).

[31] Mead characterizes rituals as "patterns of human behavior" and as "behavior that is repetitious and different from the ordinary. . . . Ritual has an extra degree of intensity" (ibid., p. 87). I do not, however, see the need to follow Mead when she goes on to link ritual intrinsically with crisis situations in life (ibid., pp. 89-90).

[32] Cf. Beattie's definition cited above, n. 29. See also Christopher Crocker, "Ritual and the Development of Social Structure: Liminality and Inversion," in Shaughnessy, ed., *Roots of Ritual*, pp. 47-86. Crocker emphasizes especially the communicative and symbolic aspects of ritual. He speaks of ritual as "essentially communication, a language in which societies discuss a variety of matters" (p. 49) and as "a statement in metaphorical terms about the paradoxes of human existence" (p. 47). A similar emphasis on ritual as "symbolic statement" is found in Edmund Leach's introduction to his *Political Systems of Highland Burma: A Study of Kachin Social Structure* (1954; Boston; Beacon Press, 1965), pp. 10-16 (in Leach's view the "symbolic statement" is one about the social order, which can be "read" by the observer as well as intuitively lived by the participant. Cf. also Leach's article "Ritual" [cited above, n. 28], p. 524*a*). Mary Douglas, to whose work we return below, also treats ritual as fundamentally a symbolic activity (*Natural Symbols* [1970; New York: Random House, Vintage Books, 1973], p. 20).

two qualifications: there can be no presumption of an intrinsic link between myth and ritual,[33] nor should "ritual," "ritualism," and "ritualist" be taken as pejorative terms referring to empty formalism or merely rote repetition of a given act (such perfunctory ritualism is described better as "ritualistic," not "ritualist").[34]

Just as it is difficult to define "ritual" as a generic concept with precision, so too it is not easy to isolate those parts of Muslim practice that qualify as "rituals." To begin with, there is no exact equivalent for "ritual" in Muslim Arabic usage. The Christian Arabic use of *ṭaqs* (pl. *ṭuqūs*) for "rite" or "ritual act" is a borrowing from Greek. The Muslim use of *manāsik* (sing. *mansik*, lit. "place of sacrifice") or of the plural forms *shi'ār* and especially *sha'ā'ir* (lit. "signs," esp. marks on sacrificial animals) is only rarely extended to Muslim or non-Muslim rites other than those of the ḥajj (e.g. *ṭawāf, sa'y, wuqūf, naḥr*).[35] The closest Muslim approximation to ritual conceptually is perhaps *'ibāda* (pl. *'ibādāt*), which means either a particular "act of worship and service" or "worship and service [of God]" in general. Thus 'ibādāt can refer to the whole range of appropriate acts for conforming life to God's will (*shar'*), but it is most often used specifically to designate the legal category in Muslim jurisprudence (*fiqh*) to which belong the major ritual and religious duties of Muslims. Some of these, notably the witnessing to one's faith (*shahāda*) and almsgiving (*zakāt*), are not properly speaking "rituals," but in a broader sense they do belong to the sphere of Muslim obligations that might be described as "rite and practice."

'Ibāda, however, as a generic concept rather than a legal classification, points to the immense degree to which Islam is understood by the Muslim to consist most fundamentally in the organization of all life, even its smallest, most mundane details, in regularized "worship and service" to God. As a contemporary manual on the legal 'ibādāt puts it, "the truth is that *'ibāda* is able to pervade (*yumkin an tantaẓima*) all human acts."[36] From the standpoint of penetration of all sectors of life by ritual or ritualized practices, Islam is arguably the most ritualistic of all traditions (including even the Jewish) in its vision of individual and collective life as perpetual 'ibāda. At both ends of the spectrum of Muslim piety—the "orthoprax" or "scripturalist"[37] (what Muslims call *salafī*, among

[33]See above, n. 21. This is not to deny, of course, that myth is often intimately related to ritual, but only to reject such a link as "original" or "necessary" in religious life.

[34]This is a basic theme of Mary Douglas's *Natural Symbols*, esp. in chap. 1, pp. 19-39. The distinction between "ritualist" and "ritualistic," the latter as a pejorative, the former neutral, is my own, not Douglas's; it allows one to distinguish, however, the empty formalism of which she speaks from her "ritualism," which is a neutral usage.

[35]See A. J. Wensinck et al., *Concordance et indices de la tradition musulmane* (7 vols.; Leiden: E. J. Brill, 1936-1969), for examples from the Hadith of the use of *manāsik* (VI, 432), *shi'ār* (III, 141*a*), and *sha'ā'īr* (III, 143*b*) for the rites of the Ḥajj. Among these, only *shi'ār* is used more frequently in other than this sense.

[36]Muḥammad Muḥammad Ismā'īl 'Abduh, *al-'Ibādāt fī al-islām* (Egypt: Maktabat Nahḍat Miṣr bil-Fajāla, 1378/1958), p. 16.

[37]See above, n. 20.

other things) on the one hand and the "folk" or popular on the other–ritual and ritualized practices give pattern and cadence to the hourly, daily, monthly, and yearly cycles of life. The full range of such practices is not easy to subsume under neat rubrics, but for our purposes a working conspectus of Muslim ritual practices across the breadth of the spectrum of piety in Islam might utilize a tripartite categorization such as the following:

I. Formal rites
   A. Major ritual duties: Ṭahāra, Ṣalāt, Ṣaum Ramadan, Ḥajj[38]
   B. *Rites de passage*: 'Aqīqa, Khitān/Khafḍ, [Nikāḥ, 'Urs], Janāza[39]

II. Ritualized devotional practices[40]
   A. Qirā'a (Tilāwa)
   B. Dhikr, Samā'
   C. Ziyāra (to tombs, shrines of saints or of imams)
   D. Invocations (e.g., Tasmiya, Taṣliya, Taslīm, Isti'ādha)

III. Periodic celebrations[41]
   A. al-'Īdān
   B. Maulid an-Nabī
   C. Lailat al-mi'rāj
   D. "Moulids" [*mawālid*] of saints; Majālis [sing. *majlis*] of imams
   E. 10 Muḥarram
   F. Lailat al-Qadr
   G. Other festivals (e.g., Lailat al-Barā'a)

[38] I.e., purification rites, ritual worship, fast in Ramaḍān, and pilgrimage, respectively.

[39] The *'aqīqa* is the hair-cutting ceremony, usually accompanied by animal sacrifice, for the newly born baby. *Khitān* is male circumcision, *khafḍ*, female excision. *Nikāḥ* is the contractual marriage, *'urs* the popular wedding celebration. *Janāza*, or *janā'iz*, is the special, simple Salat of the "four *takbīrs*" that is performed for the dead (properly, *ṣalāt al-janā'iz*).

[40] *Qirā'a*, or *tilāwa*, is the formal recitation of the Qur'ān, an activity that dominates Muslim religious life and ritual. *Dhikr* and *samā'* are the practices of "recollection" and "audition" especially cultivated among Ṣūfī groups but widely participated in at the popular level, in which litanies or Qur'ān passages are chanted or sung as a religious exercise. *Ziyāra* is the generic term for "visitation" of tombs and popular shrines. The invocations given as examples here (the "bismillāh," the blessing upon the Prophet, the "greeting with peace," the prayer for God's help, respectively) are but four of countless pious formulas with which life in a Muslim community is filled and by which it is routinized.

[41] Those cited below (A through G) are (A) the "two festivals" of the day of sacrifice during the time of Ḥajj (*'īd al-aḍḥā*) and the breaking of the Ramaḍān fast (*'īd al-fiṭr*); (B) the Prophet's birthday, 12 Rabī' al-awwal; (C) the night of the Prophet's ascension experience, 27 Rajab; (D) birth celebrations of saints and commemorations (also called *ta'āzin* [sing. *ta'ziya*] of the martyrdom of the imams (placed together because of the similar focus on particular personalities and their spiritual power and piety); (E) the fast day of Sunnis (voluntary) and the commemoration of the passion of al-Husain at Karbalā', the chief event of the Shi'i religious calendar; (F) the night of the descent of the Qur'ān; and (G) the "night

The social scientist would almost certainly find the last group of "periodic celebrations" and subgroup B of Category I, *rites de passage*, the most attractive areas of investigation, along with ziyāra to tombs and shrines (11,C) and the practice of dhikr among Sufi and other popular groups (2,B). In such practices and observances we do see the immense force of popular piety that offers the theorist or comparativist so much grist of common human religious tendencies for the mill of cross-cultural generalization. These are indeed the sectors of Muslim piety and practice in which the non-Muslim observer can most readily recognize parallels and analogies to phenomena in other religious and cultural milieus. This is by no means a denigration of their importance to any comprehensive understanding of the variegated strands of Muslim piety around the globe or of Muslim life in particular localities. Yet focus on these more popular areas of Muslim practice does not give us significant—or certainly not the most significant—access to the striking and even unique characteristics of Islam as a coherent tradition of faith and practice. It may even imply that Muslims engage in such practices because they do not find meaning in "orthoprax" observances, thereby ignoring these observances, which virtually any Muslim would identify as basic and central to being Muslim, whatever other practices he or she might also participate in.

It is in the formal ritual duties (I,A) and the closely related practice of Qur'ān recitation (II,A) (as well as, in some degree, in the many invocational formulas [II,D] that punctuate everyday life) that we must seek the *distinctive* ritual life of Muslims and the fundamentally *ritualist* orientation of Islam. The lifeblood of the community, or *umma*, flows in the repeated cycles of ṭahāra, ṣalāt, ṣaum, ḥajj, and qirā'a. These form the universally recognized backbone of Muslim practice; they are the activities to which every generation of Muslim thinkers have applied their minds in order to delineate for themselves and their fellows what it means to be Muslim. It is thus in these central practices that we can expect to find the most dependable mirror of Muslim piety, the most consistent self-image of Islam.

It is, however, unusually difficult to articulate this self-image. We have seen how chary scholars in various fields have been of addressing this image directly. Viewing Muslim ritual as little more than a variation in common Semitic practices or as a defective variety of a universal, generic religious phenomenon has been a way of avoiding confrontation with the ritual itself as it expresses Muslim faith and self-understanding. I am persuaded that the difficulties we have had in dealing with Islamic ritual on its own terms lie precisely in its uniqueness as ritual. I would locate this uniqueness in the particular character of the thoroughgoing *ritualism* that I have suggested is implicit in the pervasiveness of ritual practices in Muslim life. What I discern in the mirror of Muslim ritual is a ritualism that is unlike the ritualism of most other religious communities. Specifically, there is in the matrix of Muslim ritual what I shall call an essentially "reformational"

---

quittance," a popular festival in some parts of the Muslim world similar to new year's in other cultures.

mistrust of some of the key elements of ritualist society and religion elsewhere. Thus there seems to be a paradox at the heart of the otherwise consistently ritualist bent of Muslim piety.

This paradox became clearer to me in the course of wrestling with the large but generally not very helpful corpus of more recent ritual theory. One theoretical discussion stood out among the others because it sought to address the question of "ritualism" per se, what it connotes in religious communities, in what kinds of societies it flourishes, and what opposing tendencies or contrasts to it there are in different contexts. This discussion is that of the sociologist Mary Douglas in her 1970 work, *Natural Symbols*, especially in her introductory chapter, "Away from Ritual," where she articulates the general problem of ritualism.[42]

Douglas begins by pointing to a common modern tendency toward rejection of rituals and formality of any kind as signifying "empty conformity," meaningless formalism. This "anti-ritualism," she suggests, is both a baselessly pejorative understanding of what ritual is and also a reflection of a generally "anti-ritualist" society around us today. She seeks to show that most societies in their basic religious orientation are either "ritualist" or "anti-ritualist" in a given period—that is, that these particular orientations correlate with and reflect other societal traits and religious or social values.

Ritualism she defines as "heightened appreciation of symbolic action," which is manifested in "belief in the efficacy of instituted signs" and "sensitivity to condensed symbols."[43] By "efficacy of signs" she refers to faith in either the magical or sacramental character of ritual acts. "Condensed symbols" she uses to refer to highly complex, multivalent, but specific symbols, for example, for Christians, "atonement" or the Cross; for Jews, the *galut* ("exile") or the "holy hill of Zion."

Antiritualism is characterized for her by mistrust of symbolic, ritual acts and rejection of their sacramental or magical efficacy (i.e., interpretation of ritual as commemorative rather than efficacious in nature). Thus she sees between the Catholic and the Anglican Eucharist celebrations, for example, "a shift from the emphasis on ritual efficacy in the first, to the emphasis on commemorative rite in the second."[44] This antiritualism also gravitates toward what she calls "diffuse" as opposed to "condensed" symbols, for example, in modern humanist culture, concepts like "human values" or perhaps "social responsibility."

Douglas sees specific social origins for these two contrasting perspectives vis-à-vis ritual. Where community is a central value and communal bonds and

[42] Cf. above, nn. 32, 34. The following presentation of Douglas's ideas is based principally upon her initial chapter (pp. 19-39), in which she sets forth the general principles of her analysis of ritualism.

[43] Douglas, *Natural Symbols*, p. 26.

[44] Ibid., p. 27.

unity are strong, ritualism will flourish. Symbols and ritual action will be highly valued and some social correlates will be (1) developed ecclesiology or support of some kind of mediating institutions and authority; (2) a concept of sin and virtue involving very specific categories of external acts; (3) emphasis on formal, ritual purification and dietary restrictions; and (4) a general inclination to see meaning in external forms. Where communal bonding and authority structures are not developed, or are breaking down, antiritualism will predominate. Symbols and rituals will be denigrated as meaningless forms, and social correlates will be (1) absence of mediating authority structures and stress on individual autonomy; (2) an interiorized sense of sinfulness and virtue as "states of mind" rather than specific acts; (3) lack of stress on purificatory or dietary practices; and (4) general mistrust of external forms and symbols.

Sacramentalism (or magic) and highly complex symbolism seem to be the keys to ritualism in Douglas's scheme. She argues that attitudes about these pivotal matters ought to correlate with other generally consistent societal and religious attitudes and conditions such as those just described. This correlation should hold generally true whether one is looking at her Bog Irish Catholics of London over against the humanist English Catholic priesthood, at medieval Catholicism in contrast to the Protestant Reformation, at "high church" Anglicanism versus "low church" Anglicanism or Methodism, at orthodox Judaism over against reform Judaism, or at a tightly knit agrarian "primitive" society like the Bantu in contrast to a fluid hunter group like the Pygmy. The ritualism/antiritualism dichotomy should theoretically apply within and between socioreligious communities to groups whose differences are signaled in their attitudes to ritual efficacy and symbolic meaning.

Douglas's typology, like any typology, can hardly be expected to work everywhere equally well as a descriptive tool. Nonetheless, the general outlines of her two types of religious orientation vis-à-vis ritual and their social correlations seem to me helpful and consistent in interpreting a number of religious communities with which I am familiar. What is striking, however, is that mainstream, "orthoprax," Islam does not fit well at all into either category of her scheme. The Muslim tradition is at the core strongly ritualist by almost any standard, and virtually all of Douglas's socioreligious correlates of ritualism are traits common to Islam historically: strong communal bonding, strong traditional authorities, clear ideas of sin and virtue, emphasis on purity and dietary laws. Yet with respect to her key characteristics, ritual efficaciousness and condensed symbols, Islam does not conform well to the ritualist mold. It is of course true that at the popular level and in large measure in the special case of Shi'i practice, ritual activities such as ziyāra carry a strong element of belief in ritual efficacy (e.g., the healing power of saint's or imam's tomb) and have developed complex, "condensed" symbols (e.g., the green and red of the ta'ziya passion dramas–symbols of good and evil, martyrs and oppressors, Ḥusaynids and Marwānids, Shi'is and Sunnis). However, the main thrust of "orthoprax" Islam, in its practice as well as its theory, has been toward rejection of sacramentalism and elaborate, "condensed" symbolism (e.g., the emphasis upon performance of rites as fulfillment of duties, or the stress on very general, "diffuse" symbolic concepts such as *tauḥīd*, "declaring God's unity," or *hudan*, "guidance"). Thus at the heart of Muslim faith and practice we find a ritualism that appears to differ from ritualism in other traditions. I see its uniqueness in this regard, as I have adumbrated earlier, in what I refer to as the "reformational" cast of Muslim ritualism.

The term "reformational" is an inexact one, but I use it to connote what I see in Muslim ritual as well as Muslim thought as a pervasive and characteristic quality intrinsic to Islam. As an historical reality, Islam began as an avowed reformation of previous monotheism and pagan polytheism and has continued to cultivate ever since this reformational spirit at a very fundamental level. Its ritual action and symbolism are *systematically* set over against those of previous and contemporaneous religious traditions, especially paganism on the one hand and Judaic and Christian tradition on the other. This self-conscious effort to distinguish its faith and practice (or, from the Muslim's point of view, this work of God in distinguishing them) from other communities' faith and practice has taken two forms. The first has been a "ritualistic" approach to the sustaining and nourishing of piety and faith; the second has been a "reformational" reshaping of its ritualism in such a way as to give it a unique character that eludes most comparisons with other ritualisms.

This reformational bent in Islam rejects both sacramentalism and "condensed" symbols, as Douglas uses these terms. It is fundamentally aniconic, amythical, and commemorative or traditionalist in character. As such, it is especially evident in the moving but sparse symbolism of ṣalāt, the pragmatic quality of ṭahāra regulations, the central role of oral recitation of divine word, and the "unmythologized" character of the Ramaḍān fast. Yet even in the more elaborate and complex rites of the ḥajj we can see this reformational quality, especially in its nonsacramental character and the distinctive nature of its symbolic aspects.

The clear rejection of sacramental or magical efficaciousness of ḥajj observances is manisfested most graphically in the sacrifice at Minā on the 10th Dhū al-Ḥijja. The Qur'ān itself clearly gives this sacrifice an internalized, nonsacramental, pietistic, and ethical interpretation. Concerning the sacrifical animals, Sūra 27:37 says: "Neither their flesh nor their blood reaches God, but rather piety on your part (*taqwā minkum*) reaches Him. . . ." Sūra 22:34 stresses that the purpose of the sacrifice is "to make mention of God" (*li-yadhkurū 'sma 'llāhi*; cf. 22:36) over the beasts that God has bestowed upon humankind. Sūra 22:28, as also 22:36, commands the Muslims to "eat of them [the sacrificed animals] and feed the misfortunate and the poor." The reformational cast of these injunctions is clear; here the sacrifice becomes a symbolic act of 'ibāda and gratitude to God, not a propitiation of Him with a blood offering. In addition, the almost casual and wholly individual character of the actual sacrificial act—which is not precisely specified as to place or time nor accompanied by any ritual repetition of a sacred text–is in consonance with this antimagical, antisacramental thrust of the Qur'ānic texts.

This antisacramentalist bent is also evident in other rites of ḥajj. In a popular manāsik manual the section on iḥrām opens by stating that iḥrām "is a sign ['ibra] of intention to perform and to begin the ḥajj."[45] Modern Muslim interpretations of the meaning of the iḥrām clothing stress its symbolic "leveling" of all differences of status among Muslims.[46] Even in the taboos of the iḥrām period there is no attempt that I can find to interpret them as conveying any special power such as one might expect to find accompanying acts of abstinence. Throughout the prayers of the ḥajj there runs the theme of cleansing or purifying of sins, especially with reference to preparation for one's judgment on the Last Day, but nowhere is this seen in terms of the redemptive or absolving power of the ḥajj. Instead the petitions to God ask Him to make all the Muslim's acts such as to allow him or her to be forgiven and accepted on the Day of Judgment. In other words, they are ultimately petitions for mercy.[47]

Further, there is obvious avoidance in the rites surrounding the Ka'ba of any magical or idolatrous interpretation of acts like the sevenfold ṭawāf or the kissing of the Black Stone (*istilām*). The famous hadith ascribed to 'Umar ibn al-Khaṭṭāb and quoted in all the major collections presents this attitude graphically. 'Umar is reported to have said when he kissed the Black Stone, "By God, I know that you are only a stone, and had I not seen the Apostle of God kiss you, I would not kiss you!"[48] Tirmidhī, in his *Kitāb al-ḥajj wa-asrārihi*, writes that the pilgrim, when he goes back to the stone after ṭawāf, "kisses it, giving thanks that God has blessed him by having him follow the *sunna* of Abraham and the *sunna* of Muhammad."[49]

In these latter examples we see also the positive side of the Muslim avoidance

[45]Muḥammad Taufīq Ramaḍān, *Manāsik al-ḥajj wa'l-'umra wa-ādāb az-ziyāra* (Damascus: Maktabat al-Ghazzālī, n. d. [1395/1975?]), p. 33. Cf. Badrān Abū al-'Ainain Badrān, *al-'Ibādāt al-islamiyya muqārana 'alā al-madhāhib al-arba'a* (Alexandria: al-Ma'ārif, 1969), p. 187, where the *iḥrām* is said to be the name given to the proper intention to perform Ḥajj (*niyyat al-ḥajj*).

[46]Cf. Ahmad Kamal, *The Sacred Journey, Being Pilgrimage to Makkah* [Engl. orig. (1961) with Arabic trans.] (London: George Allen & Unwin, 1964), p. 14; S. A. Husain, *A Guide to Hajj* (Lahore: Sh. Muhammad Ashraf, 1972), p. 20; and Ali Shariati, *Hajj*, Ali A. Behzadnia and Najla Denny, trans. (Houston, Texas: Free Islamic Literatures, 1977), pp. 8-9.

[47]This general theme is evident in the prayers commonly repeated by the manuals, e.g., the common Meccan manual sold during the Hajj today: *al-Dīn wa'l-ḥajj wa'l-'umra 'alā al-madhāhib al-arba'a* (Mecca: al-Maktaba at-Tijāriyya, n. d. [c. 1977]), passim, esp. the long *du'ā'* to be prayed at 'Arafāt during the *wuqūf* (pp. 41-64, esp. 44-45). For an eloquent rendering of this basic prayer in English, see Kamal, *Sacred Journey*, pp. 69-81, esp. p. 71.

[48]Muslim ibn al-Ḥajjāj, *Kitāb aṣ-ṣaḥīḥ*, Muḥammad Fu'ād 'Abd al-Bāqī, ed. (5 vols.; Cairo, 1374-1375/1955-1956), chap. 15, hadith no. 248.

[49]Muḥammad ibn 'Alī al-Ḥākim at-Tirmidhī (d. ca. 320/932), *Kitāb al-ḥajj wa-asrārihi*, Ḥusnā Naṣr Zaidān, ed. (Cairo: Maṭba'at aṣ-Ṣa'āda, 1389/1969), p. 117.

of magicoreligious interpretations of the ḥajj rites. This aspect I call "conformative" because it is the tendency to explain all of the ḥajj observances purely as acts of proper conformity–either with divine commands or with prophetic example. One does the acts of the ḥajj not to "get" something but simply because they are to be done–either essential, required parts of the ritual (*wājibāt*) or as traditional, customary acts or ways of acting (*sunan*). Thus, in a discussion of "why" the pilgrim engages in "stoning the devils" (*ramy al-jamarāt*), a contemporary manual calls this "an action of which man can scarcely comprehend anything except that it [means] to follow God's command and to be guided by His Will."[50] This reminds us of Ghazzālī's interpretation of such acts to which we referred earlier.

This conformative quality of the ḥajj rites is a reflection of the tradionalist understanding of why one does what one does, which pervades Muslim ritual and most other areas of Muslim life. It corresponds to Mary Douglas's "commemorative" quality of ritual[51] and militates against emphasis on ritual efficaciousness of any specific nature being attached to a particular observance.

The "commemorative" character of Muslim ritualism is seen with special clarity in the way in which the Abraham myth is treated in ḥajj. The aforementioned amythical quality of Muslim ritualism is evident here in the lack of mythic continuity in the ḥajj rites as a whole. Some key observances are closely tied to the Abraham-Hagar-Ishmael cycle, but others have little or no Abrahamic reference at all, being taken purely as imitation of Muhammad's practice when he instituted the *manāsik al-ḥajj*. The 'Arafāt and Muzdalifa rites, including the major rite of the entire ḥajj, the wuqūf at 'Arafāt, have no link with the Abraham story at all. There is no sense in the flow of ritual events in ḥajj that one is reenacting a mythic paradigm (as, for example, there is in the following of the Stations of the Cross in Jerusalem).

Even in the specifically Abrahamic rites there is really no mimetic character that could bear an Eliadian interpretation as "ritual repetition" of a prototypical act of primordial, mythic time. Instead, these rites are explicitly commemorative of prototypical human acts of faith or of God's acts of mercy and guidance to His servants (Abraham, Hagar, Ishmael). Any imitation is imitation of how Muhammad commemorated these deeds of his prophetic forebears. This is made clear when one sees the lack of any text-act congruity in the prayers or praises recommended for recitation at the time of Sa'y or the sacrifice at Minā.[52] There is no

[50]Muḥammad Ramaḍān, *Manāsik al-ḥajj*, p. 92.

[51]Douglas, *Natural Symbols*, pp. 26 ff.

[52]For the Sa'y, these are primarily repeated praises and petitions for mercy, help, and blessing. See Muḥammad Ramaḍān, *Manāsik al-ḥajj*, p. 62, and *ad-Dīn wa 'l-ḥajj*, pp. 23-40. Cf. the single prayer of the final trip to al-Marwa in Ahmad Kamal, *Sacred Journey*, pp. 63-64. For Minā, there is only one short prayer of praise to be said upon entering the town, a short prayer at the time of the "stonings," and no prayers or formulas at all for the sacrifice itself. Cf. *ad-Dīn wa 'l-ḥajj*, p. 69, and Kamal, *Sacred Journey*, pp. 87-88.

statement that the worshiper sees himself or herself as *like* Hagar or Abraham, for instance, even though their actions commemorate Hagar's frantic search for water and Abraham's offering of his son as a sacrifice.

Instead of any mythical interpretation of such acts, there is only the aforementioned emphasis on conformity to tradition or on the ethical import of these commemorative acts. The latter we see especially in more modern manuals. One example, concerning the stoning rituals at Minā, points not only to the role of the stoning as reminder of Abraham's and Ishmael's faith, but says that it "expresses [the worshipers'] rejection of the attempts to lead [them] astray that they will encounter in their lives after today . . . and their battling of corruption and perversion. . . .[53] Such an interpretation, however modern, is in consonance with the whole "reformational" thrust of the ḥajj rites traditionally.

This tendency away from development of mythical symbolism and toward interpretation of these rites as diffuse symbols of obedience, piety, morality, or conformity with Islamic tradition is paralleled by the strikingly aniconic character of the ḥajj. The empty stone cube of the Ka'ba, devoid of iconography, the two unadorned rocks of Ṣafā and Marwa, the bare plains and hills of Muzdalifa and 'Arafāt, the lack of a specific place of sacrifice at Minā, the absence of any ritual paraphernalia throughout the rites, and even the marginally iconic stone pillars of the *jamarāt* are all testimony to the oft-remarked sparseness of visual symbolism in Islam. The visible simplicity of the ḥajj environment matches the simplicity of the rites themselves, in which we find no ritualistic stress on precise unison timing or on essential ritual formulas beyond the constantly repeated *talbiya.*[54] which itself in its enigmatic simplicity is a kind of diffuse symbol of 'ibāda, purity of intent, and humility before the divine omnipotence.

All in all, these various aspects of what I have termed the "reformational" quality of Islamic ritual reflect a kind of symbolical economy that we do not in most traditions associate with strong ritualism. There is a Spartan austerity to the ritual surroundings, symbols, acts, and words of the ḥajj observances that is in many ways remarkable. I am suggesting that this economy of ritual symbolism is central to the Islamic reformational urge to ward off any possibility for entry of idolatrous, ritualistic aberrations into its practice and piety.

I see the epitome of this ritual economy in the supreme rite of ḥajj, the *wuqūf* at 'Arafāt. Without 'Arafāt, no ḥajj is valid; one must at some point during the prescribed hours stand in prayer, meditation, or recitation on or near the "Mount of Mercy" on the 'Arafāt plain. Symbolically, this act has no precise mythological or theological connotations. Repentance, humility, introspection, awareness of community–these are themes of the suggested prayers for the wuqūf, but there is

[53]Muḥammad Ramaḍān, *Manāsik al-ḥajj*, p. 92.

[54]I.e., "labbaika, allahumma, labbaika," which may be rendered idiomatically "here I am, wholly at Thy service, O Lord, here I am, wholly at Thy service!"

no effort at more condensed symbolic interpretation. Here, in the sparseness of ritual action—"being there" is the only requirement—is perhaps the ultimate "reformational" symbol of the ḥajj's meaning: 'ibāda and tauḥīd. There is no *do ut des*, no elaborate symbolic drama at the heart of these rites, only the overwhelming sense of coming before God to "worship and serve" in obedience ('ibāda) and to "declare His oneness" with simplicity and sincerity (tauḥīd). The drama and the symbolism here are in the starkness of the whole, not in the elaboration of gestures, words, or visible signs.

Thus we can see in all these examples from ḥajj that however much Islam may be at base a ritualist, even "legalist" tradition of piety and practice, its fundamental, "reformational" urge to purify and to maintain worship and service of the One God has given its ritualism and ritual symbolism a quality that is perhaps unique. That the ritualism of the Pilgrimage shuns sacramental or magical efficacy and "condensed" symbols is a reflection less of Islamic societal factors, which the Douglas argument would expect, than of Muslim faith. I suspect that Muslim ritualism does not correlate fully with Mary Douglas's ritualist schema because it is a "reformed" ritualism in which sacramentalism and elaborated symbolsim have been emphatically rejected by orthoprax tradition as potential threats to pure obedience and monotheism. This appears to be one place where the uniqueness of Islamic thinking is concretely reflected in the unique aspects of its practice. Might it not even be that, *pace* Robertson Smith, Islam presents us with at least one case in which rites conform to, and indeed are formed by, ideas and faith?

There is much yet to be done to refine and probably to revise these suggestions. What I see in the way of a Muslim self-image expressed in the ritual life of Islam is a conscious *sense* of being unique, of being reformative of all less exacting 'ibāda, of clinging to a radical tauhīd in the face of less thoroughgoing monotheism as well as sheer idolatry. This "reformational" sense has, I believe, infused Muslim rituals and symbols with an unusual, distinctive quality that has led outside observers to see them as deficient in terms of their own experience and categories, which have been derived from often radically different traditions of religion and culture. Perhaps it is time that Semitists and comparativists alike turned from measuring success by the parallels and similarities that can be found between Islam and other traditions and began to work to define precisely the distinctive and *contrasting* qualities in Muslim ritual, symbolism, or whatever. All of us who study Islam from various perspectives might do well to contemplate the images of Islamic religiousness that we can find in Muslim thought and practice and try to remember, with George Santayana, that "every living and healthy religion has a marked idiosyncrasy. Its power consists in its special and surprising message and in the bias which that revelation gives to life. The vistas it opens and the mysteries it propounds are another world to live in; and another world to live in—whether we expect ever to pass wholly into it or no–is what we mean by religion."[55] Certainly Muslims in this sense "have a religion" (*lahum dīnuhum*) about which they are self-conscious, of which they are proud, and toward whose "world" they aspire. Its idiosyncrasy is evident not only in their thought but also in their practice, which necessarily mirrors that thought. Our task is at least in part to identify however we can the elements of that idiosyncrasy and to seek to appreciate it and evaluate it on its own terms.

[55] *Reason in Religion*, Vol. III, *The Life of Reason, or the Phases of Human Progress* (New York: Charles Scribner's Sons, 1926), p. 6.

INSTITUTIONALIZED LEARNING AS A SELF-IMAGE OF ISLAM

GEORGE MAKDISI

University of Pennsylvania

The proper name that best identifies the Muslim is 'Abd Allāh, God's submissive servant. In the Middle Ages, it was the name by which a Muslim was called by a fellow Muslim who did not know his real name. In the *Book of Penitents*, the characters in some of the stories were commonly addressed by this proper name, much as an American today might informally address another, whose name is unknown to him, by calling him Mac.

The Arabic lexicon explains *islām* as meaning "the manifesting of submission, and outward conforming with the law of God, and the taking upon oneself to do or to say as the Prophet has done or said."[1] Thus Islam is submission to God's will, and the Muslim is God's submissive servant, 'Abd Allāh. The verb *ta'abbada* means to devote oneself to the service of God; and to say of someone that he *ta'abbada bi 'l-Islām* means that he made himself a servant of God by following the religion of Islam. The word *'abd* commonly means a man, a human being; its plurals mean mankind and, more properly, servants or bondmen to God; in this meaning, 'abd is synonymous with *marbūb* and *mamlūk*. The proper state of God is *rubūbīya*, which commonly means ownership and, more properly, lordship, deity; and the proper state of man is *'ubūdīya*, commonly slavery, and more properly, worship, adoration, obedience with submissiveness. Man owes God *'ibāda*, that is, the doing of what God approves.[2]

Submission to God's will inheres in the meaning of the terms "'abd" and "muslim"; and an identity of meaning runs through their derivatives: the verbs ta'abbada and aslama, and the infinitive nouns 'ubūdīya and islām, and 'ibāda and islām. The Muslim conceives of himself as God's submissive servant, and sees his role as the doing of God's will, and following the example of the Prophet, the first muslim.

This is the most clearly defined image Islam has of itself, and it is nowhere

[1] Cf. E. W. Lane, *Arabic-English Lexicon* (London and Edinburgh: Williams and Norgate, 1863 ff.). s.v. *slm*.

[2] For all these terms, cf. ibid., s.v.

more clearly reflected than in the history of Islam's institutionalized learning. In Islam, law is the expression of God's will; Islamic law is a voluntarist, divine positive law. Law, in Islam, came to constitute the kernel and climax of Islamic learning. At the summit of Islam's educational system, the college of law became firmly established, and law became unchallenged as to its primacy and pervasiveness. It was only appropriate that this should be the case for Islam. Submissive obedience to God's will being Islam's vision of the proper state of mankind, this concept of 'ubūdīya was embodied in the religion's very name: Islām. Clearly the primordial and most abiding image Islam has of itself is 'ubūdīya, islām.

Orthodoxy in Islam is therefore legal, more a matter of God's law, rather than theological, which would concentrate on God Himself. When a conservative jurist and theologian of the thirteenth century was faced with the need to refute what he considered to be the rationalistic theology of a fellow Muslim of a previous century, one of the arguments he used goes to the heart of the matter that concerns us here:

> We have no need to know the meaning which God intended by His attributes; *no course of action* is intended by them, nor is there any obligation attached to them *except to believe in them*; and it is possible to believe in them without the knowledge of their intended sense. For indeed faith, with ignorance, is sound. God has enjoined belief in His angels, His scriptures, His prophets and that which He has revealed to them, though we might not know of all this except the designation.[3]

The important thing is to learn God's will and obey it. His will is revealed in His books given to His people through His messengers. The believer must obey His commands and prohibitions. In order to ascertain what to do and what to avoid doing, the simple believer seeks guidance from those who study the sacred Scriptures and derive the law from them. The first priority then in Muslim education was the education of the scholar specializing in the knowledge of God's law.

The first product of Islamic education was the mufti, produced long before the Muslim institutions of learning took shape. It was in fact the mufti's role in Islam that was later to mold, shape, and give final form to the institution that was to become the college of Islam par excellence, the madrasa.

At first a *masjid*, or non-Friday mosque, the college of law was joined later by the madrasa. The masjid was used as an institution of learning in the very first years of Islam; but from about the middle of the ninth century, and with increasing momentum, masjids were founded and organized for the express purpose of

[3] Ibn Qudāma, *Taḥrīm an-naẓar fī kutub ahl al-kalām*, ed. and trans., with introduction by G. Makdisi, *Ibn Qudāma's Censure of Speculative Theology*, Gibb Memorial Series 23 (London: Luzac, 1962), p. 22 (English pagination), p. 32 (Arabic pagination), para. 55.

producing the jurisconsult, whose first and foremost function it was to issue legal opinions to the faithful who solicited them.

The mufti was the first Muslim intellectual. He came into existence as early as the need for him arose; that is, as soon as the need arose for authoritative opinions to guide the community after the death of the Prophet. The first muftis were the Companions of the Prophet, including the first four caliphs whose special designation was "the Rightly Guided Caliphs."

From those early times and up to the first half of the twelfth century, institutionalized education put its efforts primarily into perfecting that process which produced the professional jurisconsult, the prime end product of the system.

The Image Blurred

Not all education in Islam was institutionalized, nor were all intellectuals products of the Muslim college, any more than all intellectuals of the premodern West were products of academies, or universities. Islam experienced a great awakening in the early Abbasid period with the introduction of Greek works the translation of which was energetically pursued under the caliphate of al-Ma'mūn in the first half of the ninth century. And although the traditionalist legal scholars at first shunned these books, they later found good use for some of their contents, particularly dialectic for expertise in disputation, the mechanism that became so essential in the process that led to consensus.

The introduction of Greek works brought chaos into the relative serenity of the Muslim learned scene, giving rise to rationalist movements that proved to be a thorn in the side of traditionalism. It was not long before the antagonism came to a head, producing the great Inquisition, the *miḥna*, that lasted fifteen years, in the second quarter of the ninth century.

The Inquisition was a struggle between two factions of ulama, one that advocated theology in its rationalist form, that is, the science of God, and another that advocated law, that is, the science of God's will. The former sought to speculate on the nature of God Himself; the latter insisted on the sole importance of learning and following His will. In explaining the Inquisition it has been said that criminal proceedings were introduced by the state "against acknowledged theologians who would not without reserve profess the doctrine of the 'creation of the Koran.'"[4] It was true only of those who conducted the Inquisition; they were the theologians; but those who were the object of the Inquisition, who were called upon to profess a theological doctrine, were the representatives of the law, that is, the qadis, the muftis, the *shuhūd*-notaries, and the ulama of the Prophet's Sunna, all men of the law. The question therefore is not whether these men were or were not also theologians, even traditionalist, conservative theologians–which of course

[4] I. Goldziher, "Muḥammad b. Aḥmad b. Ḥanbal," *Encyclopedia of Islam*, 1st ed.

they were, judging from their viewpoint regarding the character of the Koran—rather the question is that those singled out for subjection to the Inquisition were primarily representatives of the law, whatever else they may have been. The ulama of the Middle Ages were seldom experts in only one field of knowledge; even a jurisconsult of a conservative, traditionalist bent, could indeed be very well versed in the rationalist theology of his adversaries, if for no other reason than to hold his own against them. Part of the punishment for not subscribing to the theological doctrine of the created character of the Koran was the dismissal of these ulama from their posts as qadis and notaries.

To these conservative jurisconsults, kalam, rationalistic theology, was tainted with the foreign sciences, especially philosophy, recently come from the Greeks; whereas fiqh, law, was based on the Koran and hadith, the sacred scriptures of Islam, whose adepts were called *ahl al-ḥadīth*, the general designation of traditionalists.

The inquisitors of the miḥna demanded that their victims subscribe to their doctrine regarding the Koran. Those who refused were condemned. Many jurisconsults were flogged, many died, while others made outward profession of the doctrine to survive the ordeal. But the Inquisition finally collapsed in favor of the traditionalist jurisconsults when the Inquisition's fourth caliph al-Mutawakkil reversed the policy of persecution in the second year of his caliphate. From that time on, rationalist Mu'tazili theology was, once and for all, shorn of its political power. On the traditionalist side, there emerged the heroic figure of Aḥmad b. Ḥanbal, the great charismatic master and exponent of the Prophetic traditions, who had stubbornly weathered the long years of persecution, flogging, and imprisonment with patient endurance.

The Image Restored

Traditionalist jurisprudence resumed its course and surged ahead to win the support of political power. When the caliph al-Ma'mūn supported the kalam theologians' doctrine of the creation of the Koran, a doctrine to which he adhered, he had done so by setting the Inquisition in motion and sustaining it in a series of epistles. Two centuries later the religiopolitical scene had changed completely. In the early part of the eleventh century the caliph al-Qadir, in a parallel series of epistles, gave his support to the doctrine of the traditionalists. This series of epistles culminated in the declaration of a profession of faith, called the Qādirī Creed, *al-i'tiqād al-qādirī*. Its contents were made incumbent on all Muslims. In it were condemned all creeds opposed to the traditionalists (ahl al-hadīth), going well beyond the question of the Koran. This creed opposed extremist Shī'ism, and the two rationalist theologies that had developed in the Sunni ranks: Mu'tazilism, as well as its successor Ash'arism, in its rationalist form.

The course of events after the Inquisition helped to bring Islam's self-image back into focus. If Islam is in fact submission to God's will, then serious study should be made of the words of God and those of His messenger. And those who should command the attention and respect of the Muslim community at large are those who devote themselves to the study of the sacred Scriptures. Learning based on the Scriptures is the only learning worthy of the name; and the ulama worthy of the name are those who devote themselves to this learning. They are the leaders to be followed, for they are "the heirs of the prophets," as in fact the hadith goes: "*al-'ulamā' warathatu 'l-anbiyā'*";[5] and these ulama who are the heirs of the Prophets are the jurisconsults.

The collapse of the Inquisition and the consequent political defeat of the Mu'tazilites set in motion two developments of capital importance to the resurgence of conservative Islam. The first of these developments was the relatively rapid compilation of hadith collections; and the second, was the gradual monopolization of the masjid-mosque and its organization for the education of the jurisconsult.

These two developments were closely interconnected. Collections of traditions had already been written before, arranged either according to their contents, *'alā 'l-abwāb*, referred to as *muṣannaf, sunan, mawaṭṭa'*, and *jāmi'*, or according to their transmitters, *'alā 'r-rijāl*, and called *musnad*. The oldest book on hadith known to us is that of Makḥūl b. Abī Muslim ash-Shāmī (d. 112/730).[6] It is systematically arranged according to content. This type of collection is generally considered to have taken place in the first half of the second century of Islam (eighth of our era). On the other hand, a second type, appearing in the second half of that century, was the musnad, so-called because it was arranged according to the names of the Companions of the Prophet.[7] The first concern of the Muslim critics of hadith had been to ascertain the authenticity of the transmission of traditions through the critique of the transmitters themselves. The traditions compiled by the great hadith expert Aḥmad b. Ḥanbal, and made into a collection by his son 'Abd Allāh, are arranged according to the chain of transmitters called isnad. His collection and others like it were called musnad. Ibn Ḥanbal's *Musnad*, the best known among them, won great renown. It contains close to 30,000 traditions. Long the subject of pious reading, it has inspired a large number of secondary works from early times down to our day. The most recent of these is that of the late scholar Aḥmad Muḥammad Shākir, who devoted many years to rearranging the hadiths of this musnad in order to make their contents more easily accessible.[8]

[5]Cf. A. J. Wensinck, *A Handbook of Early Muhammadan Tradition* (Leiden: E. J. Brill, 1927), p. 234*a*.

[6]See F. Sezgin, *Geschichte des arabischen Schrifttums*, Vol. I (Leiden: E. J. Brill, 1967), p. 90, hereafter *GAS*.

[7]Ibid., p. 55.

[8]For the studies on, and rearrangements of, the *Musnad* of Ibn Ḥanbal, see ibid., pp. 504-506.

But in spite of the renown of Ibn Ḥanbal's *Musnad* and of his stature as an expert in the field (acknowledged by Ṭabarī), and in spite of the respect and profound veneration in which he was held as hero of the Inquisition, a respect and veneration that has never ceased among Muslims of all schools of law, his monumental work did not find a place among the so-called canonical collections of traditions. In itself, this fact is surprising, to say the least, given the role he played as the foremost champion of the conservative traditionalist movement. The fact that the six collections were called *ṣaḥīḥ*, sound, reliable, may imply that other collections, including the *Musnad* of Aḥmad b. Ḥanbal were not sound, that their hadiths were weak. But this could not be the case. For if Ibn Ḥanbal's *Musnad* had lacked reliability it would not have attracted some of the foremost experts on hadith to its study. Moreover, the soundness of a hadith was determined by the authoritative character of its chain of transmitters. The musnad type of collection points to the preoccupation of its compiler with the isnad, the very basis upon which reliability was determined. That the "six books" were also designated as the "sound books," *aṣ-ṣiḥāḥ*, may well be attributable to an attempt to point out that these books *should also* be considered "sound," *in spite of the fact that they were not organized according to their isnads*. Furthermore, weak hadiths were found in the two great *ṣaḥīḥ* works of Bukhari and Muslim. The hadith expert ad-Dāraquṭnī (d. 385/995) wrote a work in which he proved two hundred hadiths in the collections of Bukhari and Muslim to be weak.[9] No collections can be qualified as free of weak traditions. The criticism of traditions was a task repeatedly taken up. Consensus has never pronounced on the exclusive validity of any collection of hadiths.[10]

Many collections of the musnad type were compiled long before that of Ibn Ḥanbal. Such compilations are attributed to Abū Ḥanīfa and Shāfi'ī. Of the many musnads that have come down to us, the majority were compiled from the second Islamic century down through the period of the authors of the "six books" and well beyond them. According to Dhahabī, the best musnad was that of Ya'qūb b. Shaiba (d. 262/865) whose period falls in the middle of that of the authors of the six books. These musnads, compiled before as well as after the six books, carried the names of some of the most venerated people of early Islam. Among these musnads are those whose chains of authoritative transmitters go back to 'Ā'isha, favorite wife of the Prophet; to Bilāl, Companion of the Prophet and the first muezzin; to the Anṣār, the Medinian allies of the Prophet; to Abū Bakr aṣ-Ṣiddīq, Companion, and first of the Rightly Guided Caliphs; and to the fourth such Caliph, 'Alī b. Abī Ṭālib, cousin and son-in-law of the Prophet, whose traditions were compiled by Ibn Jarīr aṭ-Ṭabarī (d. 310/923), historian and founder

[9] See I. Goldziher, *Muhammedanische Studien* (2 vols.; Halle, 1890), II, 257; cf. F. Sezgin, *GAS*, I, 208, no. 10: *al-Ilzāmāt 'alā Ṣaḥīḥai al-Bikhārī wa-Muslim*.

[10] Cf. T. W. Juynboll, "ḥadīth," part IV: "The Collections of Tradition," *Encyclopedia of Islam*, 1st ed.

of the Jarīrī school of law. Yet none of these collections were chosen for inclusion in the six books, in spite of the veneration in which the transmitters involved were held then, and still are to this day.

This apparently surprising fact can be explained, I believe, by the important events taking place at the time; namely, the development of legal studies, and the proliferation of the masjids as colleges of law to accommodate these studies. The compilations in the six books were arranged according to chapters, for easy access to their contents. If the six books were, as is often said, canonical, that is, if they were the sole authoritative collections of hadiths, there would have been no need for students specializing in hadith to travel far and wide in the Islamic world to collect them from their authoritative transmitters. Strictly speaking, there were *no canonical books*; there were *only authoritative transmitters*. The six books were manuals of hadiths compiled for the use of students, especially useful for students of law. The advanced student of hadith in order to succeed as a master in that field, had to go beyond those books to gather the authoritative transmissions from the mouths of the living masters in that field.

The compilers of the six collections died between 256 and 303 of the hijra (870 and 915 of our era), that is to say, in the second half of the century in the first half of which the Inquisition had experienced its rise and collapse. No time was wasted by the traditionalist lawyers to step into the vacuum left by the rationalist theologians. Hadith and law were henceforth united, once and for all, in an alliance that was destined to defeat the restoration of political rationalism.

Traditionalist Islam owed its success to two of Islam's leading imams, Shāfiʻī and Ibn Ḥanbal, eponyms of the two last schools of law to survive in Islam down to modern times: Shāfiʻī, for shaping the law along traditionalist lines; and Ibn Ḥanbal, for successfully replacing the Muʻtazili philosophical theology of speculation with the traditionalist juridical theology of unquestioning submission to the sacred scriptures, without seeking to fathom their mysteries.

Thus the Inquisition brought into existence two interconnected phenomena: (1) the compilation of hadiths in collections arranged according to chapters easily used for legal studies, and (2) an increasing number of masjids devoted to these studies.

The two phenomena were eventually followed by a third; namely, the crystallization of the schools of law, and the disappearance of all others from the scene, first in Baghdad, then elsewhere. The schools of law, it is well known, had been multiplying at a rapid rate, a phenomenon inferred from their rate of disappearance: five hundred of them are said to have ceased to exist by the beginning of the tenth century. This attrition was most likely caused by the desire of conservative jurisconsults to close ranks against the rationalist forces, and thus eliminate the divisiveness inherent in the proliferation of schools of law. Attrition continued into the eleventh century when the Hanbali school emerged as the seal of the schools of law, whereas its contemporaries the Jariri and Zahiri schools ceased to exist in the Abbasid capital, their place of origin.[11]

The events of the years that followed the Inquisition clearly illustrate the losses of the rationalist movement and the concomittant gains of traditionalism. Running parallel with the masjid and madrasa were the rationalist institutions of the *dār al-'ilm* type where books on all subjects were to be found, including especially the "ancient sciences," called *'ulūm al-awā'il*, of which the caliph al-Ma'mūn was an enthusiastic adept. This type of institution continued to be founded after the Inquisition in the ninth and tenth centuries. They were all essentially libraries and were designated by the terms *dār, bait,* or *khizāna* combined with one of the following three terms: *'ilm, ḥikma,* or *kutub*. All nine possible combinations of three terms can be documented.[12] By the end of the eleventh century this type of institution disappeared with only one experiencing an ephemeral existence in the twelfth, then disappearing from the scene.

These libraries were based on the waqf, like any other institution having to do with learning. It was a repository for books of all kinds which could be read, and discussed. Some founders of these institutions set aside funds to defray the cost of ink and paper, and others provided food and lodging, for those needy seekers of knowledge coming from afar. There was no curriculum to follow, no teaching staff.[13] The sources do not name many of these libraries, but rather isolated cases of philanthropists who founded them in this or that great city in Khurasan, Iraq, and Egypt.

This type of institution, however, was not the type destined to flourish in Islam. The tenth and eleventh centuries were those in which Islam was to concentrate on the development of its colleges where law, already raised to the level of a science by the efforts of Shafi'i, was destined to reach the height of its elaboration and perfection by the end of the eleventh century. The eighth and ninth centuries were those of search and struggle from which emerged a consciousness of the direction to be taken and the determination to pursue it. The self-image of Islam in the centuries that followed the Inquisition took shape as clearly in its institutions of learning as it did in the course of historical events.

Islam, as already said, is submission to God's will. God revealed His will in His law; the college, both the masjid, and the madrasa which joined it later, emerged to teach that law. Jurisprudence, organized for systematic study, became the queen of the Islamic sciences. Theology, the science whose object was the study

[11] Cf. my "The Significance of the Sunni Schools of Law in Islamic Religious History," *International Journal of Middle East Studies*, 10 (1979), 1-8.

[12] See my *The Rise of Colleges: Institutions of Learning in Islam and the West* (Edinburgh: University Press, 1981), pp. 24 f.

[13] The tenth-century geographer al-Maqdisī cites one such institution in Basra which boasted of a kalam-expert who lectured on the subject to anyone who would listen to him.

of God Himself, rather than what God had enjoined, had no place in the curriculum. As God did not prescribe that He Himself be the object of speculation, kalam-theology was kept outside the pale. It did not, for all that, cease to be a science; but it was excluded from *institutionalized* learning. Kalam and its practitioners, the mutakallimun, and a fortiori the "foreign sciences" and its adepts, had no place in the institutionalized educational system. Those who hoped to take part in that system had to do so as jurists, or as scholars of the legitimate subjects serving as ancillaries to the study of law. Legitimacy could be obtained only through the law.

The curriculum, the methods of teaching, and the administration of education and its institutions, all point to the primacy of the law and the law professor's place of honor in the system. The system was private, individualistic, and personalist. It was private, that is, beyond the grasp of the central power. The central power, as such, had nothing to do with the foundation of institutions of learning, nor with the curriculum, nor with the methods of teaching, nor with the issuing of the licenses to teach. Institutions of learning were religious institutions, owing their origin to religious law; the teaching of the religious law and of its ancillaries was organized and administered according to the principles of that law, and the end product was destined for a religious purpose. The central power lay completely outside the system.

The Image Imbedded in Islam

The individualism inherent in this private system appears quite clearly in the legal basis of its organization, the waqf. As such it was the creation of an individual Muslim who, by an act of private charity, instituted his own *private* property for a *public* purpose, which purpose he defined according to his own wishes. The founders freedom of choice was such that its only limitation was that there be nothing in the foundation which could be construed as inimical to the tenets of Islam. And its relation to the tenets of Islam was interpreted by the jurisconsults, not by the central power. The founder could therefore choose the madhab, the school of law, his college was to represent; he could choose the professor for its chair of law; he could keep the administration of the college to himself and to his posterity down to the end of his line, or he could give it to the professor of law, or to any one else; he could decide what was to be taught in his foundation. In all of this he acted with complete freedom, including the very act of foundation itself. The system lay outside the competence of church and state. The caliph and sultan, and other officials, could, as private Muslims, found colleges, but these institutions were also controlled by the law of waqf, interpreted by the jurisconsults. The counterpart of the church was the ulama; and the ulama who held religious authority sanctioned by the religious law were, for all intents and purposes, the jurisconsults, interpreters of the law. The institutionalized system of education was under their jurisdiction.

The college of law thus had one founder, was organized for one madhab, taught by one professor of law who belonged to that madhab. This individualism was seconded by the personalist nature of the license to teach and issue legal opinions. This personal license was given by the individual professor of law to the candidate after the satisfactory defense of a thesis, or theses, in a formal disputation. In issuing this license the professor acted completely on his own personal authority. He could not be forced to grant it by any other authority, be it the central power, or even a religious body.

The final product of the college was the new professor who professed his knowledge in two ways. His primordial function was to profess opinions, legal opinions called fatwa, when they were solicited by the faithful. In doing so, he was called mufti, a giver of a fatwa, and his function was called *iftā'*; and the person soliciting the fatwa was called a mustafti, a seeker of a fatwa. The second form of professing was his teaching of the basic law course to undergraduates, and to graduates a method of arriving at legal opinions, and of defending them against the objections of adversaries. In performing this function, the professor was called mudarris, and his function or post, *tadrīs*. Thus the end product of the college of law was the training of the mufti for the ultimate purpose of issuing legal opinions and of training others for this purpose.

As Islamic law was basically individualistic, so also was its practice characterized by the freedom of the individual. The mufti, jurisconsult, was free to arrive at his legal opinion and to profess it. He was encouraged to do so by a hadith according to which he was rewarded in the Hereafter, even if his opinion proved to be wrong; and doubly rewarded if it proved to be right. The solicitor of his opinion, the mustafti, had the corresponding freedom of following the opinion of his choice; for he could ask for as many of these opinions, from as many muftis as he wished.

The system of education was also characterized by freedom: freedom of the professor, and freedom of the student. The student, after his elementary education, could enter a college of law at about the age of fifteen. The choice of college determined the madhab, or school of law, to which he would belong, since each college represented one of the madhabs. He was free to choose his madhab which could well differ from that of his father and forefathers. Moreover, he was free to change madhabs at any time, whether during his studies or in later life. He could pursue the studies of his choice, and in the order of his choice; he could concentrate on any number of subjects, in any order he desired, before or after concentrating on law. The professor was likewise free to teach a method all his own, profess his own opinions, choose his own graduates as his fellows, and set his own standards for the granting of the license to teach and issue fatwas, completely independent and free of any outside force. He too could change from one madhab to another, as in the case of one professor who changed to the Shafi'i school after being a Hanafi professor of law for thirty years.

Thus the professor's freedom to teach according to his ijtihad, his own lights, was matched by the student's freedom to learn; and the mufti's independence and freedom to profess a legal opinion was matched by the layman's freedom to follow the opinion of his choice.

What was the position of government in this setup? It is hard to see how the central power could function without coming into conflict with the ulama. These religious leaders were in the closest contact with the common people, the faithful generally. Any sustained contact with the common people with a view to influencing their voluntary action had to take the ulama into consideration. The power of the ulama came from their close contact with the people whom they advised with their legal opinions on all matters of day to day life. It was in their religious leaders that the common people put their trust; they had no trust in the central power.

This situation existed practically from the outset in Islam. Only the first four caliphs were considered as worthy of loyalty, the Rightly Guided Caliphs, *al-Khulafā' ar-rāshidūn*. The later caliphs, whether Umaiyad or Abbasid, did not enjoy such a reputation.

The central power, therefore, had to make use of the ulama in order to reach the people. It was not an easy task. The difficulty was twofold. On the one hand, the ulama were not always ready to cooperate; and on the other, those who were prepared to do so were no longer trusted by the people, and were criticized by their more cautious colleagues, resistant to losing their independence. And few and far between were those ulama who were able to have it both ways, that is to say, who could work for the central power and continue to maintain their privileged position with the people.

The Image in Recurrent Resurgence

Islamic history from its early beginnings down to our present day affords many illustrations of this perennial struggle between the spiritual and the temporal, between the ulama and the central power, a struggle whose roots lie in the absence of separation between the two orders, since the religious law embraces the whole of the Muslim's life.

One of the areas that was early utilized by the holders of power in order to secure the goodwill of the ulama, and thereby secure also that of their followers through them, was the charitable trust, the waqf. Since the waqf was a private contribution of one's personal wealth for a religious purpose, even a government official could practice this kind of philanthropy in the name of religion and secure the loyalty of the religious scholar and that of his followers in whose favor he founded a mosque-college, or a madrasa, or a sufi ribat. There are two salient examples of this type of philanthropy practiced on a very wide scale: that of Badr B. Hasanawaih who founded mosque-colleges with nearby inns for lodging the out-of-town students. He was reputed to have founded three thousand complexes of this kind during the thirty years in which he governed several provinces under the Buwaihids. The other example is that of Nizam al-Mulk, reputed to have founded a large number of masjids and ribat-monasteries and a madrasa in every city of the eastern caliphate during his thirty years as prime minister under the Saljuqs. Other institutions were founded by other holders of power, both great and small. Their foundations earned for them the gratitude of the ulama and people, and established them as generous philanthropists in the cause of religion. One must not, however, consider these foundations as public institutions, simply because they were founded by public officials. They were founded by public officials in their capacity as private individuals.

Two areas were direct government interferences in what belonged to the sphere of religion, properly speaking; namely, the functions of justice and jurisprudence, the provinces of the qadi and the mufti, respectively. When the post of qadi was created in the second Islamic century, it was an innovation, and was regarded as such by the ulama. The biographical notices abound with anecdotes pointing out that such and such a jurist refused the post of qadi. Even those who accepted it were often shown to have refused it repeatedly before accepting. For a long time the qadiship was refused by the Shafi'is; and when Suraij, the great Shafi'i jurist, accepted the post, he was criticized by his fellow Shafi'is who pointed out to him that his acceptance was an innovation in the Shafi'i madhab, that his predecessors had all refused such a post successfully, and that the custom of accepting it was practiced by the Hanafis alone. When the Caliph prevailed upon the eleventh century Shafi'i jurist, Abū Bakr ash-Shāmī, to accept the post, he did so after several refusals, but on the condition that he not be required to join in the processions of state, and that he would refuse to accept a salary for the post. This he did in order to be able to reach his legal rulings freely, without interference from the central power.

The creation of this governmental post gave the government the opportunity to deal directly with the people. Yet it was not enough to establish a rapport productive of loyalty. The people still had the jurisconsults, the muftis, who were private religious scholars, owing nothing to the government. The mufti received the license for the muftiship from another mufti. It was a closed system, beyond the grasp of government.

This situation remained in effect until the seventh/thirteenth century, when the muftiship was brought under the control of the government. And when it did, it produced the same reluctance on the part of the ulama to accept the post, as the qadiship had done before. And although private muftis continued to exist, they could not compete with the free consultations afforded by the governmental posts.

With the muftiship, for all intents and purposes, under the control of the central power, the freedom of Muslim education was dealt a fatal blow; and the process of jurisprudence which led to consensus began to deteriorate and fall into disuse, resulting in ankylosis down to modern times. Muslim education, from the thirteenth century on, gradually lost its fundamental freedom, and with it its initiative and originality. Its scholastic exercises continued to be performed, but only pro forma, shorn of their vitality, emptied of their basic significance within a system of power whose reins had been held to a great extent in the hands of the ulama. From then on, education was no longer the free and vital force it was in the community's decision-making process, consensus.

Today the tension remains what it always was, a struggle between the ulama and the central power, a struggle to find a modus vivendi between the spiritual and the temporal. The tension is plainly seen throughout the course of Islamic religious history, in the ever recurring resurgences of religious movements in Islam: from the early kharijite call of *lā ḥukm illā li 'llāh* (no judgment but that of God alone), to the call of the Muslim Brothers in modern times, *lā dustūr illā 'l-Qur'ān* (no constitution other than the Koran).

The self-image of Islam, momentarily blurred by al-Ma'mūn's Inquisition, then restored by al-Qādir's profession of faith—a self-image characterized by the basic equality of all Muslims in the eyes of the law as God's submissive servants, and by the freedom of the individual Muslim in the search for salvation by the doing of God's will, this self-image lives on in the hearts and minds of the Muslim Community, torn by the tension between the sacral and the secular. Whatever solution the future may bring, there can be no ignoring the need for Islam, *as indeed for any monotheistic faith*, to provide for the primacy of the spiritual.

THE ISLAMIC PHILOSOPHERS' CONCEPTION OF ISLAM

MICHAEL E. MARMURA

University of Toronto

I

In approaching this topic, one is immediately confronted with a pressing need for clarification. The title "The Islamic Philosphers' Conception of Islam" evokes a number of questions of which the following are perhaps the most obvious. What Islamic philosophers do we have in mind? Did these philosophers all share in one conception of Islam as the title seems to suggest? But, above all, in what sense are we using the term "Islamic" when referring to them?

Turning to the first of these questions, I am primarily concerned with philosophers belonging to what Professor Watt has aptly called "the formative period of Islamic thought." They include such major thinkers as the first of the Islamic philosophers, al-Kindī (d. ca. 866), al-Rāzī (d. either 925 or 932), al-Fārābī (d. 950), Ibn Sīnā (Avicenna) (d. 1037), and Ibn Rushd (Averroes) (d. 1198), in other words, philosophers who lived between the ninth and twelfth centuries. This is not to belittle the originality and achievements of subsequent Islamic philosophers. But the main pattern for viewing religion and religious institutions in philosophical terms was laid down and developed by philosophers belonging to the formative period. Their "conception" of Islam is quite representative.

Before turning to the other two questions, particularly the sense in which such philosophers are referred to as "Islamic," I ought to comment briefly on their relation to Greek philosophy. These philosophers, as the abundance of their commentaries on Greek philosophy attests, regarded themselves as custodians of truths arrived at by the ancients (*al-qudamā'*). At the same time, they recognized that the attainment of truth is difficult, requiring, as al-Kindī argued, not only the lifelong effort of the individual thinker, but the cooperative intellectual efforts of generations past and present.[1] Hence they regarded the quest after truth as a continuous process. Their philosophical objective, as Ibn Sīnā, reechoing al-Kindī,

[1] al-Kindī, *Rasā'il al-Kindī al-falsafiyya*, M. A. Abu Rida, ed. (2 vols.; Cairo, 1950), I, 102.

expressed it, was "to know the true natures of all things to the extent that man is capable of knowing."[2]

The Islamic philosophers were not mere passive recipients of Greek philosophy, at best repeating what had been said in classical antiquity. They commented and elaborated, criticized, sifted, refined, and adapted. They introduced distinctions and made new attempts at resolving perennial philosophical problems. They remolded concepts to forge new philosophical syntheses, stamped by the vision of their individual creators. Their metaphysics was comprehensive; their range encyclopedic. But what concerns us most here, they sought to accommodate within their conceptual schemes prophetic revelation and the institutions of Islam. Their achievement, if only in this, was remarkable.

It brings us to the second question: Can we refer to these philosophers as having "a" conception of Islam? The answer is that strictly speaking we cannot. Such a reference is only a convenient generalization that certainly calls for qualification. It would be more accurate to say that at a certain juncture in the development of Islamic philosophy a comprehensive theory of religious revelation and of the religious state was formulated in terms of which cardinal affirmations of the Islamic religion and some of its basic institutions were interpreted. The metaphysical and epistemological components of this theory were ultimately Neoplatonic and Aristotelian; its political doctrine essentially Platonic. These components, however, were remolded and rethought to present a coherent view, remarkable for its detail. The architect of this theory was al-Fārābī. His theory superseded earlier philosophical conceptions pertaining to Islam, particularly as these interpreted the Qur'ānic account of the divine act of creating the world. The theory became the dominant view among al-Fārābī's successors. For, although these successors introduced modifications, refinements, expansions, and differences in emphases, they subscribed to the basic premises of his religiopolitical theory, and their elaborations remained basically within its framework.

It is with the third question regarding the use of the term "Islamic" in characterizing these philosophers that the need for clarification becomes particularly pressing. To fully appreciate this need, we must remind ourselves of the historic conflict between Islamic theology (*kalām*) and philosophy, brought to a head in the eleventh century by the Islamic jurist and Ash'arite theologian, al-Ghazālī (d. 1111). In his *Tahāfut al-falāsifa* (The Incoherence of the Philosophers), he singled out al-Fārābī and Ibn Sīnā for his attack. He subjected twenty of their philosophical doctrines to a severe logical refutation, condemning seventeen as representing heretical innovations (*bida'*), three as expressions of infidelity (*kufr*).[3] His denunciation of al-Fārābī and Ibn Sīnā as infidels, it should be added,

[2] Ibn Sīnā (Avicenna), *al-Shifā'*: *al-Manṭiq* (Logic), Part I, *al-Madkahl* (Isagoge), M. Khuḍayri, G. Anawati and F. Ahwani, eds., revised and introduced by I. Madkour (Cairo, 1953), p. 12.

[3] al-Ghazālī, *Tahāfut al-falāsifa*, M. Bouyges, ed. (Beirut, 1927), pp. 376-377.

was not uttered for sheer rhetorical effect. It was an explicit charge made in terms of Islamic law. Thus unless one clarifies the use of the term "Islamic" when referring to such philosophers, one may well be interpreted as taking sides in this conflict.

To ward off any such suggestion of partisanship in referring to these philosophers as "Islamic," I use the term in two senses. The first is in a general cultural (and chronological) sense indicating that they belong to the civilization characterized as "Islamic."[4] This sense is suggested by the Arabic term, Islāmiyy, "Islamic," when used in certain contexts. Al-Ghazālī himself, for example, refers to the very philosophers he charges with infidelity as *al-mutafalsifa al-Islamiyyūn*, "The Islamic philosophizers."[5] Again, ash-Shahrastānī (d. 1153) devotes a part of his heresiography, *Kitāb al-milal wa an-niḥal* (Book of Religions and Sects), to *falāsifat al-Islām*, "the philosophers of Islam," where after listing a number of them he gives an exposition of Ibn Sīnā's thought.[6] That in this account ash-Shahrastānī is speaking in broad cultural terms becomes particularly evident when he includes in his listing such Christians as Ḥunayn Ibn Isḥāq (d. 873), Yaḥyā Ibn 'Adiyy (d. 974), Ibn aṭ-Ṭayyib (d. 1043), and even the sixth-century John Philoponus (Yaḥyā an-Naḥawiyy), mistakenly placed by medieval Arabic writers in the first half of the seventh century.[7]

This inclusion of Christian scholars among the Islamic philosophers is instructive. It shows that the cultural sense of the term "Islamic" does not suffice. It is too broad for our purpose. A differentia is needed to distinguish an Ibn Sīnā from an Ibn 'Adiyy, both of whom can be regarded as Islamic in the cultural sense. This brings us to the second sense in which I use the term. In its second sense, "Islamic" refers normally to those philosophers who professed themselves adherents of Islam, the religion, claiming that there is no conflict between their philosophies and Qur'ānic revelation.[8] The question of the validity or invalidity of this claim is important in itself; indeed, it is central in the history of Islamic religious thought. But it does not affect the way I use the term "Islamic" in characterizing these philosophers. For, in defining the way I use it, the concern is identification, not the passing of a judgment.

With these remarks as a prelude, I now turn to the task of indicating some of

[4]For the use of the term, "Islamicate," for "Islamic" in the cultural sense, see M. G. Hodgson, *The Venture of Islam* (3 vols.; Chicago, 1974), I, 57 ff.

[5]al-Ghazālī, *al-Munqidh min aḍ-ḍalāl*, Arabic text with French translation by F. Jabr (Beirut, 1959), p. 20 of Arabic text. The Arabic for "Islamic" appears grammatically in the genitive case as Islāmiyyīn. See also *Tahāfut al-falāsifa*, p. 9.

[6]ash-Shahrastānī, *al-Milal wa an-niḥal*, A. F. Muhammad, ed. (3 vols.; Cairo, 1949), III, 3-245.

[7]Ibid., p. 8. For the story, repeated by later Arabic writers, that the Muslim conqueror of Egypt, 'Amr Ibn al-'Āṣ, met John Philoponus see Ibn an-Nadīm, *al-Fihrist*, C. Flügel, ed. (Paris, 1871), p. 354.

[8]ar-Rāzī, as we shall shortly see, is at best a borderline case.

the ways these philosophers conceived Islam. I have already mentioned that it was al-Fārābī who systematically developed a philosophical conception of Islam into a comprehensive theory whose essentials were adopted by his successors. But before turning to this theory, I must comment briefly on the conception of Islam implicit in the thought of al-Fārābī's two predecessors, al-Kindī and the physician-philosopher al-Rāzī. For although as Islamic philosophers these two were atypical and, moreover, markedly different from each other, their thought represents trends in interpreting Islam that must not be ignored.

II

The conception of Islam encountered in al-Kindī's extant writings, although not fully developed into a comprehensive theory, is quite definite and clear. The truths arrived at through philosophy are the truths revealed to God's prophets. This idea is forcefully brought out in his discussion of the nature and history of philosophy and in his comments on the nature of prophetic revelation. His conception also manifests itself in concrete fashion in his defense of generally accepted Islamic beliefs such as the doctrines of bodily resurrection and of the world's temporal creation ex nihilo.

His major treatise, *Fī al-falsafa al-ūla* (On First Philosophy), opens with a chapter that surely must be regarded as more than an introduction to this particular work. Brief as it is, the chapter is a veritable introduction of philosophy to the world of Islam. Aristotelian and Neoplatonic ingredients[9] are recast to give a view of philosophy and its history relevant to al-Kindī's world. By definition, he tells his Islamic readers, philosophy is the knowledge of the true nature of things to the extent of man's capability. First philosophy, or metaphysics, he writes, "is knowledge of the First Truth who is the cause of every truth."[10] Knowledge of the true nature of things leads to the knowledge of their cause, the First Truth, God.

Attaining truth, he then explains, is an arduous task, requiring the cooperative efforts of philosophers past and present. It is a process that is both corrective and accumulative. "We must not," he writes, "be ashamed of deeming truth good and of acquiring truth from wherever it comes, even if it comes from races remote from us and nations different from us."[11] In a passage directed against some of

[9] See A. L. Ivry, *al-Kindi's Metaphysics* (Albany, N.Y., 1974), pp. 115 ff; "al-Kindi's *On First Philosophy* and Aristotle's *Metaphysics*," *Essays on Islamic Philosophy*, G. F. Hourani, ed. (Albany, N.Y., 1975), pp. 15-24.

[10] al-Kindī, *Rasā'il*, I, 98.

[11] Ibid., p. 103.

his contemporaries,[12] he attacks them for their spurious claim to being men of reflection (*naẓar*) and for their rejection as unbelief knowledge of the true nature of things. Such men are the ones devoid of religion, he argues. "For knowledge of things in their true nature entails knowledge of divinity, unity, virtue and total knowledge of everything beneficial and the way to it." This is the knowledge conveyed by God to His true apostles (*ar-rusul aṣ-ṣādiqa*).

This knowledge, as al-Kindī explains elsewhere,[13] is received by the apostles instantaneously. It does not come about through their seeking it, through exertion, probing, and the devices of mathematics and logic. Rather, it comes to them through God's will, "His perfecting of their souls, illuminating them for the truth; by His help, direction, inspiration and divine messages."[14] Not only is the receptivity of this knowledge confined to God's apostles, the literary excellence of its verbal expression is inimitable. It conveys its message in compact thought and succinct argument that brings home its truth directly and with ease. Al-Kindī illustrates it by giving a philosophical exegesis of verses 78-82 of chapter 34 of the Qur'ān, demonstrating how well these verses argue for the doctrines of bodily resurrection and the world's creation ex nihilo.[15]

It is al-Kindī's insistence on the doctrine of the world's creation ex nihilo with all that it entails regarding the concepts of divine causality, the world, and man that separates him from al-Fārābī and his successors. He argues for this doctrine systematically, with great vigor and detail, particularly in the second chapter of his *On First Philosophy*.[16] His position—recently defended in the light of modern mathematical theories of the infinite[17]—rests on two pivotal points. The first is that an actual infinite quantity is impossible. The second is that past events, since they existed, constitute an actual quantity and hence cannot be infinite. Moreover, he argued, motion or change is an essential characteristic of physical body. Body by definition is in motion. Since the world's past existing motions cannot be infinite, its existence cannot precede these motions. Creation is not the setting into motion of an already existing static universe. A static universe, for al-Kindī, is a contradiction in terms. The world's creation at a finite moment in the past from the present is hence ex nihilo.

Al-Kindī's philosophy was thus in harmony with generally accepted Islamic beliefs. He did not reinterpret these beliefs to affect such a harmony. In this he differed from al-Fārābī and his successors. It is thus ironic that as an Islamic philosopher he was atypical. He had, it is true, some philosopher followers, but they were overshadowed by al-Fārābī, Ibn Sīnā, and their successors.

[12] Ibid., pp. 103-104.
[13] Ibid., pp. 372-373.
[14] Ibid., p. 373.
[15] Ibid., pp. 373-376.
[16] Ibid., pp. 106-122.
[17] William L. Craig, *The Kalām Cosmological Argument* (London, 1979), pp. 19-36, 61 ff.

The other atypical Islamic philosopher, al-Rāzī, advocated a doctrine of the world's creation in time, but not out of nothing. In this and in his cosmogony in general he was greatly influenced by Plato's *Timaeus*.[18] This Cosmogony is for the most part in total opposition to basic Islamic beliefs. On the other hand, al-Rāzī's conception of the Godhead is in some respects very Qur'ānic. To see both the negative and the positive sides of his philosophy in relation to Islam, we must sketch very briefly the main outline of his cosmogony and refer to his celebrated myth of creation associated with it.[19]

There are five eternal principles: matter (atoms); space; time; the world-soul; and God. Creation is God's act of imposing order on disorganized matter, thereby enabling the world-soul to unite with matter, to become individuated, forming particular living beings. The created world began at a finite moment in time and will continue to exist for a finite period of time, after which the order imposed on matter ceases and the five elements revert to their original state. During the world's finite ordered existence there is transmigration of souls to higher and lower levels. God endows men with reason, an emanation from Himself, to awaken their souls to seek their original abode, away from matter. This awakening is achieved through philosophy, of which all men are capable, although many willfully refuse to pursue it. The end of the created world comes about when reason prevails and all individual souls disengage from matter, reuniting to form once again one world-soul, leaving matter in its original state of disorder.

In this scheme the world-soul is neither an emanation from God, nor is it dependent on Him ontologically. There is a period in which transmigration takes place, but ultimately there is no individual immortality. The soul's "awakening" is achieved through philosophy. Not only would prophets be superfluous, but their existence, according to al-Rāzī, would be inconsistent with divine wisdom and compassion. If God were to reveal His truths to men, He would have to reveal them to all men. To favor one individual or one people with prophethood would be unjust. The false belief that God has spoken through prophets has caused nothing but strife and war. That these aspects of al-Rāzī's philosophy are un-Islamic is obvious, needing no elaboration.

On the positive side, al-Rāzī's conception of the Godhead is in certain respects Qur'ānic, as is seen in his answer to two questions raised by his account of creation. The first is: Why was the world created at one particular moment of time and not at any other? The second is: Why was the world created at all?[20]

[18] See M. Fakhry, "A Tenth-Century Arabic Interpretation of Plato's Cosmology," *Journal of the History of Philosophy*, 6 (1968), 15-22.

[19] Γ r an interpretive discussion of this myth, see L. F. Goodman, "Razi's Myth of the Fall of the Soul: Its Function in his Philosophy," in Hourani, *Essays On Islamic Philosophy*, pp. 25-40.

[20] *Rhazes Opera Philosophica Fragmentaque qaue Supersunt*, P. Kraus, ed. (Cairo, 1936), pp. 282-286; see also, pp. 202-212, 309-310.

The answer to the first question is that it is precisely because the divine act is voluntary that one moment of time was arbitrarily chosen for creation. For, if–as some have maintained–a preponderant (*murajjiḥ*) was needed to determine this choice, then in reality it would not have been a free choice. God's act would have been determined. Hence, to affirm creation in time at a moment arbitrarily chosen by God is to affirm the divine attribute of will.

In answering the second question, ar-Rāzī resorts to myth. The world-soul became enamored of matter, desiring to unite with it. Matter, however, resisted the soul's activity of attempting to give it the form needed for affecting this union, leaving the soul in great affliction. God, who is both omnipotent (*qadīr*) and compassionate (*raḥīm*), intervened on behalf of the soul, imposing on matter the needed form. His act of intervention is the world's creation. This reply has to be contrasted with Plato's answer to the same question in the *Timaeus* (30), namely, that God created the world because He is good and has no jealousy and desired that all things be as like Himself as possible. The world's creation in ar-Rāzī's account, on the other hand, is due to God's compassion and is enacted through His power, two attributes repeatedly affirmed in the Qur'ān.

Thus although in many ways ar-Rāzī's philosophy is radically opposed to fundamental Islamic beliefs, it nonetheless affirms quite positively the divine attributes of will, power, and compassion. Even his rejection of prophethood, the most conspicuous of his un-Islamic views, contains an egalitarianism which is perhaps closer to the spirit of Islam than the Platonic elitism encountered in al-Fārābī and his successors. Ar-Rāzī, however, was a maverick, and we must now turn to the more representative philosophical conception of Islam encountered in the writings of al-Fārābī and his followers.

III

If al-Kindī and ar-Rāzī pioneered the philosophical venture in Islam, al-Fārābī gave Islamic philosophy its direction. This is specially true of his conception of religion and of his political theory which was dependent on it. For this conception became the basis of the religious and political thought of his philosopher successors. It should be remarked, however, that in his philosophical discussions of religion[21] he does not make direct references to Islam, the prophet

[21]We are thus excluding treatises attributed to al-Fārābī which are not strictly philosophical expositions such as the *Du'ā' 'aẓīm* (A Magnificent Invocation) and *Min al-as'ila al-lāmi'a wa al-ajwiba al-jāmi'a* (Brilliant Questions and Comprehensive Answers). The authenticity of these works, particularly the second, is not certain. These works are included in al-Fārābī's *Kitāb al-milla wa nuṣūṣ ukhrā*, M. Mahdi, ed. (Beirut, 1968), pp. 87-92, 93-115.

Muhammad, or the Qur'ān. Nor does he mention by name any other religion. This reluctance to point to the particular is typical of al-Fārābī and is quite consistent with his striving after the theoretical and demonstrative ideal of making his discussion as universal as possible. On the other hand, it seems to us clear that his conception of religion, or rather, "the virtuous religion" (*al-milla al-fāḍila*),[22] represents his conception of the Islamic religion as it is ideally meant to be. It manifests itself perhaps most explicitly in the centrality of the prophet and revelation to his religious and political philosophy. The prophet is not merely the recipient of revelation, but is also the statesman, the leader, and founder of the virtuous political community. It also manifests itself in other ways in his writings: for example, his identification of the Active Intelligence (*al-'aql al-fa''āl*), the last of the celestial intelligences in his emanative scheme, with the Qur'anic "The Faithful Spirit" (*ar-rūḥ al-amīn*) and "The Holy Spirit" (*rūḥ al-quds*),[23] and his discussion of the role of such religious sciences as *kalām*, "Islamic theology," and *fiqh*, "Islamic law," in the state.[24] To this one must add what is obvious, the historical circumstance that al-Fārābī, after all, was part of the medieval world of Islam.

His conception of Islam, as one would expect, is philosophical. It involves his metaphysics, epistemology, and psychology (all largely Aristotelian and Neoplatonic) and his Platonic theory of the state. If one is to single out one proposition in his philosophy that sums up his conception of revealed religion, it would be the statement that religion is the imitation of philosophy.[25] The term "imitation" (*muḥākā*) is not to be understood in a derogatory sense. It refers—as we shall shortly see—to the special epistemic function of man's faculty of imagination. Put in another way, religion gives the same truth as philosophical truth but in a language that the nonphilosopher can understand. For it gives the particular example, the particular instant, the symbolic image of philosophical truth, whether this truth is the abstract universal in the realm of theory or the more tangible norm in the realm of practical action. The reception of this revelation, as we shall see, involves both the prophet's rational soul (theoretical and practical) and his exceptionally strong imaginative faculty.

This theory of prophethood and revelation is best understood within the framework of al-Fārābī's emanative cosmology. The world proceeds from God in a series of successive existents, a hierarchical chain of being where the closer the existent is to God, the higher is its value. From God a first celestial intelligence

[22] As distinct from nonvirtuous religions. The expression *al-milla al-fāḍila* is used in al-Fārābī's *Kitāb al-milla*, pp. 43, 44, for example.

[23] Al-Fārābī, *as-Siyāsa al-madaniyya*, F. M. Najjar, ed. (Beirut, 1964), p. 32.

[24] Al-Fārābī, *Ihsā' al-'ulūm*, Uthman Amin, ed. (Cairo, 1949), pp. 107-113.

[25] M. Mahdi, *Alfarabi's Philosophy of Plato and Aristotle* (New York, 1962), p. 44; al-Fārābī, *Kitāb arā' Ahl al-Madīna al-Fāḍila*, A. Nader, ed. (Beirut, 1958), pp. 88-95, 102-104.

emanates and from this intelligence a series of successive celestial dyads proceeds. Each dyad consists of an intelligence and a body. The first of the celestial bodies is the starless outermost sphere of the heavens, followed by the sphere of the fixed stars, then the spheres of the planets. Interposed between the planets is the sphere of the sun. The last of the celestial bodies is the sphere of the moon. The celestial intelligences, ten in number, terminate with the Active Intelligence. From it, the last of the celestial intelligences, emanates the terrestial world, the world of generation and corruption.

The terrestial world is also hierarchically structured. At the lowest point in the normative scale of existence is prime matter, the underlying matter common to all material existents. It is followed by the four elements. As these elements acquire more complex forms they ascend in the order of being until they reach man. Man, by virtue of his possession of a rational soul, represents the highest form of species in the terrestrial world. But there is a hierarchy within this species, since the rational capabilities of men differ. Man's highest perfection manifests itself in the philosopher-prophet who stands as the link between the terrestrial and celestial worlds. For in the act of receiving revelation, the prophet's rational soul unites with the Active Intelligence.

Al-Fārābī explains the nature of revelation and the manner of its reception in terms of the Aristotelian division of the rational human soul into the theoretical and the practical and the function of the imaginative faculty in relation to this division. The function of the theoretical faculty is the acquisition of abstract universal knowledge whereas the function of the practical faculty is to deliberate on courses of action. The imaginative faculty stands in an intermediary position between sensation and the rational soul. Thus, as a nonintellectual faculty it cannot acquire abstract knowledge. Nor can it acquire the rational practical principles in terms of which particular courses of action are deliberated and enacted. It can, however, imitate both types of rational knowledge, theoretical and practical, forming sensory particular images that either symbolize this knowledge or give concrete examples of it.

The Active Intelligence plays a vital role in man's acquisition of rational knowledge. By its illuminary action, akin to the action of light on colors, it transforms particular images, initially acquired through sense perception, into immaterial forms. The rational soul, hitherto an intellect only in potentiality (*'aql bi-l-quwwa*), becomes now "the actual intellect" (*al-'aql bi-l-fi'l*). A higher stage is reached when the actual intellect becomes the object of its own knowledge. The rational soul then becomes "the acquired intellect" (*al-'aql al-mustafād*). In the case of rare, exceptional individuals, namely prophet-philosophers, a still higher state of cognition is attained. This is when the acquired intellect receives the Active Intelligence, resulting in a composite in which the acquired intellect acts as the matter, the Active Intelligence as the form.[26]

[26] al-Fārābī, *Kitāb ārā'*, p. 103; *as-Siyāsa*; p. 79.

Al-Fārābī refers to the prophet who has attained this state as "the human in which the Active Intelligence has indwelled (*ḥalla*)."[27] The indwelling, he points out, is in both the theoretical and practical divisions of the prophet's rational soul which now becomes flooded with the intelligible knowledge from the Active Intelligence. This knowledge overflows from the rational soul on to the prophet's imaginative faculty which now performs its imitative function. It produces imitative images that either symbolize or give particular examples of both theoretical and practical knowledge. The images representing theoretical knowledge are expressed in assertive and descriptive language relating to God and His creation. The representations of practical philosophy are expressed in prescriptive language, constituting the revealed law.[28] In other words, the prophet's imaginative faculty translates rational knowledge into a language which the nonphilosopher can understand. This is the revealed word.

The political aspects of this concept of revelation as the imitation of philosophy are Platonic. Only the few are capable of acquiring rational philosophical knowledge and hence the majority of men must not be addressed in philosophical language. It is true, al-Fārābī's prophet is Islamic in that he is the recipient of revelation and is the founder and leader of a religious community. But he is also Plato's philosopher-king. Al-Fārābī's prophet must be a philosopher. A necessary condition for the establishment of a "virtuous" political community is that its first ruler must be a prophet-philosopher. Subsequent rulers need not always be prophet-philosophers, although normally they must be philosophers or have a philosopher share the rule. In one work, al-Fārābī speaks of legal rulership, *ar-ri'āsa as-sunniyya*, where a ruler, versed in the law, but who is not a philosopher, may lead a virtuous community.[29]

But why must the founder of the virtuous political community be a philosopher? The reason is that in addition to revealing the divine law, such an individual must be endowed with exceptional intellectual powers, theoretical and practical, necessary for establishing the virtuous political community. To take his theoretical powers first, it is through them that he attains knowledge of the true nature of things, including the true nature of happiness. For happiness is the good in itself and is realized only through the virtuous political community. Again, through his theoretical powers he is able to attain perfect knowledge of the cosmic order, of the structure of the universe. It is the model on which he must organize society. For society must be like the cosmic order, hierarchical, rational, and harmonious. It must consist of various levels, each performing its special function, each serving a higher level, the whole ruled by reason which is represented by the prophet-philosopher and the law he reveals. Theoretical knowledge,

[27] al-Fārābī, *Kitāb ārā'*, p. 104.
[28] al-Fārābī, *Kitāb al-milla*, pp. 46-47.
[29] Ibid., pp. 56, 60; also an allusion to this type of leadership in *as-Siyāsa*, p. 81.

however, though necessary, is not sufficient. The prophet-philosopher must exercise his practical virtues, namely, his "deliberative virtues, moral virtues, and practical arts."[30] He must use these to mold the character of the youth and the multitude through "the method of persuasion and imagination." He must direct the nonphilosophical majority by appropriate means of persuasive speech and exemplary deeds. He must also apply the law to new circumstances. In brief, he must educate, organize, direct, and lead.

Al-Fārābī's political philosophy is comprehensive and detailed. (We have only touched on some of its basic features.) Its thesis that revelation is the imitation of philosophy has far-reaching implications. It means that it is only the philosophers, always a minority, who can understand religious language on the conceptual level. It also means that there can be no real conflict between philosophy and generally accepted Islamic beliefs based on the language of revelation. Conflicts between the two can only be apparent, ultimately resolvable once religion is interpreted philosophically.

The explanation of prophetic revelation in terms of the then current Plotinian and Aristotelian metaphysical and psychological categories is certainly a remarkable intellectual achievement. But it is also a convenient theory for an Islamic philosopher as it allows him a free hand, so to speak, in philosophizing about the nature of God and His creation. In terms of this theory of interpretation, al-Fārābī's doctrine that the world is the eternal effect of an eternal cause becomes consistent with scriptural accounts of creation. Again, his doctrine that individual immortality is confined to the souls of only certain sections of humanity becomes reconcilable with scriptural statements on the hereafter.[31] For, in the final analysis, it is religion that must accommodate itself to philosophy and not the other way around.

IV

Al-Fārābī's concept of religion as the imitation of philosophy with its corollary that the majority of mankind must not be addressed in philosophical language was adopted by such thinkers as Ibn Sīnā, Ibn Ṭufayl (d. 1184) and Ibn Rushd. We have singled out these three thinkers, not only because of their adoption of al-Fārābī's concept of religion, but also because in their treatment of it they convey quite explicitly that the religion they are discussing is primarily Islam.

[30] Mahdi, *Alfarabi's Philosophy of Plato and Aristotle*, p. 13.

[31] For al-Fārābī the souls of the citizens of "ignorant cities" simply disintegrate after death. See *Kitāb ārā'*, pp. 118 ff.

A fourth important and influential successor and follower of al-Fārābī was Ibn Bājja (d. 1138). Although in his extant writings relating to political thought he makes some direct references to Islam, these are sparse and given in passing.[32] For this reason, we shall confine ourselves to the three philosophers we have singled out, our purpose being to indicate very briefly how they reiterate al-Fārabī's concept of religion in a context that is now quite explicitly Islamic.

To turn first to Ibn Sīnā, a comparison between his theory of prophecy and that of al-Fārābī is beyond our scope here. Suffice it to say that although there are differences in their respective accounts of the manner in which prophets receive revelation, their concept of what constitutes this revelation remains the same. Ibn Sīnā simply re-expresses the Fārābian theory that religion gives philosophical truth in the language of image and symbol. He re-expresses this in his psychological writings, in Book X of the *Metaphysics* of the *Shifā'* and in his treatise, *Fī ithbāt an-nubuwwāt* (On the Proof of Prophecies). In the last two works, he reaffirms al-Fārabī's principle that philosophy must not be divulged to the public. The prophet, he tells us in the *Metaphysics*, must not only avoid addressing the masses in philosophical language, but he must refrain from indicating to them that there is knowledge that is being kept away from them:[33]

> Nor is it proper for any man to reveal that he possesses knowledge he is hiding from the vulgar. Indeed, he must never permit any reference to this. Rather, he should let them know of God's majesty and greatness through symbols and similitudes derived from things that for them are majestic and great, adding this much–that He has neither equal, nor companion, nor likeness. Similarly, he must instill in them belief in the resurrection in a manner they can conceive and in which their souls find rest. He must tell them about eternal bliss and misery in parables they can comprehend and conceive.

Implicit in this passage is another need for symbolism, namely to conceal from the uninitiated what they are incapable of understanding. "It has been said," writes Ibn Sīnā in his *On the Proof of Prophecies*, "that a condition the prophet must adhere to is that his words should be symbols and his expressions hints." Referring to "the foremost Greek philosophers and prophets," he tells us that they made use of symbols for concealing their views from the uninitiated. Then returning to the use of symbols as the only way of communicating with the

[32] Ibn Bājja, *Rasā'il Ibn Bājja al-falsafiyya*, M. Fakhry, ed. (Beirut, 1968), p. 207, for example.

[33] Avicenna, *Healing: Metaphysics* X, M. E. Marmura, trans., in *Medieval Political Philosophy*, R. Lerner and M. Mahdi, eds. (New York, 1963), pp. 100-101 (corresponding to Ibn Sīnā, *ash-Shifā': al-Ilāhiyyāt*, G. Anawati, S. Dunya and S. Zayid, eds., revised by I. Madkour [2 vols.; Cairo, 1960], pp. 2, 443).

commonality, he asks: "How could the prophet Muhammad (May God's prayers and peace be on him) bring [theoretical] knowledge to the uncouth nomad, not to say to the whole human race considering that he was sent a messenger to all?"[34]

This direct reference to the prophet Muhammad (not the only one in this treatise) is one of the indications that when discussing religion, Ibn Sīnā is discussing primarily Islam. In *Metaphysics*, X, of the *Shifā'*, he uses what is basically a Fārābian, Platonic concept of the state to interpret and place within it Islamic teaching, ritual, and institutions.[35] The obligations of prayer, pilgrimage, and when necessary holy war, the prohibitions of gambling and usury, marriage and divorce (treated in a legal context that is entirely Islamic), the caliphate (with a reference to 'Umar and 'Alī) are all discussed within this Fārābian framework. Ibn Sīnā also devotes the second and longer part of his treatise *On the Proof of Prophecies* to philosophical interpretations of Qur'ānic verses and Islamic traditions.[36] In effect, he provides (to his own satisfaction) a concrete demonstration of al-Fārābī's theory that religion is the symbolic representation of philosophical truth. What is of special significance here is that the religious language Ibn Sīnā interprets philosophically is either Qur'ānic or taken from Islamic tradition.

A more dramatic illustration of al-Fārābī's theory that religion is the imitation of philosophy and the dictum that philosophy must be confined to the few capable of understanding it is provided by Ibn Ṭufayl in his philosophical tale, *Ḥayy Ibn Yaqẓān*. Ḥayy, the hero of the tale, grows up from infancy, reared until boyhood by a roe, on an island uninhabited by other humans. Endowed with exceptional physical and intellectual powers, he undergoes a process of self-education, first on the practical, then the scientific and philosophical levels, to finally attain the highest form of knowledge, the mystical vision of God and of the intelligible order emanating from him. On a nearby island, a community adhered to a monotheistic religion revealed to one of the ancient prophets–a religion that presented the true objects of knowledge in the form of imitative images that symbolized them.[37] It was a community of religious literalists, however, with the exception of the pious Asāl who was wont to probe the inner meanings of revelation. He thus sought seclusion and traveled to Ḥayy's island seeking it, there to encounter Ḥayy.

Asāl teaches Ḥayy language. He discovers that Ḥayy is one of the rare philosophical saints who, unaided by men, had attained the highest truth of which

[34] Avicenna, "On the Proof of Prophecies," M. E. Marmura, trans., in *Medieval Political Philosophy*, p. 116 (corresponding to Ibn Sīnā, *Fī ithbāt an-nubuwwāt*, M. E. Marmura, ed. [Beirut, 1968], p. 48).

[35] Avicenna, *Healing: Metaphysics* X, in *Medieval Political Philosophy*, pp. 99-111; Ibn Sīnā, *ash-Shifā': al-Ilāhiyyāt*, II, 441-459.

[36] Avicenna, *On the Proof of Prophecies*, pp. 116-121; Ibn Sīnā, *Fī ithbāt annubuwwāt*, pp. 48-61.

[37] Ibn Tufayl, *Ḥayy Ibn Yaqẓān*, L. Gauthier, ed., 2d. ed. (Beirut, 1936), p. 136.

Asāl's religion was but a symbolic copy. In his turn, Ḥayy recognizes Asāl's religion to be true, finding nothing in it to contradict what he had witnessed.[38] Ḥayy, however, desires to go to Asāl's island to raise its people to a higher understanding of their religion. He thus insists against Asāl's initial dissuasions that they both go. They both visit the island and Ḥayy begins to teach the more advanced of the community the inner meaning of their religion. He soon becomes painfully aware of their total incapacity to understand him. Learning for himself the dictum that the nonphilosopher must not be addressed philosophically, he adjures them to disregard everything he told them and to continue with their literalist understanding of their religion as before. He and Asāl then travel back to their island to lead the life of mystics. In this narrative, Ibn Ṭufayl does not state that the religion is Islam, but the context of the tale is Islamic as the narrative is constantly informed with quotations from the Qur'ān.

It is with Ibn Rushd that we have a treatise devoted exclusively to the relation between philosophy and Islam. Not only is the work concerned with the relation of Qur'ānic language to philosophy, but it approaches the question from the standpoint of Islamic religious law. This treatise is his *Kitāb faṣl al-maqāl wa taqrīr ma bayn ash-sharī'a wal-falsafa min al-ittiṣāl* (The Decisive Treatise, Determining the Nature of the Connection between Religion and Philosophy).[39] It is a legal defense of philosophy which also challenges the legal and philosophical grounds for al-Ghazālī's condemnation of al-Fārābī and Ibn Sīnā as infidels.

In this work, Ibn Rushd develops a theory of scriptural interpretation which—as I see it—is essentially Fārābian, an expansion on ideas inherited from al-Fārābī and from his disciple Ibn Bājja. He argues that philosophy is the contemplation of existents inasmuch as they indicate the creator. Basing himself on Qur'ānic utterances urging man to contemplate existents as a manifestation of divine wisdom and power, he maintains that philosophy provides the perfect method for executing this divine injunction. The study of philosophy is hence commanded by the divine law. It is, however, an obligation confined to those who have the capacity to pursue it, prohibited for all others. Men's capacities differ and each Muslim must study the manifestations of divine power according to his intellectual capacity.

Most men do not transcend in their intellectual capacities the level of rhetorical reasoning and should pursue the divine injunction on this level. Similarly, there are those who reason on the dialectical level, a small group identified by Ibn Rushd with the Islamic theologians, *al-mutakallimūn*, and they must understand scriptures on their level. The philosophers are the minority. They are the demonstrative class and must pursue the divine injunction on the level of demonstrative reasoning.

[38] Ibid., pp. 144-147.

[39] Ibn Rushd, *Kitāb faṣl al-maqāl*, G. F. Hourani, ed. (Leiden, 1959).

Since Islam's divine law is true, Ibn Rushd argues, and since it commands the demonstrative class of men to study philosophy, there can be no conflict between scripture and philosophy.[40] When one encounters what appears to be a conflict, it indeed is only an apparent conflict, resolvable by taking the scriptural utterance as metaphor and interpreting it in a manner consistent with demonstrative truth and correct Arabic usage. Its philosophical interpretation is only allowed the demonstrative class, identified by Ibn Rushd with those "well grounded in knowledge" mentioned in the Qur'ān.

We need not go further into the way Ibn Rushd expands on this to classify the types of Qur'ānic statements in terms of levels of interpretation. The central point that concerns us is his argument that when there is an apparent conflict between scripture and philosophy, it is scripture that has to be understood metaphorically and interpreted by the demonstrative class philosophically. It is really a restatement, within an Islamic legal context, of al-Fārābī's position that it is religion that must accommodate itself to philosophy and not the other way around. Hence, as with al-Fārābī, Ibn Rushd's theory of interpretation allows the philosopher considerable latitude in his metaphysical thinking about God, the world, and the destiny of the human soul. Moreover, it gives sanction to the philosopher to utter different interpretations of certain scriptural doctrines, depending on the level of understanding of the people he is addressing.

To say this about the Fārābīans does not necessarily mean that they formulated their theory of religion simply as a means for providing themselves with a form of protection for their philosophical pursuits. There is, as we see it, no compelling reason to doubt that they were fully convinced that their conception of Islam was in harmony with the Qur'ān. The question, as we see it, is not that of their sincerity. Al-Ghazālī, for example, did not attack al-Fārābi and Ibn Sīnā for being insincere in their belief in God and prophethood. He attacked them because, as he thought, they had a wrong conception of God and prophethood. The conflict pertained to the nature of the Godhead. It reflected the tension between two concepts of God. One, espoused by the philosophers, derived essentially from Greek philosophy. It was largely a concept of God as mind with its emphasis on divine knowledge as universal and conceptual. The other was a Qur'ānic concept which did not confine its emphasis to divine knowledge, but also stressed such attributes as life, will, power, speech, hearing, and seeing.

What these Islamic philosophers were attempting to achieve, however, is understandable, regardless of whether or not one agrees with their conclusions. They viewed themselves, as we have mentioned earlier, not only as the inheritors and preservers of earlier philosophical truths, but as continuing the quest after "the true nature of things." At the same time, they were part of a culture that

[40] Ibid., p. 13.

was Qur'āno-centric, a culture whose ethos was religious. The Qur'ān and the mission of the prophet were the central facts of their history. As metaphysicians they could not bypass such facts. Here they were in search of "the true nature" of what was at the core of their way of life. Their interpretation of Islam philosophically must hence be viewed in part as an attempt at self-understanding. Whether in this attempt they hit the mark, completely missed it, or achieved something in between is another matter. As an intellectual feat, however, their attempt remains very impressive.

THE SUFIS AND THE *SHAHĀDA*

ANNEMARIE SCHIMMEL

Harvard University

One fine morning in 1955, I encountered a bus driver in a service station in Bursa. When he learned that I was teaching history of religions in the Ilâhiyat Fakültesi (Faculty of Islamic Studies) in Ankara he asked: "Hanīm, can you explain to me something? We say that Islam has five pillars: the profession of faith, prayer, alms tax, fasting, and pilgrimage. But to my feeling the *shahāda* is the basis of Islam and not just one part of it!" His question showed the deep concern of the simple Muslim for the importance of the shahāda, even though he was certainly not aware that he stood in a long tradition in which the problem of the relation between *islām* and *īmān* had been discussed in every possible detail.[1]

Among Muslim mystics, al-Ḥakīm at-Tirmidhī (d. 892) seems to have been one of the first to discuss the meaning of the shahāda in its connection with islām and īmān: īmān means, for him, that man should give himself completely to whatever God orders for him (*ḥukm*), whereas in order to be a *muslim* he is obliged to fulfill his ritual duties which he knows through God's order (*amr*). Both īmān and islām are based on a contract in which it is stated that God is the Lord and man the servant, a contract that has found its briefest expression in the words *lā ilāha illā Allāh.*[2] Thus, the shahāda is the root of both islām and īmān, and four centuries after Tirmidhī, Maulānā Rūmī blamed the qadis for calling a man a *mu'min* because he *pronounces* the shahāda without existentially

[1]Toshihiko Izutsu, *The Concept of Belief in Islamic Theology: A Semantic Analysis of "īmān" and "islām"* (Tokyo: The Keio Institute of Cultural and Linguistic Studies, 1968), p. 68. He quotes al-Bāqillānī's famous statement: *"Al-islām 'ala khams,"* "Islam rests upon five (things)."

[2]Berndt Radtke, *Al-Ḥākim at-Tirmidhī: Ein islamischer Theosoph des 3./9. Jahrhunderts* (Freiburg: Klaus Schwarz, 1980), pp. 78-81. See also 'Alī ibn 'Uthmān al-Jullābī al-Hujwīrī, *The "Kashf al-Maḥjūb:" the Oldest Persian Treatise on Sufism* (London: Luzac–Leiden: Brill, 1911, repr. 1936 and often), chap. XVII, pp. 286 f f.

participating in its meaning. Only such participation ought to constitute true īmān.[3]

The formula *lā ilāha illā Allāh* can indeed be regarded as the very center of Islamic life and thought: The two basic religious attitudes—the prophetic and the mystic—can be expressed by its words. Prophetic monotheism is exclusive, mystical monotheism, inclusive. The prophetic "No!" is intended to cut man off from every interest in things besides God and is a precondition for the proper "Yes." As Nathan Söderblom formulates it: "For [without such a No] all that denies and destroys, degrades and delays what is right and good would be allowed to remain unattacked and unabolished. That is why a No is necessary in the moral warfare of the individual, in the evolution of religion, and in the history of the race."[4]

This prophetic "No!" stood at the beginning of Islam, and it was in its light that the shahāda was understood by Muslims. Later developments in Sufism, however, led to interpreting the same negation in a mystical way, namely as pointing to the all-inclusive nature of the Divine besides which nothing has real existence.

The shahāda has numerous aspects. It soon gained a special sanctity so that Sharafuddīn Manērī in fourteenth-century Bihar told his disciples that even if man's sins would fill ninety-nine sheets to be put on the scales at Doomsday, one single sheet with the words of the shahāda would outweigh them.[5] In popular piety the repetition of the formula for meritorious purposes became similarly important.

On another level one may think of the fascinating calligraphic forms of the shahāda with its eleven vertical strokes, which largely contributed to the development of various types of decorative writing in Islam and could grow into mandala-like forms.

The poets of the Muslim world never tired of inventing new interpretations of the shahāda: Sanā'ī (d. ca. 1131) saw the *lā* in its graphic form as a broom by which everything besides God could be swept away,[6] and Rūmī took over

[3] Jalāluddin Rūmī, *Mathnawī-i Ma'nawī*, ed. and trans., with commentary, by Reynold Alleyne Nicholson, Gibb Memorial Series, n. s. Vol. IV (8 vols.; London: Luzac, 1925-1940), lines 2175-2177 (hereafter *M*, quoted with volume and line). In *M*, I, 292, Rūmī says:

M and *u* and *m* and *n* are not a badge of honor:
the word *mu'min* [believer] is only for description.

[4] Nathan Söderblom, *The Living God: Basic Forms of Personal Religion*, Gifford Lectures (London: Oxford University Press, 1933), p. 298.

[5] Sharafuddin Maneri, *The Hundred Letters*, Paul Jackson S.J., trans., Classics of Western Spirituality (New York: Paulist Press, 1980), p. 105. For a full treatment of this *dhikr* see Abū Ḥāmid al-Ghazzālī, *Iḥyā' 'Ulūm ad-Dīn*, Vol. I (Bulaq, 1289/1872-3), pp. 264-269.

[6] Abū'l-Majd Majdūd Sanā'ī, *Ḥadīqat al-ḥaqīqa wa sharī'at aṭ-ṭarīqa*, Mudarris Rażawī, ed. (Tehran: Chāpkhāna-i Sipihr, 1329sh/1950) p. 139.

this image.[7] Other religious poets interpreted it as a weapon comparable to 'Alī's famous two-edged sword, Dhū'l-faqār, and Jāmī (d. 1492) went even further by likening it to a crocodile that swallows everything besides God.[8] Rūmī, on the other hand, did not only repeat the image of the "dagger of *lā*" but experienced it as a torrent, carrying away everything that might distract man's heart,[9] or as a fire that burns both worlds.[10]

In the Sufi orders the shahāda became one of the most important constituents of the *dhikr*, for according to a *ḥadīth*, it is the noblest dhikr of all. It was soon accompanied by rhythmical breathing and strictly defined movements of the head, and often ended, in dhikr gatherings, with the repetition of only the last *h*, the letter of the Essence, *huwiyya*, which comprises everything else.[11]

The dialectical form of the shahāda lent itself to different mystical interpretations for, as Richard Hartmann has stated correctly in his survey of Qushairī's *Risāla*, the inner life of the Sufi largely swings between two poles.[12] The shahāda is the model for this constant movement which leads man from the depth of ignorance to the knowledge of God, but which also expresses the constant interplay of Divine *jalāl*, majesty, and *jamāl*, beauty, of *'adam*, nonexistence, and *wujūd*, existence, of *sukr*, intoxication, and *ṣaḥw*, sobriety, of *qabḍ*, pressure, and *basṭ*, expansion, and, most importantly, *fanā*, annihilation, and *baqā*, remaining in God. Each is part of life, for only the constant change between systole and diastole, of taking in the breath and releasing it again (as in the dhikr of the shahāda), makes life possible; it manifests itself, as Iqbal would say, in *khalwa*, solitary meditation, and *jilwa*, manifestation.

Without negation life cannot go on: "From the *lā* you go upward, *bālā*," says

[7] Jalāluddīn Rūmī, *Dīwān-i kabīr ya Kulliyāt-i Shams*, Badī'uzzamān Furūzānfar, ed. (10 vols.; Tehran: University Press, 1366sh/1957 ff.). Hereafter *D* with number of poem and line, 1876/19776.

[8] Maulānā 'Abdur Raḥmān Jāmī, *Silsilat adh-dhahab*, in *Haft Aurang*, Aqā Murtaẓā and Mudarris-i Gīlānī, eds. (Tehran: Kitābfurūshī-i Sa'dī, 1338sh/1958), p. 18.

[9] Rūmī, *D*, 152/1743; *lā* as a sword that slays the lover, *M*, III, 4098; cf. also *M*, V, 589.

[10] Rūmi, *D*, 155/1768. In *M*, IV, 859, he gives a lively description of the power of this negation: "Once man has realized that there is no god but God, the emerald appears to him as worthless as leek, human beauties like rotten onions, and the radiant moon looks like a black pot."

[11] See Cyprian Rice, O. P., *The Persian Sufis*, 2d ed. (London: Allen and Unwin, 1969), p. 92, a quotation from Najmuddīn Dāyā-i Rāzī. Other statements about the *dhikr* of the *shahāda* in the Kubrawiyya order in Nūruddīn 'Abdurraḥmān-i Isfarāyīnī (1242-1317), *Kāshif al-Asrār*, Hermann Landolt, ed. and trans., (Tehran: McGill University in collaboration with Tehran University, 1980), pp. 20-27 of the introduction; also p. 8, an account of the *shahāda* to drive away evil spirits. An excellent survey of the technique of this *dhikr* in Richard Gramlich, *Die schiitischen Derwischorden*, Vol. II (Wiesbaden: Steiner, 1978), pp. 391-403.

[12] Richard Hartmann, *Al-Ḳuschairīs Darstellung des Sufitums* (Berlin: Mayer & Müller, 1914), p. 8.

'Aṭṭār,[13] while Rūmī asks the Beloved to consider him a *lā*, a nonentity, and transform him into *illā*, in other words, to make him participate in the Divine Unity.[14] The lā and illā of the shahāda have been taken by the mystical poets to point particularly to the contrast of *kufr*, infidelity, and *īmān*, faith, which are, as Sanā'ī says in the beginning of his *Ḥadīqat al-ḥaqīqa*, only "doorkeepers at God's gate"[15] and who, as Rūmī continues, are both lovers of Divine glory, *kibriyā*.[16] Some mystics have compared the word lā to tresses (a fitting comparison when one looks at its graphic form!) which hide the superresplendent, unqualified Face of God, "and everything is vanishing save the Face of God" (Sura 28.88).[17] Rūmī's interpretation of the shahāda is even more meaningful: God is the kernel of everything, and infidelity and faith are His rinds. Infidelity, symbolized by the lā, is the outer rind, which is dried up and of no use but to be thrown in the fire, whereas faith, illā, is the inner peel, which is constantly kept fresh and fragrant by its contact with the Essence.[18] In visual terms, the *h* of Allah, the "letter of the Essence," forms the center around which the words of the shahāda grow, as it were, to reach the point of utter distance in the lā (see illustration).

The constant flow of movement implied in the shahāda was interpreted by the mystics of the Ibn 'Arabī school as pertaining not only to the worshiper who

[13]Farīduddīn 'Aṭṭār, *Dīwān*, Sa'īd-i Nafīsī, ed. (Tehran: Kitābkhāna-i Sanā'ī, 1336 sh/1957), p. 141.

[14]Rūmī, *D*, 1912/20116; cf. the refrain of the *Chakkīnāma* ("millstone poem," in which the grinding of flour is used to exemplify religious topics), quoted by Richard M. Eaton, *Sufis of Bijapur* (Princeton: Princeton University Press, 1978), p. 161:

> Say *lā ilāh*, dwell in the *illā Allāh*.

[15]Sanā'ī, *Ḥadīqat al-Ḥaqīqa*, p. 60.

[16]Rūmī, *M*, I, 2446; the next line reads:

> Brass and silver are both servants of this alchemy

i.e., both worthless and valuable matter can be transformed into divine gold.

[17]For the whole problem see: Carl W. Ernst, "Faith and Infidelity in Sufism: Ecstatic Expressions and Their Repercussions in Medieval Islamic Society," Ph.D. diss., Harvard University, 1981. The image of the "tress" as connected with the negation and with Iblīs occurs in 'Ainulquḍāt al-Miyānjī al-Hamadhānī's *Tamhīdāt*, 'Afīf 'Uṣairān, ed. (Tehran: University Press, 1341 sh/1962), pp. 117-118.

[18]Rūmī, *M*, IV, 3281 f f. The eighteenth-century Indian mystic Nāṣir Muḥammad 'Andalīb has described the way of the Sufi from the beginning of the word *Allāh* through its various letters until the soul rests in the *h*, surrounded by its luminous circle (see Annemarie Schimmel, *Pain and Grace* [Leiden: Brill, 1976], p. 131). The Sufis were well aware that the word *Allāh*, contrary to all other names of God, yields a meaning even when letter by letter is taken away: when the initial *alif* is removed, *llh* (*lillāh*) "for God" remains; if one then takes away the first *lām*, *lh* (*lahu*) "for Him" remains, and if the second *lām* is removed, *h*, the letter of ipseity, "He," remains, and all mysteries are contained in this final *h* (see Abū Naṣr as-Sarrāj, *Kitāb al-Luma' fī't-Taṣawwuf*, Reynold Alleyne Nicholson, ed. [London: Luzac, 1914], p. 89). For other mystical interpretations of *Allāh*, out of which the *shahāda* as it were grows, see Jean Canteins, *La Voie des Lettres* (Paris: Albin Michel, 1981).

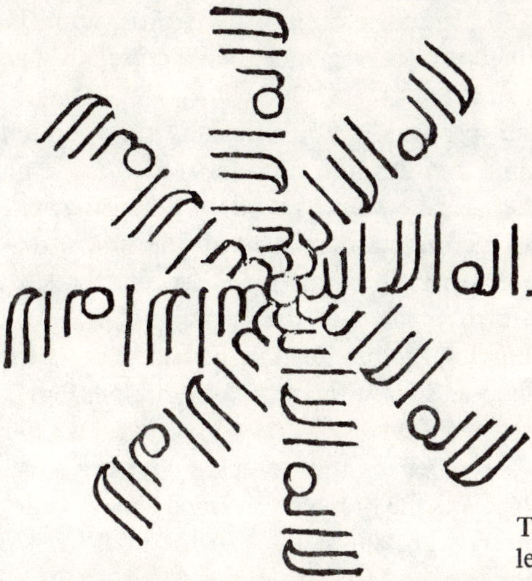

The shahāda, centered on the essential letter *h*, with the *lā* as the "outer rind."

experiences the shahāda in his life and in his dhikr, but to the whole cosmogonic process: life is a constant divine breathing, lā ilāh meaning that everything in the colorful world of created things is perishable, that nothing is worthy of worship and, in the last consequence, that nothing has existence besides God. Taking in the breath in the illā Allāh means that everything returns into the unfathomable abyss of Divine existence.[19]

These various interpretations make the *kalima*, as the shahāda is often called, extremely important for the life of the mystic. During spiritual education, the sacred formula had to be recited in seclusion, for the Sufis knew that the dhikr of the shahāda had a wonderful power over their hearts. Najmuddin Dāyā-i Rāzī, the Kubrawi mystic (d. 1256) explains in poetical words that this dhikr is "the good tree" mentioned in the Koran (Sura 14.24), and "when this tree reaches the fullness of perfection, the blossoms of contemplation appear on the tips of the branches and from these gradually emerge the fruits of revelations and supernatural visions. One of these fruits is the station of *tauḥīd*."[20] This is the station of which Sulṭān Bāhū, the Panjabi mystic of the later seventeenth century, sings

[19] See Rice, *The Persian Sufis*, p. 64; cf. also in general Henry Corbin, *Creative Imagination in the Sufism of Ibn 'Arabi*, Ralph Manheim, trans. (Princeton: Princeton University Press, 1969).

[20] Rice, *The Persian Sufis*, p. 96, quoting Najmuddīn Dāyā-i Rāzī.

in an unforgettable image, which fits well into Najmuddīn Dāyā's description: "Allah the jasmine bush will grow in the heart when the gardener [*murshid*] waters it with the water of negation and affirmation," in other words, with the shahāda, so that it finally fills everything with its fragrance, being closer to man "than his jugular vein" (Sura 50.16).[21]

The "Sufi saint of the twentieth century," the North African Darqawi master Aḥmad al-'Alawī, to whom Martin Lings has devoted his fine study, made his disciples repeat the kalima 75,000 times, for he knew, as did all Sufis, that this dhikr was necessary to cleanse the heart before man could reach the full realization of God. He makes this clear with al-Ghazzālī's words: "When the thoughts are muddled with other than God, thou hast need of the negation *lā ilāh*, but once thou hast withdrawn from all things in contemplation of Him who is the life of all, thou takest rest in: 'Say Allah, and leave them to their idle prating!'" (Sura 5.91).[22]

For similar reasons, Najmuddīn Dāyā symbolizes this process under the image of the lā ilāh as a sergeant-at-arms who cleans the Presence chamber, man's heart, so that the king Illā Allāh can dwell there, ruling supreme.[23] As the *ḥadīth qudsī* says: "My heavens and My earth do not contain Me, but the heart of My faithful servant contains Me."

Sharafuddīn Manērī takes up, like Sufis before him, the ḥadīth qudsī: "*Innī lā ilāha illā anā*. . . . Verily, there is no god but I, so worship Me; whoever from among you brings the witness 'There is no god save God' enters My castle, and whoever enters My castle is secure from [eternal] punishment." This divine saying occurs also in al-Ghazzālī's *Ihyā' 'ulūm ad-dīn* and seems to have been very popular in the Islamic world after 1200.

Manērī also uses the image of a fortress into which the novice enters. Here, in the stronghold of the Lord,

> his heart is put at ease. Wisdom demands that a fortress should be constructed out of words of both denial and affirmation so that, when travelers along the way to Unity enter it, they will feel secure from what can obstruct their way: their ego and Satan. When the world of divine Unity has been disclosed to the inner vision of the novice, he finds that any being that has come into existence through creation is "other," and he perceives that the denial of "other" is a precognition for attaining Unity.

[21] Sultan Bahoo, *Abyāt*, Maqbool Elahi, ed. and trans. (Lahore, 1967), no. 1 (letter *alif* of the *sīḥarfī*, "golden alphabet"). Sulṭān Bāhū (d. 1692) from Jhang district in the southern Punjab was a Qādirī Sufi and therefore used the *shahāda* as his *dhikr*, as was customary in the Qadiriyya.

[22] Martin Lings, *A Sufi Saint of the Twentieth Century*, 2d ed. (London: Allen and Unwin, 1971), pp. 85, 113.

[23] Rice, *The Persian Sufis*, p. 94.

Manērī then goes on to show, as had many Sufis before him, that even the shahāda and its positive statement is not complete: "For legal scholars, denial comes after affirmation, whereas lexicographers state that affirmation comes after negation. For a Sufi, both denial and affirmation are idolatry," for they each require three parts: the thing affirmed, the affirmer, and the act of affirmation (the same holds true for denial). Manērī quotes Sanā'ī's famous verse:

> Beyond denial and affirmation there lies desert in which not even "you" exist.
> Having crossed the wilderness of "There is no god" and reached the Kaaba of "but God" they taste the drink of "He is the Beginning and to Him do we return. . . ."[24]

This statement by a fourteenth-century Indian Sufi leads us to the very secret of the shahāda as perceived by the Sufis. Sarrāj devotes no less than seven pages of his *Kitāb al-Luma'* to the *bāb at-tauḥīd*,[25] and Hujwīrī, like many others, speaks of the threefold tauḥīd which man has to experience.[26] Indeed, the whole history of Sufism can be seen as a movement from the simple statement that God alone is man's goal to the conviction that it is God alone who acts, and finally, that God alone has true existence.[27] Abū Bakr ash-Shiblī (d. 945), noted for his daring definitions, states in one of his aphorisms: "He who learns an atom of the science of tauḥīd carries the heavens and the earth on one hair of his eyelashes"[28] because everything is so minute and insignificant compared to God.

It was apparently al-Kharrāz in the late ninth century who for the first time expressed the central Sufi idea that true personality belongs to God alone, and that only God has the right to say "I,"[29] an idea that was put in plain words by Shiblī: "No one has ever said 'God' but God." The Sufis were here on good Koranic ground, for Sura 3.16 states: "God gives witness that there is no god but He," which means, "He Himself gave witness of His Oneness, *waḥdāniyya*."[30]

Louis Massignon has drawn the attention of scholars to a grammatical problem that the early Sufis encountered while meditating upon the shahāda:

[24] Maneri, *Hundred Letters*, letter no. 40, pp. 152-154. Isfarāyīnī has composed a whole treatise on the *ḥadīth qudsī* of the citadel (see Landolt, *Kāshif al-asrār*, p. 18, p. 44; Persian text Annexe A, part 5, no. 7).

[25] Sarrāj, *Kitāb al-Luma'*, pp. 28-35.

[26] Hujwīrī/Nicholson, *Kashf*, pp. 278 ff.

[27] For the whole problem see the fine study by Richard Gramlich, S.J., "Mystical Dimensions of Islamic Monotheism," in Annemarie Schimmel and Abdoldjavad Falaturi, eds., *We Believe in One God: The Experience of God in Christianity and Islam* (London: Burns and Oates, 1979), p. 136.

[28] Sarrāj, *Kitāb al-Luma'*, p. 35.

[29] Paul Nwyia, S.J., *Exégèse coranique et langage mystique* (Beirut: Dar al-Machreq, 1970), p. 249.

[30] Sarrāj, *Kitāb al-Luma'*, p. 42: *shahida li-nafsihi bi'l-waḥdāniyya*.

> It has been pointed out . . . that the *shahāda*, "There is no divinity—except God" should not be thought of as a complete and homogeneous judgment, but as an "exception" *istithnā'*, in other words, a condensed parable, and that as such, this heterogeneous sentence could have a useful purpose and a meaning, without having, a priori, either an intrinsic convincing force (logic) or an intrinsic (real) sacramental efficacy. . . .
>
> . . . .
>
> The early Muslim grammarians maintained, out of a fideistic position, that the sentence is homogeneous and had claimed that what the negation of the first member is aimed at is the real existence (*wujūd*) of the divinity, not the pure idea (essence, *māhīya*) of the divinity in itself. This gave the *shahāda* an immediate ritual efficacy sanctioned by various *ḥadīth* cited in Muslim and Bukhari.[31]

The feeling of "ritual efficacy" was certainly strong in the mystical tradition expressed by the Sufi orders who felt that the formula in itself has a religious value.[32] Ḥallāj however, as Massignon continues, followed those grammarians who saw in the shahāda a shift in a condensed parable, from virtual divinity (of hypothetical gods) to actual and real Divinity (of God):

> Ḥallāj agreed with this, and he forbade his disciples to waste their time reciting or meditating on the *shahāda*, because it gave them neither a logical proof for the intelligence nor a real grace for the heart. Only God is capable of making us articulate and decompose the *shahāda* with the intention of transference which renders it legitimate by helping us to become conscious of the mystery of His unity in the very operation of His act. He makes us first deny our self in our heart in order that He may then affirm Himself there by His presence. . . .[33]

[31] Louis Massignon, *La Passion d'al-Ḥosayn ibn Manṣour al-Ḥallāj*, 2d ed. Vol. III, (Paris: Gallimard, 1975), pp. 44 f., Herbert Mason, trans., in Merlin L. Swartz, ed. and trans., *Studies on Islam* (New York and Oxford University Press, 1981) p. 144.

[32] Landolt (*Kāshif al-Asrār*, p. 30) speaks of the role of the shaikh as the one who, by teaching the novice the formula of the *dhikr*, truly initiates him: "If this function of the shaikh is indispensable in order to make the *dhikr* become an 'arrow of the King,' it is also true that the nobility of this 'weapon' is lastly derived from the fact that the sentence *lā ilāha illā Allāh* contains in itself a purifying and theophanique power, a light, which is so often mentioned by our Isfarāyīnī as its very secret. . . ."

[33] Massignon/Mason in Swartz, *Studies on Islam*, p. 146. Massignon also discusses Iblīs's twofold negation as defined by Rūzbihān-i Baqlī (*Sharḥ-i Shaṭḥiyāt, Commentaire sur les paradoxes des Soufis*, Henry Corbin, ed., Bibliothèque Iranienne, 12 [Tehran and Paris: Institut d'Etudes Iraniennes, 1966], p. 528), and he speaks of the inverse relation of the *lā*

Indeed, there is no way for Ḥallāj to accept that by reciting the shahāda man can prove in a real way that God is unique.

How could he profess this unity? "There is no one who acts but God." Man "should act, but he should know at the same time that he is not the subject of the action, but rather the place in which the divine action, which he does not cause but rather receives, is made manifest," to quote Junaid.[34] Since man cannot really act, he is also, as Richard Gramlich says correctly, "unable to make a profession of faith. He can not or should not *be*—so also he can not or should not be a monotheist. . . . To be a monotheist would be a transgression against mystical monotheism. For there is only one true monotheist: God Himself, and that is clearly recognized by Muslim mystics."[35] Shiblī has time and again repeated this very feeling which had been expressed by his friend Ḥallāj throughout his whole life, namely that real tauḥīd is impossible: whoever expresses it is a heretic (*mulḥid*), whoever points to it is a dualist; whoever is silent about it is ignorant, and whoever imagines that he has reached it has no results, just as the one who thinks he is near to it is in reality far away, and the one who points to it is an idol worshiper.[36] Manērī expresses the same fact with the often used metaphor of the animal that falls into a pile of salt and becomes salt itself: likewise the worshiper immersed in the shahāda is finally taken out of himself and "made a mere nothing so that only God Himself would remain, and man would be simply a sign in the middle"[37] (a definition closely related to Junaid's saying

---

of the negation and the *al-* of the definite article in Arabic, a relation summed up by Ernst, "Faith and Infidelity," p. 65: "Iblīs was thus prevented from seeing the deification (unification) of Adam, because he refused to accept unknowing. Here Ḥallāj has been playing with the grammatical meaning of *ma'rifa* and *nakira* as signifying not only gnosis and unknowing, but also the definite noun and the indefinite noun in Arabic grammar. The definite noun, of which one has knowledge (*ma'rifa*), is preceded by the definite article *al-* (*alif-lām*), while the word "no" (just the reverse, *lā* or *lām-alif*) denies the existence of something when it is followed by the indefinite (*nakira*). If the full meaning of negation had been grasped by the excessively literal Iblis, he could have followed the path of negation to its ultimate conclusion." For only after realizing the *lā ilāha* one can reach the definite knowledge of *illā Allāh*, of the divine presence.

[34] Gramlich, "Mystical Dimensions," p. 141.

[35] Ibid., p. 143. Abū Bakr ash-Shiblī says: "The confession of oneness is in reality the property of Him who is confessed as the One, according to its external form; it is the ornament of him who confesses the oneness" (Abū'l-Qāsim 'Abdul Karīm al-Qushairī, *Ar-Risāla fi't-Taṣawwuf* [Cairo: Dār al-kutub al-'arabiyya al-kubrā, 1330 h/1912], p. 125, in *Bāb at-Tauḥīd*). Cf. also the saying of Aḥmad-i 'Uliyyān-i Nasawī in Landolt, *Kāshif al-asrār*, text p. 50; "As long as man does not become God, he can not commemorate God," to which Isfarāyīnī adds the comment that this Sufi approaches the truth "through the window of *kufr*, infidelity."

[36] Sarrāj, *Kitāb al-Luma'*, p. 30.

[37] Maneri, *Hundred Letters*, p. 155. For the image of the salt mine see 'Aṭṭār, *Dīwān*, ghazal no. 516, and 'Aṭṭār, *Muṣībatnāma*, Nūrānī Wiṣāl, ed. (Tehran: Zawwār, 1338sh/1959),

that the true *muwaḥḥid* is "a figure in the hands of God, a figure over which His decrees pass. . . ."[38]

The Sufis went so far as to confess that "the essence of *shirk*, polytheism, is that you think you are without *shirk*"[39] (for even the assumption of a different entity for the muwaḥḥid constitutes polytheism). Because the Sufi sees nothing in the two worlds except God, even Sufism may be called idolatry, "since it is the safeguarding of the heart from the vision of the other, and there is no 'other'."[40] These ideas were summed up in Anṣārī's oft-quoted lines with which he closes the *Manāzil as-sā'irīn*:

> No one confesses the One as the One,
> For everyone who confesses Him as the One, denies Him. . . .[41]

The mystical interpretation of the shahāda could also take a different turn, as Massignon has pointed out. For the followers of Ibn 'Arabī the shahāda is, according to Jāmī's interpretation,

> a regular and homogeneous proposition with a single subject. It is a universal negative linked to a particular affirmative, E.I., "there are no gods, excepting from them God"; this complete proposition, according to the rules of logic, by simple conversion (*dalīl al-khilāf*) becomes, thus, AO: "there are gods, without excepting God from them. . . . " All forms may be adored, for each one manifests a design of the Unique. Ibn Kamālpāshā, Kawrānī, and Nābulusī even wrote that the great mass of believers must be made to see that this monism is the only acceptable interpretation of the canonical *shahāda*.[42]

This may well be true for the more philosophically minded later Sufis, yet, even in many cases in which the shahāda has been interpreted in a "technically" monistic

---

p. 15; Rūmī, *M*, II, 1344, and *M*, VI, 1858, further *D*, 3041/32343, and *D*, 3100/33057, and his Tarjī'band no. 10/34985; Khwāja Mīr Dard, "Dard-i dil," no. 161, in *Chahār Risāla* (Bhopal, 1310 h/1892-1893).

[38] Hujwīrī/Nicholson, *Kashf*, p. 282.

[39] Ibid., p. 39.

[40] Thus Shiblī, quoted in Rūzbihān-i Baqlī, *Sharḥ-i shaṭḥiyāt*, paragraph 162.

[41] Abū 'Abdallāh-i Anṣārī, *Manāzil as-Sā'irīn*, Serge de Laugier de Beaureceuil, ed. and trans. (Cairo: Institut Français d'Etudes Orientales, 1962); see also Gramlich, "Mystical Dimensions," p. 144. It may have been a result of such ideas that Sarmad, the mystical poet of Judeo-Persian origin at the Mughal court, pronounced only the first half of the profession of faith, claiming that he would be a sheer hypocrite if he pronounced the affirmation as long as he had not freed himself completely from the state of negation. Yusuf Husain, *L'Inde Mystique au Moyen-Age* (Paris: Adrien Maisonneuve, 1929), p. 96.

[42] Massignon and Mason, in Swartz, *Studies on Islam*, p. 147.

sense, one will have to think of Whinfield's warning: "Oneness of being is not a rational hypothesis but the result of an overwhelming spiritual vision."[43] Jāmī, concerning whom Whinfield made this remark, indeed states in his *Lawā'ih*:

> Unification consists in unifying the heart–that is to say, in purifying it and expelling from it attachment to all things other than the "Truth" Most Glorious, including not only desire and will but also knowledge and intelligence. In fact, one must quench desire of all things hitherto desired, and cease to will what one has hitherto willed, and also remove from the intellectual vision all concepts and all cognitions, and turn away the mind from all things whatsoever, so that there remains no consciousness or cognition of aught save the "Truth" Most Glorious.[44]

The cognition of nothing but Him, that is what the true lover experiences in the end–just as when Majnun felt that he had become one with Laila, or when Hīr in Panjabi folk poetry finally cries out:

> *Ranjhā Ranjhā kar dē ninh meñ apē Ranjhā huī*
> Saying Ranjhā Ranjhā in my mind, I myself have become Ranjhā.

Rūmī has often alluded to this loving tauḥīd, as in his wonderful description of Zulaikhā, who referred with each and every word to her beloved Yūsuf,[45] or even more outspokenly in the famous story of the man who knocked at his friend's door and was sent away because he said "I." Only after answering the beloved's question, "Who is there?" with the words, "It is you, O beloved!" was he admitted into the Presence because "there is no room for two Is in the narrow house."[46] To repeat Kharrāz's statement once more, only God has the right to say "I."

[43] Maulānā 'Abdur Raḥmān Jāmī, *Lawā'iḥ*, Edward Henry Whinfield and Mirza Humanmad Ḳazwini, ed. and trans. (London 1906, new ed. London: Theosophical Publishing House, 1978), Introduction p. 4.

[44] Ibid., No. 10.

[45] Rūmī, *M*, VI, 4043 f f.

[46] Rūmī, *M*, I; 3063 f f. Rūmī continues with the description of the "two-colored lasso," i.e., the letters *k* and *n*, which constitute the creative word *kn* [*kun*, "Be!"] and distract man from the essential unity which is achieved when one undergoes the *ṣibghat Allāh*, the "baptism" or "coloring of God" (Sura 2.138, see *M*, I, 766; *M*, II, 1345). In other examples pertaining to the seeming duality that hides the essential unity he speaks of the squint-eyed person who claims that there are two moons (*M*, II, 3637) or, in a humorous vein, of the squint-eyed man who saw two bottles instead of one and promptly smashed the one actual bottle (*M*, I, 326 ff.). This image is taken over from 'Aṭṭār and Sanā'ī; for this set of ideas see Annemarie Schimmel, *The Triumphal Sun: A Study of the Works of Mowlānā Jalāloddīn Rūmī* (London: Fine Books, and The Hague: East-West Publications, 1978), p. 238.

This stage is not reached by meditating on grammatical formulas, as the theoreticians of Sufism might think, but by suffering, by "burning oneself before God."[47]

Who knows God? Someone who is saved from the *lā*.
And who is saved from the *lā*? The lover who has seen affliction, *balā*![48]

This passionate statement by Rūmī stands in contrast with the more theoretical approach of many of his contemporaries and Sufis of later times. There are variations of the simple words of the simple words of the shahāda such as *lā maujūda illā Allāh*, "there is nothing existing save God," which became one of the central claims of post-Ibn 'Arabī Sufism. There is also the daring formula used (probably for the first time) in 'Irāqī's *Lama'āt* and still current in some Turkish mystical circles: *lā ilāha illā 'l-'ishq*, "There is no deity save Love." Generally accepted in mystically minded Islam is the shortened form known from the Koran, *lā ilāha illā huwa*, *hū* being considered as the essential part of the word *Allāh*. In prayer, Sufis might attest *lā ilāha illā anta*, "There is no deity save You." The shift from the more theoretical acknowledgment of God's unity to a personal confession can be witnessed especially in mystical prayer poetry, such as the great encomia at the beginning of 'Aṭṭār's epics. The ecstatic repetition of the variation *lā ilāha illā anā*, "There is no deity save Me," which appears like a typical *shaṭḥ* in which the speaking subject seems to be God, not the human being, was used by the Shaṭṭārī order in India.

Suhrawardī Maqtūl, the Master of Illumination (d. 1191), gives another list of formulas which the faithful appropriate during their gradual annihilation in God: beginning with the tauḥīd of the common people, *lā ilāha illā Allāh*, it leads to the tauḥid of the elite, *lā huwa illā huwa*, "There is no he but He," which means the negation of all ipseities. The next step, *lā anta illā anta*, "There is no thou but Thou," is the negation of all thous but still implies a certain feeling of duality. The final formula is *lā anā illā anā*, "There is no I but I," which indeed harks back to Kharrāz's statement that no one can say "I" but God. At this point the worshiper is no longer even an instrument through which God speaks but has become immersed in the ocean of the eternal Essence where no attestation of any kind is possible.[49]

Even though existential tauḥīd was considered the goal for the true muslim and mu'min, many felt a certain danger in a "monistic" interpretation of the

[47] Rūmī, *M*, I, 3008.
[48] Rūmī, *D*, 2406/15415.
[49] Shihābuddīn Yahya Sohrawardī Maqtūl, *Oeuvres Philosophiques et Mystiques*, Vol. II, *Les Oeuvres Persanes*, Seyyed Hossein Nasr, ed. and intro.; Prolégomènes, analyses et commentaires par Henry Corbin, Bibliothèque Iranienne, 17 (Tehran and Paris: Institut d'Etudes Iraniennes, 1970), "Ṣafīr-i sīmurgh," Persian text pp. 365-365, French interpretation p. 100.

shahāda. Was not wrongly interpreted tauḥīd the reason for Iblīs's fall? He had refused to prostrate himself before Adam (Sura 2.29) because he took too literally the Divine Will that no one should be worshiped but God, declaring, as Ḥallāj put it, *juḥūdī laka taqdīs* ("My rebellion means to declare Thee holy")[50] and had overlooked the divine element which God had placed into Adam by breathing into him. Thus, Satan became "more monotheistic than God," to use Hellmut Ritter's apt formulation,[51] and even though one current in Sufism took his unflinching monotheism as an example of true love,[52] many Sufis, and certainly all orthodox Muslims, were aware of the dangers of the "Iblisian tauḥīd."[53]

Overstressed tauḥīd could lead to dangerous antinomianism. It could blur the borderlines that separate Islam from other religions, and might wipe out the difference between Moses and Pharaoh or between Abū Ḥanīfa and Hanuman, as the most daring Sufis in Sindh and the Punjab exclaimed in their ecstatic songs.[54] There was only one way to avoid the sweeping generalizations of some of the later Sufis, and that was to stress the second half of the shahāda, the words *Muḥammad rasūl Allāh*. Martin Lings quotes a telling example from Shaikh al-'Alawī, whose attitude is typical of the greatest interpreters of truly Islamic Sufism:

> In *lā ilāha illā Llāh* all being is comprised, that is, Universal Being and particular being, or being and that which is metaphorically said to exist, or the Being of the Truth and the being of creation. The being of creation cometh under *lā ilāha* which meaneth that all save God is naught (*bāṭil*), that is, denied, not to be affirmed, and the Being of the Truth cometh under *illā*

[50] Al-Ḥusain ibn Manṣūr al-Ḥallāj, *Kitāb aṭ-Ṭawāsīn: texte arabe avec la version persane d'al-Baqli*, Louis Massignon, ed. and trans. (Paris: Geuthner, 1913), pp. 41-55. See also Annemarie Schimmel, *Mystical Dimensions of Islam* (Chapel Hill, N.C.: University of North Carolina Press, 1975), pp. 194-196.

[51] Hellmut Ritter, *Das Meer der Seele: Gott, Welt und Mensch in den Geschichten Farīduddīn 'Aṭṭārs* (Leiden: Brill, 1955), p. 538.

[52] Peter J. Awn, "Iblīs in Ṣufi Psychology," Ph.D. diss., Harvard University, 1978, discusses the various aspects of mystical satanology in detail. Following Ḥallāj, Aḥmad Ghazzālī represents Iblīs as the chamberlain of the *lā ilāh* and Adam as the chamberlain of *illā Allāh*, while 'Ainulquḍāt sees Iblīs and his "black light" as the tress of the Beloved (the *lā*, see n. 17) and Muhammad as the mole and cheek of the Beloved; he urges man to proceed from the black tress to the mole and cheek of Muhammad's light which, however, still is something created and therefore implies duality, which has to be, finally, transgressed. See Ernst, "Faith and Infidelity," pp. 142-146 (discussing 'Ainulquḍat's *Tamhīdāt*, pp. 116-118); Awn, "Iblīs," pp. 199-212.

[53] Rūmī, *M*, III, 801, uses the story of Hārūt and Mārūt to show the dangers inherent in "intoxicated *tauḥīd*."

[54] The most outspoken representative of this kind of Sufi poetry (which was interpreted, understandably, as being "wildly pantheistic") are Bullhē Shāh (d. 1752) in the Punjab and Sachal Sarmast (d. 1826) in Sind; in their verses in Panjabi, Sindhi, and Siraiki similar statements can be found on almost every page.

> *Llāh*. Thus all evils come under the first half, and all that can be praised cometh under the second half.
>
> All being is comprised in the affirmation of Oneness, *lā ilāha illā Llāh*, and thou must comprise it also in naming the noblest of the slaves [in saying *Muḥammadun Rasūlu Llāh*, Muhammad is the Apostle of God].
>
> This second testification compriseth the three worlds: Muhammad denoteth the World of the Kingdom, that is, the sensible world, and the reference to his Apostlehood is a reference to the World of the Dominion, the inner world of the secrets of abstract conception, and this is mediate between the ephemeral and the Eternal, and the Name of Divinity pointeth unto the World of the Domination, the Sea from which both sense and conception are brought forth.
>
> *Rasūl* . . . is indeed the mediator between the ephemeral and the Eternal, since without him existence would be brought to nothing; for if the ephemeral meeteth the Eternal, the ephemeral vanisheth and the Eternal remaineth. When the Apostle was placed in his exact relation unto both, then was the world ordered, for outwardly he is a lump of clay, and inwardly he is the Caliph of the Lord of the Worlds.
>
> In short, the meaning of the affirmation of Oneness is not complete, nor is its benefit all-embracing, without the affirmation of Oneness in Essence, Qualities, and Actions. This affirmation is to be understood from the saying *Muḥammadun Rasūlu Llāh*. [55]

This sounds almost like an illustration of Nathan Söderblom's remark that, "The Prophet is an effect of God's activity."[56] It is indeed the Prophet who gives Islamic Sufism its peculiar character, as it is the second half of the shahāda which makes the Muslim community a specific and well-defined *umma*.

The general notion of outsiders, however, seems to be that the Prophet has little, if any, value in the mystical tradition of Islam, and the remarks which the learned Hindu Lilaram Watanmal wrote in 1889 in his study of Shāh 'Abdul Laṭīf, the grestest Sindhi Sufi poet, are typical of the approach of many Hindu and certainly also some Christian interpreters of Sufism: "Shah Laṭīf, too, has in his *Risālō*, in several places, impressed on his hearer the necessity of believing in Mahommad (sic) as a prophet and something more. . . . The orthodox Mahommadans might well believe him as the chief prophet of God. But the Sufis can *not*, consistently with their pantheistic doctrines, say that the prophet Mahommad is the only medium of salvation. . . . "[57] These patronizing remarks as to what a Sufi

[55] Lings, *A Sufi Saint*, pp. 145 f.

[56] Söderblom, *The Living God*, p. 224.

[57] Lilaram Watanmal, *The Life of Shah Abdul Latif* (Hyderabad [Sind], 1889), p. 38. The useful book by Lajwanti Ramakrishna, *Panjabi Sufi Poets* (London and Bombay: Oxford University Press, 1938), contains numerous remarks of this kind, which are rightly criticized by

can and ought to believe are certainly off the mark. To be sure, one knows that an early mystic like Rābi'a al-'Adawiyya (d. 801) was so overwhelmed by her love of God that she claimed that there was no room left in her heart for the love of the Prophet, and similar sayings are related from other early Sufis as well.[58] But even Bāyezīd Bisṭāmī (d. 874-875), the ecstatic Iranian mystic, asked God at the end of his flight through the heavens, "What am I to do?" God spoke to him: "Abū Yazīd, thou must win release from the 'thou-ness' by following My beloved. Smear thine eyes with the dust of his feet and follow him continually!"[59] In other words, he is advised to go back to the Prophet who indeed is the living witness of God's unity, and whose words and actions mark the very borders of the Muslim community which his example had shaped.

Almost at the same time as Bāyezīd received the Divine admonition to go back to the Prophet, al-Kharrāz in Baghdad was blessed with a dream appearance of the Prophet (an aspect of Islamic piety which allows important insights into the working of the Muslim religious experience). Being asked whether he, Kharrāz, loved him, he gave Rābi'a's answer of a century earlier and was told by Muhammad, "He that loves God must have loved me."[60] One can well agree with R. A. Nicholson's remark that "during the Middle Ages the person of Mohammad stands in the very center of mystical life of Islam."[61]

With this development we witness the same attitude that always brought Christian mystics back to meditate on the doctrine of the Incarnations, which was "the only safeguard against the pantheism to which they always tend."[62] For

---

Johann Fück in his review article, "Die sufische Dichtung in der Landessprache des Panǧab," *Orientalistische Literaturzeitung*, 43 (1949), col. 1-11.

[58] For her see Margaret Smith, *Rābi'a the Mystic and Her Fellow-Saints in Islam* (Cambridge University Press, 1928). The most famous case is of Shiblī who said when the Prophet's name was mentioned in the call to prayer: "If You had not ordered it I would not mention anyone besides You in the call to prayer" (Qushairī, *Risāla*, p. 17). About the aversion of some Sufis to exaggerated veneration of the Prophet in early times see Fritz Meier, *Abū Sa'īd-i Abū 'l Ḫair*, Acta Iranica, 3ième sér, Vol. IV (Leiden: Brill, 1976) p. 238.

[59] Hujwīrī/Nicholson, *Kashf*, p. 238. Bāyezīd allegedly claimed: "My banner is greater than that of Muhammad" when the famous tradition was mentioned that at Doomsday "mankind would gather under Muhammad's banner," Rūzbihān-i Baqlī, *Sharḥ-i shaṭḥiyāt*, para. 74.

[60] Farīduddīn 'Aṭṭār, *Tadhkirat al-auliyā*, Reynold Alleyne Nicholson, ed. (2 vols.; London: Luzac and Leiden: Brill, 1905-1907), I, 67, cf. also II, 41.

[61] Reynold Alleyne Nicholson, *The Idea of Personality in Islam* (Cambridge: Cambridge University Press, 1923), pp. 6 f. For the development of the veneration of Muhammad see Tor Andrae, *Die person Muhammads in glaube und lehre seiner gemeinde* (Stockholm: P. A. Vorsted, 1918), still the unsurpassed classic; Annemarie Schimmel, *Und Muhammad ist Sein Prophet: Die Verehrung des Propheten in der islamischen Frömmigkeit* (Cologne: Eugen Diederichs, 1981).

[62] Evelyn Underhill, *Mysticism: A Study in the Nature and Development of Man's Spiritual Consciousness* (1911; repr. New York: E. P. Dutton, 1961), pp. 120-121.

the Muslim, the figure of Muhammad, the "servant of God," *'abduhu*, plays a role similar to that of Jesus in Christian mysticism: he guarantees that the Sufis do not irretrievably lose themselves in the Ocean of God.

The veneration of the Prophet in mystical circles, which implies meditation upon the second half of the shahāda, had begun soon after the Prophet's death. Muqātil (d. 767) interpreted the Light Verse (Sura 24.35) as pertaining to the Prophet through whom the Divine light shines as through a glass.[63] At the same time the numerous Koranic statements about and allusions to the Prophet and his specific role as well as the traditions handed down from earlier generations were elaborated in popular and in mystical piety. Muhammad's historic life was seen "as an epitome–or if you will, an exhibition–of the essentials of a spiritual life."[64] Was he not sent *raḥmatan lil-'ālamīn*, as "Mercy for the worlds" (Sura 21.107) to quicken dead hearts as rain quickens the seemingly death earth? Was he not *ummī*, "illiterate," (Sura 7.157-158) and thus able to communicate to his community the Divine word without any "intellectual" admixture?[65] His hegira became the model of man's leaving this material world to reach the final station of glory, and the sighing palm trunk was a perfect example for the faithful who would lament once they were separated from their beloved Prophet. The mystics experienced their own *mi'rāj* but never forgot that their flight through the heavens into the Divine Presence could take place only in the spirit while Muhammad performed his heavenly journey in body *and* spirit: a sign of his absolute superiority which proved to the mystics that the highest rank one's soul can reach is equal to that which the Prophet's body could attain.[66] Muhammad became the Perfect Man, *al-insān al-kāmil*, a position that was theoretically elaborated by

[63] Nwyia, *Exégèse coranique*, pp. 93-94.

[64] Underhill (*Mysticism*, p. 121) makes this statement about the role of Christ in Christian mysticism, but it can be used verbatim to express the role of the Prophet in Islamic mysticism, and in Muslim piety in general.

[65] The translation of the word *ummī* has been a matter of dispute. It probably meant a member of a community which, contrary to the Jews and Christians, had not yet received a revealed scripture. However, in mystical circles it soon came to denote the illiteracy of the Prophet, which made him an immaculate vessel for the divine revelation: just as Mary had to be a virgin to be the vessel for the divine Word in its incarnation, thus Muhammad had to be unlettered to be the vessel for the divine Word in its "inlibration" (as H. A. Wolfson called it). Islamic poetry, particularly in the Persianate tradition, is filled with verses in praise of the *ummi* who could not read or write but was able to read the letters of the Well-Preserved Tablet, and who could wipe out all previous libraries.

[66] The fact that the Prophet returned to this world to implement God's orders here was understood as pointing to his very special role, for according to Hujwiri he thus remained "subject to the ordinances of the religious law, to the end that the proof of God may be established" and is thus the model of the true *muwaḥḥid* (Hujwīrī/Nicholson, *Kashf*, p. 283). Muhammad Iqbal, *The Reconstruction of Religious Thought in Islam* (Lahore: Ashraf, 1930 and often) begins the fifth chapter of his book with the famous saying of the Indian Sufi 'Abdul Quddūs Gangōhī (d. 1538) who stated that he would never have returned if the

Ibn 'Arabī and his successors, particularly 'Abd al-Karīm al-Jīlī, who addressed him in high-flown poetical words as did almost all Muslim poets in every language from Swahili to Urdu and Turkish.[67]

To be sure, Muslims are always reminded that the Prophet was and remained a human being, "God's servant," even during his most wondrous experience, as is attested by the Koranic use of *'abduhu* in the two passages which are interpreted as relating to his heavenly journey and dialogue with God at a distance of "two bows length and nearer" (Sura 53.1-14, and Sura 17.1). They knew that his unique, lofty position must not be confused with Christian statements about Jesus, as Būṣīrī (d. 1298) states very clearly in his *Burda*,[68] a poem which is a veritable compendium of medieval concepts connected with the Prophet, and has gained a sanctity of its own in all Islamic countries from Senegal to South India. But the concept of the *ḥaqīqa muḥammadiyya*, the primordial archetype of Muhammad, out of which practically all creation emerged and to which the mystic traveler hoped to return, tremendously enhanced the importance of the Prophet in the systems of Ibn 'Arabī and his followers. In them Muhammad becomes the temporal manifestation of the first created principle and the one who reflects the sum total of the Divine Names. Any mystic who sought to attain union with him, *fanā' fī'r-rasūl*, had to pass through the stages of all the previous prophets whose qualities were described, often enigmatically, in Ibn 'Arabī's *Fuṣūṣ al-ḥikam.*[69] The role of the *shaikh* or *pīr*, who, united with the *ḥaqīqa muḥammadiyya*, becomes the center on which the disciple's concentration focuses, belongs to this strand of mystical veneration of the Prophet and deserves special study.[70]

The idea of the "light of Muhammad," probably growing out of his appellation in the Koran as *sirājūn munīr*, "a shining lamp" (Sura 33.46) and elaborated in Muqātil's interpretation of the Light Verse as pertaining to Muhammad, permeates

---

experience of the *mi'rāj* had been granted to him; based on this remark Iqbal discusses the different attitudes of prophet and mystic, as they had been defined in the West, somewhat earlier, in the works of Nathan Söderblom and Friedrich Heiler.

[67] See Reynold Alleyne Nicholson, *Studies in Islamic Mysticism* (Cambridge: Cambridge University Press, 1921), pp. 86-87. Numerous examples from the various literatures in Islamic areas in Schimmel, *Und Muhammad ist Sein Prophet*.

[68] Al-Būṣīrī, *Al-kawākib ad-durriyya fī madḥ khair al-bariyya*; Vincenz von Rosenzweig-Schwannau, *Funkelnde Wandelsterne zum Lobe des Besten der Geschöpfe*, (Vienna, 1824); C. A. Ralfs, *Die Burda*, with German, Persian, and Turkish translations (Vienna, 1860); René Basset, *La Bordah du Cheikh al-Bousiri* (Paris, 1894).

[69] The *Fuṣūṣ al-Ḥikam* are now available in a reliable translation by R. J. W. Austin, *The Bezels of Wisdom*, Classics of Western Spirituality (New York: Paulist Press, 1981).

[70] The role of the shaikh as the true representative of the Prophet became most important in Islamic orders; for a very interesting example see Schimmel, *Pain and Grace*, pp. 78-80, about the case of Khwāja Mīr Dard whose statements about his inseparable union with his faṭher, a *sayyid*, who was also his mystical guide, are highly revealing.

all later poetry and prose. It was particularly important in the work of Sahl at-Tustarī (d. 896)[71] who developed light mysticism into a comprehensive system which certainly inspired his disciple Ḥallāj's superb description of the Prophet in his *Kitāb aṭ-ṭawāsīn.*[72] Folk songs speak of the light of Muhammad as do sophisticated mystical theoreticians. Ibn Isḥāq's description of the light that filled the world at the Prophet's birth is the centerpiece of *maulid* literature, and the *qawwāls* in Indo-Pakistan repeat over and over again:

> *Muḥammad sham'-i maḥfil būd shabgāhī ke man būdam*
> Muhammad was the candle of the assembly in that nightly place where I was![73]

Did not the Koran state that God and the angels utter blessings over the Prophet (Sura 33.56), and did God Himself not address Muhammad with the words of the famous ḥadīth qudsī, *laulāka laulāka mā khalaqtu 'l-aflāka*, "If you hadst not been I would not have created the spheres,"? so that the Prophet is often called simply "the lord of *laulāka*"? According to mystical circles in Iran in the late twelfth century God proclaimed *Anā Aḥmad bilā mīm*, "I am *Aḥmad* without the *m*" that is, *Aḥad*, or One." This ḥadīth qudsī has permeated poetry and both mystical and nonmystical writing in the eastern part of Islamdom to our century.[74]

Muhammad is also the *shafī'*, the intercessor at Doomsday, who, contrary to all other prophets, will intercede for his whole community.[75] The mystical, almost mythical qualities of the Prophet seem to be overwhelming in later mystical thought and poetry. The folk poets admonished their listeners:

> You are the maidservant in your dervish's house:
> Mention Allah and the Prophet's name in every breath.[76]

[71] Gerhard Böwering, *The Mystical Vision of Existence in Classical Islam: The Qur'ānic Hermeneutics of the Sufi Sahl at-Tustarī (d. 283/896)* (Berlin: Walter de Gruyter, 1980). A fine poetical example of this idea is the introduction of 'Aṭṭār's *Manṭiq uṭ-ṭair*, Dr. M. Jawād Shakūr, ed., 2d ed. (Tehran: Kitābfurūshī-i Tehrān, 1962), pp. 18 f., where the poet describes the column of the Light of Muhammad which performs the ritual prayer in pre-eternity before everything is created out of it.

[72] Ḥallāj, *Kitāb aṭ-ṭawāsīn*, Ṭāsīn as-sirāj, pp. 11-12, Arabic text.

[73] Attributed to Amīr Khusrau (d. 1325); S. M. Ikrām, *Armaghān-i Pāk* (Karachi: Idāre-i maṭbū'āt-i Pākistān, 1953), p. 128.

[74] For this *ḥadīth qudsī* and its role in later literature see Schimmel, *Mystical Dimensions*, pp. 224, 419, and idem, *The Triumphal Sun*, pp. 166, 286.

[75] Muhammad's role as *shafī'*, intercessor, seems to have developed very early even though it is not explicitly mentioned in the Koran; it is often connected with his heavenly journey during which he implored God to have mercy on his community. See also Taede Huitema, *De voorspraak (shafā'a) in Islam* (Leiden: Brill, 1935).

[76] Eaton, *Sufis of Bijapur*, p. 171.

The names given to the Prophet (from Aḥmad to Ṭāhā, Yāsīn, Bashīr, Munīr, and many others) were and still are used for children so that they may participate in his *baraka*,[77] and the repetition of the formula of blessing over him (*ṣalawāt-i sharīfa, durūd*) became in a number of mystical fraternities an important form of dhikr, repeated hundreds of thousands of times or used immediately after the *basmala* at the beginning of every work. It is this constant remembrance of the Prophet which makes Sufism so distinct from other mystical currents. One of the outstanding mystical poets and thinkers of Delhi in the eighteenth century, Khwāja Mīr Dard, has even coined the phrase: "Humanity consists of Muhammadanism."[78]

It is typical of the Muslim world view that as a counterweight against all-too-sweeping expressions of mystical utterances pertaining to the Unity of Being, trends developed which were called by their founders *ṭarīqa muḥammadiyya*. Not only in Mīr Dard's works do we find the proud claim to be a *muḥammadī-yi khāliṣ*, a "sincere Muhammadan" and to walk in the Muhammadan Path (which his father, Muḥammad Nāṣir 'Andalīb, had founded around 1734). We also observe similar developments in Ottoman Turkey and in North Africa.[79] In fact most of the orders that were founded in the eighteenth and early nineteenth centuries laid special emphasis upon the Prophet as their "beautiful model," *uswa ḥasana*, as he is called in Sura 33.21. This appellation forms the central statement for the development of the *imitatio Muhammadi* by following his normative *sunna*. The Sanusiyya, the Tijaniyya, and particularly the Mirghaniyya orders have produced a great number of invocations and prayers directed to the Prophet, who was their only true guide in life as well as their constant spiritual companion.[80]

Despite this intense veneration of the Prophet among Sufi orders, the Muslim orthodox, legalistically minded circles always doubted whether Sufis should be accepted as true Muslims. Such doubt was concerned, in the first place, with

[77] August Fischer, "Vergöttlichung und Tabuisierung der Namen Muhammad," in Helmuth Scheel and Richard Hartmann, eds., *Beiträge zur Arabistik, Semitistik und Islamkunde* (Leipzig: Harrassowitz, 1944). See also Max Horten, *Die religiöse Gedankenwelt des Volkes im heutigen Islam* (Halle: Niemeyer, 1917), pp. 15 ff.,; Schimmel, *Und Muhammad ist Sein Prophet*, pp. 97-107.

[78] Khwāja Mīr Dard, *'Ilm ul-kitāb* (Delhi, 1310h/1891), p. 432.

[79] For the development in India see Annemarie Schimmel, "The Golden Chain of Sincere Muhammadans," in Bruce B. Lawrence, ed., *The Rose and the Rock: Mystical and Rational Elements in the Intellectual History of South Asian Islam* (Durham, N.C.: Duke University Press, 1979). The term *ṭarīqa muḥammadiyya* already occurs in early sources, thus Isfārāyīnī around A.D. 1300 states that the *ṭarīqat-i muḥammadī* has reached him in uninterrupted succession, from hand to hand, from 'Alī ibn Abī Ṭālib; see Landolt, *Kāshif al-asrār*, text p. 19. Even a short Arabic treatise on the duties of the *murīd* by 'Aziz al-Uskudārī (d. 1698) claims to teach the *ṭarīqa muḥammadiyya* (Princeton, Yahuda Collection Ms. Nr. 2841, fols. 97*b*-103*b*).

[80] A fine survey in Constance E. Padwick, *Muslim Devotions* (London: SPCK, 1961).

those Sufis who overstressed the first part of the shahāda to point to the all-embracing Unity of Being, and who, in their poetry, often voiced their contempt for the handbooks of traditional Muslim education such as *Kanz Qudūrī Kāfiya*.[81] From verdicts by Ibn Taimiyya (d. 1328) to contemporary Muslim scholars in Egypt or Pakistan, one finds statements comparable to that issued in the *Majallat al-Azhar* about thirty years ago in a review of the works of Louis Massignon and Louis Gardet: "Islam is extremely precise of what a Muslim is and what not. Now the great majority of those whom the orientalists call Muslim mystics have nothing in common with Islam."[82]

In order to keep the balance between the two parts of the shahāda and between the "mystical" and the "prophetic" interpretation of its words we turn, in the end, to a man who has been acknowledged as one of the leading exponents of modern Islam, even though he too was the target of attacks from various factions; a philosopher who is one of the few Muslim thinkers that has integrated Western philosophy skillfully into his work on the reconstruction of religious thought; a poet who combines true "mystical" feeling with sound criticism of post-Ibn 'Arabī trends in Sufism. This man is Muḥammad Iqbāl, about whom Kenneth Cragg once wrote that he "expresses the meaning the *shahāda* has come to hold for some modern Muslims."[83]

[81] It was common among Sindhi, and to a lesser degree Panjabi, poets to ridicule the three major works that were taught in Indian madrasas, i.e., 'Alī al-Muttaqī al-Burhānpūrī's (d. 1567) *Kanz al-'ummāl*, the handy collection of Prophetic *ḥadīth*; Qudūrī's (d. 1094) handbook of Ḥanafī *fiqh*, and the grammatical poem, the *Kāfiyya*, by Ibn Malik (d. 1274). The first verse in this style is attributed to Qāḍī Qādan of Sehwan (d. 1551), but is probably later since it is doubtful whether the *Kanz* was already popular during his lifetime in India. The most pleasant expression of the contempt for the written, legalistic word (which goes together with the stress on the Prophet's quality as *ummī*," unlettered") is by Sachal Sarmast, "Waḥdatnāmō," in *Risālō Sindhī*, 'Uthmān 'Alī Anṣārī, ed. (Karachi: Sindhi Adabi Board, 1958), p. 34:

> Had the mollas once tasted the syrup from the Indus of Love,
> *Kanz Quduri Kafiyya* would have floated on the waves;
> They would have said Farewell to syntax and no longer cared for grammar.

See also Schimmel, *Pain and Grace*, p. 202. Even Iqbāl claims in *Armaghān-i Hijāz* (Lahore, 1938), p. 143:

> Whosoever knotted *lā ilāh* [*illā Allāh*] into his mind,
> Has left the fetters of school and molla.

[82] *Mağallat al-Azhar*, Rajab 1372h/April 1953, pp. 892-893, quoted in R. Caspar, "Muslim Mysticism: Tendencies in Recent Research," in Swartz, *Studies on Islam*, p. 183 n. 34.

[83] Kenneth W. Cragg, *The Call of the Minaret* (New York: Oxford University Press, 1956), p. 64 Iqbāl's interpretation of the *shahāda* has been dealt with in extenso in Annemarie Schimmel, *Gabriel's Wing: A Study into the Religious Ideas of Sir Muhammad Iqbal* (Leiden: Brill, 1963), pp. 86-171. Iqbāl's strongest statement is found in *Asrār-i khūdī* (Lahore, 1917), line 81:

> When I say "I am a Muslim," I tremble
> Because I know the difficulties of the profession *lā ilāha illā Allāh*."

Indeed, one can understand Iqbāl's thought best by returning time and again to his statement that "the ideal of the Muhammadan umma is the preservation and propogation of tauḥīd."[84]

Tauḥīd therefore forms the center of Iqbāl's theology and poetry: Muslims should be true witnesses of tauḥīd in this world, being one nation, or umma; turning to one place of worship, following one Prophet, and relying upon one book, thus manifesting in the world the Unity of God.[85] As early as 1910 he wrote: "As a political force we are perhaps no longer required; but we are, I believe, still indispensable to the world as the only testimony to the Absolute Unity of God."[86]

Iqbāl's concept of the shahāda with its negative beginning is in a certain way reminiscent of a definition of Paul Tillich who speaks of the "love-power unit which destroys what is against love."[87] It is not the mystical, inclusive "No," which Iqbāl advocates, but the true prophetic "No," which is the precondition for reaching the illā: lā is a starting point from which man can wander toward the Divine. It is the beginning of a road that will never be traversed completely, for to reach the illā Allāh in the mystical sense would mean, as we mentioned earlier, man's complete annihilation in God, whereas Iqbāl constantly stresses the importance of separation and longing as well as the necessity of returning to the world, activated by the experience of speaking to God in the intimate, person-to-person relation of prayer (which repeats the experience of the Prophet during his heavenly journey). It is the way leading from lā to illā that matters for him, and just as the classical mystical poets had described la as a broom or a sword, Iqbāl, too, uses this imagery and speaks of the constant strife which is inaugurated by uttering the lā:

> To say No in front of everything besides God is life;
> From this strife, creation is refreshed,[88]

as he says in a rather late Persian poem.

[84] *Rumūz-i bēkhūdī* (Lahore, 1917), p. 195.

[85] In his *Jāvīdnāma* (Lahore, 1932) Iqbal introduces as representatives of true *tauḥīd* both Abū Dharr, the poor companion of the Prophet, who had been regarded as a model for the Muslims at least since Sanā'ī's days (see *Dīwān*, p. 363) and Bāyezīd Bisṭāmī, who appears as the model Muslim in Rūmī's *Mathnawī* (*M*, V, 3358 ff.), but he also mentions the mighty Seljuk rulers Sanjar and Töghrul.

[86] *Stray Reflections: A Notebook of Allama Iqbal*, Javid Iqbal, ed. (Lahore: Ashraf, 1961), no. 13, p. 15.

[87] Paul Tillich, *Love, Power, and Justice* (New York and London: Oxford University Press, 1954), p. 47.

[88] *Pas che bāyad kard* (Lahore, 1936), p. 19.

We have honor from the *lā ilāh*,[89]

for it is "the turning point of the world, the material of our mysteries . . . the sword in the hand of the believer, the chain armor that protects the faithful."[90]

Since the shahāda comprises all these aspects, Iqbāl combines his political as well as his theological ideas with this formula. According to Islamic tradition, Pharaoh was drowned in the state of lā without proceeding to the illā.[91] For Iqbāl, however, there are two more representatives of the stage of lā: one is Nietzsche, who used the "dagger of lā" to cut off the fancies of Hellenized Christianity and to unmask the weakness of Christian culture. With a sentence that was used among the Naqshbandis[92] to point to Ḥallāj's weakness, Iqbāl states that Nietzsche would have been able to proceed to the illā provided he had found a spiritual guide from the Islamic tradition instead of "placing his pulse in the hand of European physicians."[93] An analogous case is that of the Russian nation which, after the October Revolution, bravely shouted its lā against the old order, against Tsarism and outworn religious and social forms but has never taken the final step of accepting Islam and implementing its basically correct ideas of social justice in the Islamic framework by fulfilling the conditions of the illā Allāh—by attesting that there is no deity *Save God*.[94]

Along with Iqbāl's poetical and sometimes surprising if not shocking interpretations of the first part of the shahāda goes his stress on the second half. In this he proves himself a good successor to the "sober" mystical tradition. It would be difficult to find any other poet in modern times who has sung as many glowing verses in honor of the Prophet as has Iqbāl.[95] Muhammad's name is radiant before the community and illuminates the world. Iqbāl sees the Prophet both as the primordial figure of light and as the model of spiritual poverty, *faqr*: in a powerful hymn put into Ḥallāj's mouth, he describes him as the true "servant of God," *'abduhu*, and sees him at the same time as the only guide of his community, the exemplar for political and social decisions. He is the caravan leader who brings

[89] *Asrār-i khūdī*, line 1607.

[90] *Rumūz-i bēkhūdī*, p. 161.

[91] See Ritter, *Meer der Seele*, p. 74.

[92] The Naqshbandi master Muhammad Zamān of Luñwārī (d. 1781) said: "If Ḥallāj had lived now, one of our children would have shown him the way" Hotchand M. Gurbaxani, *Luñwāriā ja lāl* [Karachi: Educational Publishing Company, 1934], p. 97). Sayings of this kind seem to have been quite popular among Indian Naqshbandis.

[93] For Nietzsche see *Jāvīdnāma*, lines 1373 ff.; *Payām-i Mashriq* (Lahore, 1923, repr. S. M. Ashraf, Lahore, 1958), pp. 238, 241; *The Reconstruction of Religious Thought*, pp. 194 f. For the whole question see Schimmel, *Gabriel's Wing*, pp. 323-327.

[94] "Afghānī's Message to the Russian People" in the Sphere of Mercur, *Jāvīdnāma*, pp. 27-28.

[95] Annemarie Schimmel, "The Place of the Prophet in Iqbal's Thought," *Islamic Studies*, I, 4 (1962), pp. 111-130.

souls to the central sanctuary in Mecca and in whose caravan Iqbāl sees himself playing the role of the caravan bell.[96] Besides all this he is the fragrance of the hundred-petaled rose, a reference to the Muslim community.[97] The fact that Muhammad is called in the Koran "the seal of the prophets" (Sura 33.40) is for Iqbāl, as for all Muslims, "the factor which accurately draws the line of demarcation between Muslims and non-Muslims and enables one to decide whether a certain individual or group is part of the community or not. . . ."[98] Iqbāl is thus indeed an excellent translator of the meaning of both parts of the shahāda, combining in an unusual way the mystical and prophetic elements of classical Islam.

It is certainly more than an accident or a superficial rhetorical play that in his *Jāvīdnāma* (1932) he has chosen the person of Ḥallāj to sing the most important and revealing hymn to the Prophet, for it was Ḥallāj who had pondered the shahāda to its full consequence. Not only did he create the superb praise of the Prophet in his *Kitāb aṭ-ṭawāsīn*, he also knew that true mystical tauḥīd cannot be achieved as long as there is a difference between a speaker and the object of his speech, or between a seeker and the object of his search.

> From saying "One" you do not become a monotheist—
> The mouth does not become sweet from saying "sugar"! [99]

Thus sang the Moghul heir apparent Dārā Shikōh in the middle of the seventeenth century. His favorite Sufi, Ḥallāj, gave public testimony to his desire to realize perfect tauḥīd by making God alone utter the shahada. By becoming a *shahīd*, martyr, to Divine love, he was at the same time a true *shāhid*, witness, to the annihilation of the human, transitory "I" before the eternal Divine "I", which the Sufis experienced as the last consequence of the shahāda.

[96] *Bāng-i darā* (Lahore, 1924). It is the last line of Iqbāl's famous *Tarana-i milli*, the "National Song;" the title of the whole collection, *Bāng-i darā*, is derived from this programmatic line.

[97] *Asrār-i khūdī*, lines 395 f.

[98] This statement was directed against the Qadianis and their claims that Mirzā Ghulām Aḥmad was the recipient of some continuing revelation. See *Speeches and Statements of Iqbal*, compiled by "Shamloo" (Lahore: Ashraf, 1945), p. 108.

[99] Dārā Shikōh, in Bikrama Jit Hasrat, *Dara Shikuh: Life and Works* (Santiniketam, 1953), quatrain XIX, p. 151.

ISLAM IN MODERN EUROPE

DAVID KERR

Center for the Study of Islam and Christian-Muslim Relations,
Selby Oak Colleges, Birmingham

THE BACKGROUND

Among the many writings of Professor Montgomery Watt whose distinguished career as scholar of Islam we celebrate and honor by this conference, there is his volume–the fourth in the Islamic Surveys series–on the *History of Islamic Spain*, written in collaboration with Professor Pierre Cachia.[1] Published in 1965 this book has long since established itself as a basic reference work for at least English-speaking students interested to follow the course of Islam's earliest experience of physical presence in Europe, from the early eighth to the late fifteenth century. Beyond the historical analysis of conquest, penetration, and dynastic succession, the book's greater interest lies in its discussion of, and reflection upon, the intellectual and artistic achievements of the period, as Muslim culture mediated through Arabs and Berbers interacted with that of Latin Christendom to produce–in the words of the authors–"a genuine symbiosis of indigenous and adventitious elements of the population with their respective cultures."[2]

Professor Watt returned to this subject, in wider panorama, in a series of lectures given in the early 1970s at the Collège de France, subsequently published under the title *The Influence of Islam on Medieval Europe*–ninth in the Islamic Surveys series.[3] The focus of this book is less upon the physical presence of Muslims in Europe than upon the civilizational impact that the Muslim world effected upon medieval Latin Christendom in the fields of commerce and technology, science, and philosophy, and the complex attitudes toward Islam which this produced in the European mind. Having argued that "Because Europe was reacting against the influence of Islam it belittled the influence of the Saracens and exaggerated its dependence on its Greek and Roman heritage," Professor Watt

[1] M. Watt, *A History of Islamic Spain*, Islamic Surveys, 4 (Edinburgh, 1965).

[2] Ibid., p. 169.

[3] M. Watt, *The Influence of Islam on Medieval Europe*, Islamic Surveys, 9 (Edinburgh, 1972).

concluded his lectures with the challenge: "So today an important task for us Western Europeans, as we move into the era of the one world, is to correct this false emphasis and to acknowledge fully our debt to the Arab and Islamic world."[4]

This challenge may serve to direct our thoughts to the subject with which I propose to deal, I fear rather rashly, in this lecture on "Islam in Modern Europe"–in which the Europe of our attention will be the continent as a whole (excluding the Soviet Union and Turkey other than by passing reference), and the Muslims, not only Arabs and Berbers, but in greater number Turks, Slavs, Tartars, Indians, Pakistanis, Bangladeshis, East and West Africans . . . indeed people from nearly all the major regions of what we recognize traditionally as "the Muslim world." My purpose is to attempt an impressionistic survey of the varied and therefore complex situation of the estimatedly 13 million Muslims living in Eastern and Western Europe today, and to reflect on how they see their identity as Muslims. What are the situations in which they are living? What problems and potentialities does their contemporary experience of Europe create? How, in this important situation of Muslim minority existence, do they understand themselves as Muslims and Islam as their religious way of life?

Questions such as these are coming to be recognized as of increasing importance within Europe today, as I imagine is comparably so in the United States and North America as a whole where the Muslim population is estimated in the region of some 6 million. I confine myself to the European situation where issues arising from the increasingly permanent presence of Islam as the second largest religious grouping within the continent, as within most individual European states, are finding their way into the deliberations of governments, political parties, industry, educational systems, and religious and cultural bodies–in a phrase, the pillars of Europe's establishment. One would wish to be able to include the universities within this generalization, and most particularly the academic centers of Islamic studies, but, alas, one cannot since, with but rare exception, they continue in the traditional mold of Islamic study within the perspective of "Orientalism." As a result, very little research has yet been done on Islam in modern Europe, and scholarly interest thus far has tended to look at the Muslim communities as examples of ethnic minorities under the disciplines of sociopolitical or economic analysis.[5] Instructive as such studies can be, they

[4] Ibid., p. 84.

[5] E.g., N. Abadan-Unat et al., *Turkish Workers in Europe, 1960-1975; a Socio-Economic Reappraisal* (Leiden, 1976); M. Anwar, *The Myth of Return: Pakistanis in Britain* (London, 1979); R. Donia, *Islam under the Double Eagle: The Muslims of Bosnia and Hercegovina, 1878-1914* (New York, 1981); U.-B. Engelbrektsson, *The Force of Tradition: Turkish Migrants at Home and Abroad* (Gothenburg, 1978); W. Lockwood, *European Moslems: Economy and Ethnicity in Western Bosnia* (New York, 1975); A. Michel, *The Modernization of North African Families in the Paris Area* (The Hague, 1974); R. Rist, *Guestworkers in Germany* (New York, 1978).

are inadequate if they ignore, or unless they are complemented by, equal interest in the "religious" aspect of contemporary Islam in Europe–careful though we must be in applying the term "religious" in its Western sense to Islam which sees itself in Europe, as much as in the traditional Muslim world, as a comprehensive way of life. To date, I know of only one academic center which addresses itself to research on Islam in Europe in this sense–in the city of Birmingham in the British Midlands, with a Muslim citizenship in excess of 25,000.[6]

Professor Watt regrets in his book on Islamic Spain that the gaps in our knowledge of that subject are so vacuous that conclusions can be no more than provisional. How much more, then, must this same regret apply as a caveat with respect to any observations we may hazard about the situation of Islam in the rest of European history? If we treat the Arab-Berber Muslim presence in medieval Spain and Sicily[7] as the first phase of Islamic experience of Europe, what we know of it would seem to be in abundance by comparison with the near total absence of scholarly investigation of what we could identify as the second phase: the long history of Muslim presence in Eastern Europe. What do we know, for example, of the small and apparently tight-knit community of Muslims of Turkish extraction who were settled in the Danube basin by the tenth century, though it was significant enough for a mention by Yaqūt al-Hamawī (d. 1229) in his geographical reference book, *Mu'jam al-Buldān*, on account of his having met some Hungarian Muslim students traveling in Syria?[8] Still in pre-Ottoman times, how little has been studied of the character of Muslim life in northeastern Europe during the period of the Mongol Khanate of the Golden Horde, the most westerly of the Mongol-dominated regions which took shape in the thirteenth century while Berke and his successors flourished in what Chaucer termed "Sarray in the land of Tartarye."[9] Already by the tenth century mosques were being built in Constantinople for use by Slavs and Turks who, though soldiers in service of the Christian Emperor, were granted permission to perform Islamic worship and to name the Caliph in the *khutbah*.[10] But not until the Ottomans' conquest of Constantinople in 1453 and their subsequent westerly movement through the Balkans into central Europe does our historical view of Islam in this part of the continent begin to find a sharper perspective, though it is only recently that we have been provided with a reliable bibliographical reference of the works of Bosnian Muslim authors of this long period by the industry of Dr. Smail Balic, Keeper of the Oriental Books at the Austrian State Library

[6] See *Research Papers: Muslims in Europe* (Centre for the Study of Islam and Christian-Muslim Relations, Selly Oak Colleges, Birmingham, U.K.), March 1979– (continuing quarterly).

[7] A. Ahmad, *A History of Islamic Spain*, Islamic Surveys, 10 (Edinburgh, 1975).

[8] S. Balic, ed., *Die Muslims in Donauraum* (Vienna, 1971), p. 17.

[9] See J. Saunders, *A History of Mongol Conquests* (London, 1971), pp. 155-162.

[10] Balic, *Die Muslims in Donauraum*, p. 3.

in Vienna.[11] On the basis of his possibly unique research into this field of Islamic history, Dr. Balic, himself a Muslim of Bosnian descent, firmly refutes the notion of Islam in Eastern Europe being the product of Ottoman imperialism and states his opinion that long before the appearance of the Ottomans, "a large part of the indigenous population had adopted Islam entirely of their own free will for the specific reason that it helped them in many ways to safeguard their own national characteristics, and to express their own cultural and sociopolitical identity in their own ways."[12]

How interestingly this conclusion tends to converge with that of Professor Watt about Islamic Spain, but how much more frustrating that the comparisons have as yet been so little researched. Let us bear Dr. Balic's opinion in mind, however, as we turn now to what we might call the third and most recent phase of Muslim settlement in Europe: the migration of some 6 million Muslims into Western Europe since World War II, mainly from Asia and Africa. The statistics usually given indicate 2 million Muslims in France, mainly from North Africa, 1.7 million in the Federal Republic of Germany, mainly Turks, 1.2 million in the United Kingdom, mainly from Pakistan, Bangladesh, India (Gujerat, or by way of East Africa) and from her former African colonies, the Middle East, and Malaysia, and some 200 thousand Indonesians, Turks, and Moroccans in the Netherlands. Smaller Muslim migrant populations are to be found in the Nordic countries, Belgium, Italy, and Spain. But while the highest incidence of modern Muslim settlement in Western Europe is by migration from Asia and Africa, our picture would be incomplete without noticing the substantial number of Eastern European Muslim migrants (in addition to Turks) from the Yugoslav Republic of Bosnia and Hertzegovina who comprise the largest group of Muslims in Sweden (8,000), the second largest after the Turks in West Germany (120,000), and are estimated to be the third largest element in Muslim community, after Turks and Pakistanis, in Denmark.[13]

The terms "migrant" and "migration" are potentially misleading in that they suggest impermanence, and as used of Muslims would seem to relegate Islam in Western Europe to the status of a merely transitory phenomenon. Let me risk being repetitious in reiterating that it is yet too early to state firm conclusions, but clearly the trend is away from "migration" toward "immigration" in the sense that the migrant communities, among which the Muslims are numerically preponderant, are increasingly coming to see themselves as being permanently settled in Western Europe. To be sure, the original motive in these

[11] S. Balic, *Die Kultur der Bosniaten* (Vienna, 1978).

[12] S. Balic, "Eastern Europe: The Islamic Dimensions," *Journal of the Institute of Muslim Minority Affairs* (King Abdulaziz University, Jeddah), 1, 1 (May 1979), 29.

[13] All population statistics in this paper are taken from J. S. Nielsen, "Muslims in Europe: An Overview," *Research Papers: Muslims in Europe* (Centre for the Study of Islam and Christian-Muslim Relations, Birmingham, U.K.), 12 (December 1981).

postwar migrations was largely economic, and therefore seen as short-term, as several Western European countries actively encouraged migrant workers to provide the additional manpower needed in the process of industrial expansion in the 1950s and 1960s. The term "man"-power is used advisedly in that the migrants were admitted majoritatively as single males who were prepared to forego the comforts of family life in order to achieve economic betterment for the benefit of the families they had temporarily left in their countries of origin. During this first phase of postwar migration, therefore, little interest was shown by Muslims (or by other ethnic groups, for example, Caribbeans, Hindus, Sikhs in Britain) in community organization, but a second phase was introduced by the implementation of legal restrictions upon migration to Britain in the early 1960s, and upon the use of migrant labor in member states of the European Common Market in face of industrial recession in the early 1970s. The relevant legislation limited the access of single male workers, but allowed for the entry of the dependents of male workers already resident in Western Europe. The resulting change in patterns of migration has given rise to a deeper sense of permanence within the migrant population, and interest is therefore turning beyond that of purely economic gain to issues of the identity of the migrant communities as ethnic and religious minorities permanently resident in Western Europe. In the case of Muslims in Britain this development can be traced, for example, by the proliferation of locally based and national organizations which sprang up after the first Commonwealth Immigration Act in 1962, resulting in the formation in 1970 of the Union of Muslim Organizations in Great Britain and Eire with the purpose of securing "the survival of their religious and cultural identity in a non-Muslim environment."[14]

Thus, while it is tempting to contrast the contemporary situation of Muslims in Western and Eastern Europe along the lines of foreign migrants and indigenous populations, this must be tempered by the fact that in Western European countries we are now, after roughly thirty years, moving into what might be termed the second generation of Muslims, most of whom have been born in Western Europe which therefore they regard to be their actual home, however much the parent generation might continue to live in the uncertain position, evocatively expressed in the title of the study by a Muslim author, Muhammad Anwar, of Pakistanis in Britain by the phrase *The Myth of Return*.[15] Any comparison would also have to bear in mind that migration is not limited to the experience of Muslims in Western Europe alone, to the exclusion of the East. For example, there has in recent years been a significant incidence of Muslim migration to the German Democratic Republic where as many as 15 thousand Algerian Muslims work under

[14] "Union of Muslim Organizations," *Impact International* (London, 9-22 April 1976), p. 42, hereafter *Impact International*.

[15] See n. 5, above.

short-term contracts between the Algerian and East German governments. Nor within Western parts of Europe is Muslim settlement a recent phenomenon in its entirety. About 10 percent (5 thousand) of the Muslim community in Austria are indigenous Europeans of Bosnian descent, and most of the 150 thousand Muslims in Greece are Turks who remained in western Thrace at the time of the retraction of Turkish frontiers, their character been legally decreed by the Greek Constitution as "Muslim" in order to indicate a religious rather than ethnic or national minority.[16] In Britain several small groups of Muslims were already resident in the nineteenth century. Gujerati Indian and Yemeni Arab seamen took shore jobs in London, and yet more significantly in the provincial parts of Cardiff, South Shields, and Liverpool where the Yemenis in particular organized a remarkably coherent community structure around *zawiyah* centers faithful to the 'Alawi *tariqah* which had spread to Yemen from North Africa.[17] British universities attracted Muslim students from the then imperial colonies, numbers of whom settled in Britain for professional reasons and tended to make common cause with a few, somewhat eccentric members of the lesser aristocracy who converted to Islam often as a result of imperial service overseas; this alliance accounts for the first purpose-built mosque in Britain in 1889 (Woking, south of London) which operated fairly effectively as a center of Muslim missionary activity in London during the early part of the twentieth century, though under the opprobrium of Lahori Ahmadi affiliations.[18] Similar histories could be told of Germany,[19] of France[20] and the Netherlands,[21] each with extensive imperial involvement in the Muslim world of the nineteenth century, and for other reasons of Finland, where a small community of Tartar Muslim traders from the Crimea had established itself in Helsinki by the end of the nineteenth century, from where they maintained commercial links with European Russia through other Tartar Muslims who settled in Poland at about the same time.[22]

[16] J. Nielsen, "Forms and Problems of Legal Recognition for Muslims in Europe," *Research Papers: Muslims in Europe* (Centre for the Study of Islam and Christian-Muslim Relations, Birmingham), 2 (June, 1979), 6-7 (translated and reprinted as "Europas Muslime: Ihr Rechts-Status," *CIBEDO Dokumentation* [Cologne],4 [Sept. 1979]).

[17] For an account of the founder of this order, see M. Lings, *A Sufi Saint of the Twentieth Century: Sheikh Ahmad Al-'Alawi, His Spiritual Heritage and Legacy*, 2d ed. (London, 1971).

[18] M. Ally, "The History of the Muslim Community in Britain," M. A. thesis, University of Birmingham, 1981, p. 38.

[19] M. Abdullah, "Old Relations, New Community," *Impact International*, pp. 34-35; cf. idem, *Geschichte des Islams in Deutschland* (Graz, 1981).

[20] See Centre d'Information et d'Etudes sur l'Emigration Mediterranéenne, *L'Islam en France* (Paris, 1978).

[21] See S. Theunis, *Ze Zien Liever Mijn Handen dan Mija Gezicht: Buitenlandse Arbeiders in Onsland* (Het Wereldvenster, Baarn, 1979); cf. *Moslims en Christenen in Nederland* (Nederlandse Zendingstraad, Amsterdam), pp. 35-40.

[22] S. Syrjanen, "Submission to Conference of European Churches' Consultation on 'Islam in Europe'" (Salzburg, 1978) (unpublished).

While it is clear, therefore, that there are significant differences in the contemporary situation of Muslims in Eastern and Western Europe, these should not be overgeneralized or exaggerated. It should be emphasized that the contemporary situation in both regions of Europe must be set against the background of the first two stages of Islamic presence in Europe which remind us that there has been an Islamic history in the making in the European context continuously since the early part of the eighth century: in Spain where, as Professor Watt has shown, there was creative interaction between Muslim and Christian cultures, the effects of which survived the expulsion of Muslims from the Iberian peninsula in the late fifteenth century, though they have been belittled in the historical memory of later Europeans; and, from about the tenth century, in Eastern Europe where Islam has been, in Dr. Balic's view, an important factor in the shaping of the national identity of the Albanians, Bosnians, and others. The contemporary settlement of Muslims in Western Europe can only be regarded as novel in the most relative terms, therefore, and it would be gravely misleading to view the entire experience of Muslims in modern Europe through the perspective of post-World War II migratory trends. What is most clearly common to the present-day situation of Muslims in both Eastern and Western Europe is that both find themselves living as substantial minorities in non-Muslim societies in which secularism is the order of the day, be it in terms of the official ideology of the socialist republics of the East, or in the working principle that religion must be relegated to the private sphere of the individual, as we find in the West. In either case Muslims feel themselves confronted by problems of community identity, and it is to them that we must now turn.

The Problem

Secularism and the problems of secularization are a preoccupying debate in the welter of Muslim writing–magazines, newspapers, tracts–in Europe today, and it is principally within the context of this debate that Muslims are working out their conceptions of their future in the West.[23]

For many Muslims, of course, secularization does not represent any problem at all, for they may already have renounced what, in Western terms, we would identify as a religious affiliation to Islam, and would therefore accept the attribution of being "Muslim" no more than in the sense of belonging to a socio-political grouping. This is officially the case, most strikingly, in two instances of Muslim majority presence or plurality in Eastern Europe: in Albania, the only European state with a majority Muslim population and the only one that

[23]For up-to-date survey, see *Abstracts: European Muslims and Christian-Muslim Relations*, J. Nielsen and S. von Sicard, eds. (Centre for the Study of Islam and Christian-Muslim Relations, Birmingham, U.K.), September 1979– (continuing twice-yearly).

officially declares itself to be atheistic; and in the federated Republic of Bosnia and Herzegovina in Yugoslavia, part of whose population is described officially as "Muslim in the ethnic sense," on a par with other constituent ethnic groups—Croats, Serbs, and Macedonians. In the city of Zagreb, the chief Imam admits that less than half of the 100 thousand Muslim population have any devotional adherence to Islam. A comparable situation in the West pertains among the large populations of Turkish migrants as, for example, in the Federal Republic of Germany where estimatedly 30 thousand of the overall Turkish community have ideological allegiances ranging from Bulent Ecevit's Republican Party leftward toward various atheistic Marxist groups.

On the other hand, however, slightly less than half of the Muslim population of Zagreb *do* desire to practice Islamic *'ibadāt*, and it may be part of what is cautiously described as a religious revival among Muslims in Eastern Europe, of which there is evidence also in the Soviet Union where the religious orders (*turuq*) are said to be powerful underground.[24] To return to the West German situation, we must recognize the presence of powerful anti-Kemalist organizations which, as in Turkey, react strongly against secularizing tendencies within the Muslim population or as represented by the state: an example is the Sülaymanli group, loyal to the revivalist teaching of Sheikh Sülayman Hilmi Tunahan (d. 1959) which has effectively spearheaded a self-help campaign by Muslim parents to provide religious education in Qur'an schools for their children, thus creating one of the most controversial disputes within the Turkish community in West Germany.[25] In the United Kingdom one of the most articulate voices within the Muslim intellectual and leadership elite—and within the Union of Muslim Organizations—is that of the disciples of Abu'l 'Ala Maududi (d. 1979) whose writings are widely available in English as well as Urdu, and inspire several British-based Muslim organizations sympathetic to his Jama'at-i-Islami movement to produce their own literature which is stridently critical of secularization.[26]

Among the mass of literature dealing with this issue, much of which is written

[24] See A. Bennigsen and C. Lemercier-Quelquejay, "Muslim Religious Conservatism and Dissent in the USSR," *Religion in Communist Lands*, 6, 3 (Autumn 1978), 155-159; the same authors more fully in *Les Musulmans Oubliés: l'Islam en URSS aujourd'hui* (Paris, 1981); passim; cf. M. Broxup, "Islam and Atheism in the North Caucasus," *Religion in Communist Lands*, 9, 1-2 (1981), 40-46.

[25] M. Abdullah, "Muslim Religious Education in the Federal Republic of Germany: The Qur'an School Debate," *Research Papers: Muslims in Europe* (Centre for the Study of Islam and Christian-Muslim Relations, Birmingham, U.K.), 4 (December 1979), 12-29 (translated and reprinted from German original "Weshalb Koranschule," *CIBEDO Dokumentation* [Cologne], 3 [June 1979]).

[26] See K. Ahmad and Z. Ansari, eds., *Islamic Perspectives: Studies in Honour of Sayyid Abul A'la Mawdudi* (Islamic Foundation, U.K., 1979), esp. last chapter written by the editors, "Mawlana Sayyid Abul A'la Mawdudi: An Introduction to His Vision of Islam and Islamic Revival," pp. 359-383. Khurshid Ahmad was formerly Director General of the Islamic

more emotionally than critically, the most thoughtful analysis of which I am aware is that of Professor Ali Merad, a Muslim intellectual from Algeria who has made his home in France. In an unpublished lecture given to a conference held in Salzburg in 1978 under the auspices of the Conference of European Churches on the Theme of "The Church and Muslims in Europe," he emphasized that Muslim experience of secularization in Europe is not radically new since all Muslim societies have been faced by the processes of secularization since the nineteenth century. "The contemporary history of Islam," he opines, "is that of a slow but inexorable penetration of Muslim society by ideas and by cultural, social and political models which are of secularist provenance." We are all familiar with the reactions it has produced within the Muslim world between secularists and traditionalists, the masses and the ruling elites, and Professor Merad sees these broadly to be replicated in the contemporary experience of Muslim in Europe, as illustrated by the examples I have offered. But Professor Merad points to one important difference, and I paraphrase his argument: However severe these tensions have been (in Muslim societies), notably when a government uses its juridical power and other means of coercion in order to impose its policy of secularization (e.g., the Kemalist regime in Turkey), the impact of the process of secularization on the Muslim way of life is attenuated by a variety of factors which pertain to the density and homogeneity of the social fabric, to the inertia of the body of the community whose reactions of refusal cannot always be controlled by the political power. The sociocultural environment thus plays the role of a sort of protective screen, or filter, in the sense that the symbols of Islamic identity at the social level cannot be abolished overnight simply as the result of a political will. . . . In such a situation the experience of secularization may be irritating, it may be constraining, but it is not necessarily traumatic. By contrast, however, the social environment in the secular societies of Europe bears little trace of an Islamic way of life, culture or tradition, and has no reference to those symbols which form Muslim consciousness at the deepest level. In such a social context the Muslim feels not only to be cast into anonymity, but finds himself or herself condemned to suffer the fate of the exile, or of the person reduced to the status of outsider in his or her own country.[27]

In this lucid way Professor Merad points to the sense of marginalization which Muslims in Europe, whether "religious" or "cultural," suffer alike, either by virtue of their recent migration from their countries of origin, often from rural

---

Foundation, Leicester, U.K., which is actively engaged in the work of *da'wah* in Britain through the publication and distribution of books, pamphlets, and the like reflecting the views of Mawdudi (see "The Islamic Foundation," *Impact International*, pp. 41).

[27] A. Merad, "Quelques observations sur la position du musulman dans une société pluralistique," unpublished paper presented to the Conference of European Churches' Consultation on "Islam in Europe," Salzburg, 1978, pp. 4-5.

situations in, for example, Anatolia or Pakistan where the traditional symbols of Islamic society remain strong, or by virtue of the social and political revolutions which have taken place in European countries which they may have inhabited for centuries. In neither case do Muslims have the means of participating in the political process, and they are hard pressed to preserve their personal or communal identity at all. Reviewing the predicament of religious Muslims in Eastern Europe, Balic concludes pessimistically that "Islam as religious consciousness is a kind of agony where the younger generation is concerned; the impact-basis of Islamic tradition grows narrower every day, and so the situation of Muslim communities in eastern Europe is not a very hopeful one."[28] Among the evidences he adduces is the example of Bulgaria where for several years pressure has been exerted to eradicate what are regarded as "foreign names" among the Muslim population, including the name Ishmael (Ismā'īl), although "Christian" Biblical names are accepted as being Bulgarian. Yugoslavia, as already mentioned, permits Bosnian Muslims to exercise what are termed their "national rights," but it was only in 1978 that the Islamic theological college in the Bosnian state capital of Sarajevo was reopened after its closure during World War II. And it is in Sarajevo also that we find, in exile, the only *madrasah* in southeastern Europe which still teaches in the Albanian language, the regime of Tirana having prohibited any form of religious Islamic expression within Albania.[29]

But is the situation, as perceived by Muslims themselves, essentially better in the Western democracies? We would, of course, like to think so, given the democratic and humanitarian principles that we claim to defend, and clearly Muslims appreciate the attitudes of toleration which are in marked contrast to the situation in much of Eastern Europe. There is a large difference, however, between toleration and acceptance, and it is precisely here that Professor Merad sees the greatest paradox in Western societies which, to him, seem unprepared and therefore unwilling to extend democratic principles to facilitate the exercise of political, cultural, moral, and spiritual values on the part of immigrant communities—and perhaps most particularly in the case of Muslims in view of the deeply ingrained Western prejudice against Islam which Professor Watt has analyzed in his study of *The Influence of Islam on Medieval Europe*.[30]

Furthermore it is well known that Islam needs to express itself in terms of community (*'ummah*),[31] and the trend of post-World War II Muslim migration

[28] Balic, "Eastern Europe: The Islamic Dimension," p. 30.

[29] Ibid., p. 31; cf. "Yugoslavia and Albania," *Impact International*, pp. 32-33.

[30] Watt, *The Influence of Islam on Medieval Europe*, pp. 72-77; cf. N. Daniel, *Islam and the West: The Making of an Image* (Edinburgh, 1960); R. Southern, *Western Views of Islam in the Middle Ages* (Cambridge, Mass., 1962).

[31] E.g., *Surat āl-'imrān*, 104: "And let there spring from you a community (*'ummah*) who invite to goodness, and enjoin right conduct and forbid indecency. Such are they who are successful."

to Western Europe indicates a clear correlation between the growth of Muslim family life and the need of Muslim families to associate with one another within a wider community through which to experience and express their corporate identity. I have already alluded to this in distinguishing the two phases of post-war migration. In the United Kingdom, the second phase began with the first legal restrictions on immigration in 1962. Over the next five years, of the Pakistani Muslims entering the country the number of dependents of male workers who had been admitted in the 1950s was more than double that of new male workers gaining admission–52 thousand as against 22 thousand. The reconstitution of Muslim family life in Britain created community concerns as represented by the plethora of Muslim organizations which sprang up in the 1960s, and in the numbers of mosques or prayer houses that were created–they being the most obvious "pillars" of Muslim community. There are no reliable statistics on the number of Muslim places of worship in Britain, and estimates range between three hundred and one thousand, but whichever figure is nearer the truth it is generally agreed that two-thirds of the mosques have appeared since 1962. The same phenomenon is evident on the European mainland, though the second phase of Muslim migration did not begin until the early 1970s following the legal restrictions on labor importation in 1973-74. Since then there has been a rapidly increasing incidence of marriages among Turkish workers in Germany with a sharp reduction of remittances of income being sent back to Turkey as wages are now kept in Germany to finance the requirements of family life. A 1975 survey of how Turkish workers in Germany occupied their spare time showed that less than one percent attended worship, while it is now estimated that there are as many as 700 mosques in West Germany.[32]

Accepting these observations as indexes of the growth of Muslim aspirations for community expression in Western Europe, we can appreciate why the distinction between sociopolitical affairs in the public sector and religion as a private concern, fundamental to secular principle in the West, is seen by Muslims to assure their toleration as individuals while at the same time isolating, and thereby subtly suppressing, the cultural and moral factors pertaining to Islamic community upon which effective Muslim participation in Western society must depend. Moreover, the distinction is seen to be rather more theoretical than real in view of the fact that many Western European countries acknowledge a state church or provide legal guarantees and privileges for their indigenous churches, and may extend other forms of recognition to the Jewish communities.

With only three exceptions, however, Western European countries have so far been unwilling to confer any form of legal recognition upon their Muslim

[32] Arbeitsring Ausland für Kulturelle Aufgaben, Einstellung Türkischer Arbeitsnehmer in der Bundesrepublik Deutschland (Cologne, March 1975); cf. "Die Presenz des Islam in der Bundesrepublik Deutschland," *CIBEDO Dokumentation* (Cologne), 9 (December 1980).

communities on a par with Christian churches and Jewish communities–the exceptions being Greece, Austria, and Belgium. In Greece and Austria it has been a matter of inheriting or reactivating earlier legal provisions. Under the terms of the post-World War I treaties of Sèvres (1920) and Lausanne (1923), the Muslim population of Western Thrace was accorded legal recognition as a religious community under a then arch-mufti who was held responsible under the Greek constitution for the jurisdiction of all matters relating to *shari'ah* family law and religious foundations (*awqāf*), though in other matters the Muslims of Western Thrace are subject to the jurisdiction of the Greek courts.[33] In Austria, legal recognition had been given in 1874 and 1912 to the Muslim population of the pre-World War I Hapsburg Empire, with a mufti in Vienna and a codification of Hanafi family law in German. With the disintegration of the Empire and the creation of the Federal Republic the reduced Muslim population was no longer able to take advantage of the 1912 legislation, and their legal association was anyway dissolved by the Germans in 1939. Not until 1979 was it finally reactivated after a ten-year campaign by the Muslim Social Service Organisation, with the result that the Muslim community now receives tax concessions, access to the media, and provision for religious education in the state school system.[34] Only in Belgium, among European countries of recent Muslim migration, has legal recognition been accorded to the Muslim community, on a par with Christians and Jews, by legislation promulgated in 1974 which acknowledges the Islamic Cultural Centre in Brussels as having overall responsibility for Islamic religious affairs, with power to delegate to provincial bodies.[35]

At least two applications for similar legal status are currently being considered by Länder administrations in West Germany, and the Union of Muslim Organisations in Britain has appealed to the British Government to recognize *shari'ah* family law, but so far without success.[36] The constitutional and legal problems involved in this issue are enormously complex and raise details that I have no competence to discuss. It would appear, however, that the difficulties have as much to do with the fragmentary character of Muslim leadership in Europe as with the manifest ambiguities of current European thought about the ethnic and religious plurality of European society. In the religious tradition of Islam, which has never developed patterns of representative leadership analogous to those upon which Western democracy operates, it is very difficult for Muslims to represent themselves effectively in Western societies. In Britain, where a reasonably coherent leadership has evolved within the Union of Muslim Organisations, there

[33] Nielsen, *Forms and Problems*, pp. 6-7.
[34] Ibid., pp. 2-5.
[35] Ibid., pp. 9-11.
[36] Ibid., pp. 11-17.

is still much evidence of internal competition within the Muslim community among different religious schools of thought (viz. Brelvis, Deobandis, and Wahhabis), and between them and other bodies that aspire to leadership in terms of the national and ethnic backgrounds of the immigrants. The same problems exist in other West European countries, perhaps more acutely in the absence of the substantial professional class of Muslims who tend to provide leadership in Britain. And in the Netherlands the situation pertains where Muslims have to operate under the legal restriction that only a native Dutchman can serve as a registered official of any organization, which effectively limits Muslim leadership to the small number of European converts. Some progress has been made in sorting out such leadership problems since the inauguration, in 1973, of the Islamic Council of Europe which, from its base in London, seeks to develop and coordinate Muslim leadership throughout Europe, to represent Muslim concerns before European governments, and to provide a connection with the international Muslim world particularly through its link with the Organisation of the Islamic Conference in Jeddah. But, significant as the Council already is, one cannot help but feel that the distance between it and the grass roots communities it aspires to represent may foster the very same problems with which Western participatory democracies are faced at a time when those who are represented demand a greater control upon their representatives.

A positive sign is that one of the two working commissions of the Islamic Council of Europe is concerned with Islamic education for Muslim children, youth and adults, the priority being given to this issue reflecting the need most urgently felt within the local communities of Muslims to provide for the transmission of Islamic knowledge to new generations of European Muslims. I have already alluded to the difficulties faced by Eastern European Muslims in this regard, and in the West the problem is threefold: first, for the majority of the older generation of immigrant parents, the very concept of religious education as we know it in the West is alien since they have probably never learned Islam as an objectified set of beliefs and practices, but experienced it as the cement of an integrated cultural and social structure, and in this sense find it very difficult to extrapolate the core of religious teaching from the cultural context in which they have known it as a way of life; second, the younger or second generation of children live in a tension between two cultures, that of their parents within the family, and that of the state school where their Western education tends to subvert the traditional values of their parents; last, but by no means least, in the state schools themselves a critical debate continues as to how best to evolve an educational curriculum which would meet the needs not only of Muslim children but also of other religious and ethnic minorities. Nowhere are the problems of pluralist societies more sharply or emotionally exposed than in education, but equally education is probably the most important ingredient in the upbuilding of a sense of identity and the reality of community among Muslims in Europe, as it has been for Jews who have given priority to the development of their own schools and colleges.

Many Muslims wish to do the same, although, apart from the Qur'an schools which provide a rudimentary and conservatively traditional type of Islamic education, Muslim schools are almost as rare in Western Europe as they are in the East.

It has been my contention, following Professor Merad's line of argument, that because the problem of secularization is not per se novel to Muslims in Europe, their widely expressed anxieties about what many see to be the dangers of secularism should not be interpreted as inability to cope with the reality of modern Europe, as is sometimes suggested. The problem is, rather, that they find themselves exposed to the secularizing and materialist pressures of Europe without what Professor Merad calls the "protective screen" of familiar symbols of Islamic identity which serve to filter the process of secularization. Dr. Balic predicts rather pessimistically what he sees to be the likely future of Muslims in Eastern Europe, though the recrudescence of Islam in Central Asia may well have its impact on Muslims in the Soviet Union and Eastern Europe. Of the West Professor Merad also speaks with a degree of pessimism, but as Muslims strive to develop the pivotal institutions of Islamic community–family, mosque, and education–in Europe, there is reason by the terms of Merad's own analysis, to expect that they will be able to engage with the forces of secularization in a manner that could facilitate their evolving an Islamic identity appropriate to contemporary Europe because they no longer feel traumatized by it.

CONCEPTIONS OF THE FUTURE

Evidence that some politically active Muslim intellectual leaders are beginning to think in the direction suggested by my foregoing comments is to be found in *Muslim Communities in Non-Muslim States*,[37] which contains the papers given at an international seminar held in London in 1978, hosted and organized by the Islamic Council of Europe in conjunction with the Organisation of the Islamic Conference's Department of Muslim communities in Non-Member States. The purpose of the seminar–the first of its kind–was to initiate discussions that would develop a conceptual framework for analysis of the problems encountered by Muslims in minority situations, and to initiate an ongoing review of the actual living conditions of Muslim minorities. Both these concerns are now reflected in the *Journal of the Institute of Muslim Minority Affairs*[38] produced by the University of King Abdul Aziz in Jeddah as a consequence of the seminar, and now in its second issue.

[37] Islamic Council of Europe, *Muslim Communities in Non-Muslim States* (London, 1980).

[38] Published by the Institute of Muslim Minority Affairs, King Abdulaziz University, Jeddah; vol. 1, no. 1 (Summer 1979); vol. 1, no. 2 (Winter 1979); vol. 2, no. 1 (Summer 1980); vol. 2, no. 2 (Winter 1980); vol. 3, no. 1 (Summer 1981).

Muslims in Europe are by no means an exclusive concern of these publications whose purview is the one-third of the world's total Muslim population who live in minority situations, but it is clear that the European situation and the position of Muslims in the West more generally stand high in their priority. They firmly aver the value for the Muslim world as a whole of the 300 million Muslims living as minorities, and insist that while their situations may call for the support of Muslim majorities, their experiences as minorities may also have a positive bearing upon the life of the 'ummah as a whole. Due emphasis is given to the need of Muslim minorities to preserve or transplant their Islamic identity, and here it is seen that the moral and material support of Muslim majorities can be appropriate since, as the much quoted prophetic hadith states: "Muslims are like one body; if a part of the body hurts, the whole body is sick." But caution is expressed against the notion of Muslim minorities being simply "enclaves in a foreign soil," to be regarded by Muslim majorities as "overseas territories." Their destiny is acknowledged to be inseparable from that of the Muslim world as a whole, but, to quote the Secretary General of the Islamic Conference, Dr. Ahmadou Karim Gaye, "all actions which aim . . . at strengthening the cultural identity of these communities have to be taken within the framework of their national societies and without prejudice to the fact that each one belongs to its own country."[39]

Dr. Syed Abedin, a staff member of the Institute of Muslim Minority Affairs in Jeddah, develops this point in such a way as to suggest how Muslim minority experience can be valuable to the 'ummah as a whole, particularly at a time when, as he says, "the categories of power, prosperity, vision and leadership have again come to be conjoined with the category of Islam."[40] What, he asks, is the value of the Muslim communities that, as in the minority situations in Europe which we have described, do not possess the attributes of sovereignty? In answer to this question he proposes, seemingly with the Muslim minorities in India and Europe particularly in mind, that they should be encouraged to develop their own analyses of their identity, by balancing what he terms "doctrinal" aspects against "behavioural" aspects in the search for definitions of "Islam" and "Muslim" which would be appropriate both to their unquestionable, though critical, participation in a non-Islamic state, and to their membership in the universal 'ummah. "This would require," he argues, "that we seek a new definition of Islamic culture which spells out clearly its doctrinal base,

[39] A. Gaye, "Muslim Minorities: A Framework," in *Muslim Communities in Non-Muslim States*, pp. 3-4.

[40] S. Abedin, "The Study of Muslim Minority Problems: A Conceptual Approach," in ibid., p. 19.

that we make this the core of our identity, and that we adapt ourselves in those behavioural aspects of our lives which do not compromise or isolate this core."[41]

Several contributors agree that the current concern for Muslim identity in Europe, in order that it be legitimate in terms of Islamic ideal, must be conceived not as an end in itself but as an expression of the universal mission of Islam. As such it is an issue of *da'wah*, and as clearly as da'wah expresses the universality of Islam, so in modern times it requires Muslims to exercise their *'ijtihad* in interpreting Islam to face new challenges in such a way as will not only preserve and develop their Islamic identity but also contribute from the resources of Islam to the needs of any particular society. This cause will not be advanced, many recognize, by dwelling self-defensively upon traditional intolerance of Islam in the West, though some take the view that "Muslim countries should make their relationship with the non-Muslims of the world a function of the way these countries treat their Muslim minorities."[42] But, argues one contributor to the debate, "It would be entirely different if we emphasised being human creatures of the one God as the common irrevocable bond, and projected Islam not as the religion of one of the many contending human groups but as the 'natural religion' of all."[43]

Ideas such as these, promising as they are, presuppose a level of intellectual sophistication which, as we have seen, the majority of Muslims in Europe have yet to attain. But this factor is recognized, at least implicitly, in the emphasis given by the International Seminar to issues of education for Muslim minorities, and by the formal recommendation of the creation of "an International Muslim University of Science and Technology that would enable Muslims from all parts of the world, and particularly from Muslim communities in non-Muslim states, to pursue advanced modern knowledge and research within the framework of Islamic belief and in consonance with the spirit of Islam."[44]

In the meantime the concern for Islamic identity in Europe and the West may be seen to oscillate between two poles of thought within the general perspective I have just summarized. On the one hand, many Muslims are evidently attracted by the model of the *dhimmi* status that is accorded, classically at least, to non-Muslim believers living within the 'ummah, guaranteeing their right to preserve and express their religious identity as a community, though in a manner consonant with the interests of the Islamic state to which they are loyal; by reversal this could be a paradigm for the participation of Muslim minorities in non-Muslim

[41] Ibid., pp. 24-25.

[42] M. Ali Kettani, "The Problems of Muslim Minorities and Their Solutions," in ibid., pp. 106-107.

[43] M. Siddiqi, "Muslim Communities in Non-Muslim States," review article in *Journal of Institute of Muslim Minority Affairs*, 1, 2 (1979), 2,1 (1980), 206.

[44] Islamic Council of Europe, *Muslim Communities in Non-Muslim States*, p. 168.

states, as argued in both volumes by Professor Ismail al-Faruqi of Temple University mentioned above.[45] Professor al-Faruqi envisages this paradigm in terms of a creative tension between Islamic values embodied in an ideologically conscious Muslim community and its critical participation in the life of a non-Muslim society, and in no way does he give conceptual support to a tendency, evident among some of the more tradition-bound sections of the Muslim immigrant populations of Western Europe, toward a tacit "ghettoism."

On the other hand, Professor Ali Merad, whose views on the marginal position of Muslims in contemporary Europe I have already mentioned, asks whether there is not spiritual and ethical value in what he terms their "solitude," which could positively inspire the type of community to which as Muslims they must aspire. With the Quranic motif of Abraham explicitly in mind, he calls Muslims in Europe to accept to be for the time being the solitary bearers of the Quranic revelation and of their heritage of faith, so as to demonstrate through ethical engagement with the problems of modern European society that "Islam is not tied to the destiny of empires and ideological systems . . . nor to nations, nor to a cultural community . . . but that the Muslim community is a community of people where fellowship exists in a communion of faith . . . open to all other people amongst whom it has the vocation of being 'an intermediate community' (*'ummatan wasatan*, Sura 2,143)–a community for the service of the well being and peace of humankind." On these grounds Professor Merad concludes that "by the principles which define the vocation of the Islamic community, and therefore the personal mission of each of its members, Muslims should be well prepared to involve themselves in the pluralist societies of our times and to co-operate loyally with them, the more so since the spiritual families which compose them belong to the community of the People of the Book."[46]

In this view Professor Merad echoes those of his teacher, Louis Massignon, and in a striking way calls us back to the spirit behind what Professor Watt, in his study of Islamic Spain, calls "a genuine symbiosis of the indigenous and adventitious elements of the population with their respective cultures." If–as I have argued that we must–we refuse to limit our consideration of the contemporary situation of Muslims in Europe to the categories of "migration" or "oppression," but set it within the context of a continuing history of Muslim presence in Europe which began in the eighth century, then there is, I believe, no compelling reason to disavow that "a genuine symbiosis of the indigenous and adventitious elements of the population" could be achieved again. The social and economic conditions in which this religious-cultural symbiosis must develop are likely to be widened if,

[45] I. Faruqi, "The Rights of Non-Muslims under Islam: Social and Cultural Aspects," *Journal of Institute of Muslim Minority Affairs*, 1,1 (Summer 1979), 90-102; cf. *Muslim Communities in Non-Muslim States*, p. 168.

[46] Merad, "Quelques observations," p. 8.

as seems probable, Turkey enters in full membership of the European Economic Community within the next ten years. As this happens we may hope that Europe and the West may be liberated from their prejudicial views of Islam into the one world of which Professor Watt has written, and that Muslims throughout the world may likewise be released from the torments of their traumatic experience of Europe over the past two centuries.

INDEX